Franklin
on
Franklin

Franklin

on

Franklin

Paul M. Zall

THE UNIVERSITY PRESS OF KENTUCKY

Publication of this volume was made possible in part
by a grant from the National Endowment for the Humanities.

Editorial and Sales Offices: The University Press of Kentucky
663 South Limestone Street, Lexington, Kentucky 40508–4008

04 03 02 01   5 4 3 2 1

Library of Congress Cataloging-in-Publication Data

Franklin, Benjamin, 1706–1790.
     [Autobiography]
  Franklin on Franklin / [edited by] Paul M. Zall.
       p. cm.
    The first twenty-three chapters are based on Zall's recovery
    of Franklin's first draft of his autobiography, and the last six
    chapters are derived primarily from Franklin's correspondence
    and journals.
    Includes bibliographical references.
    ISBN 0–8131–2201–5 (acid-free paper)
    1. Franklin, Benjamin, 1706–1790. 2. Statesman–
United States–Biography. I. Zall, Paul M. II. Title.
E302.6.F7 A2 2001a
973.3'092–dc21   00–012055

FOR MARTIN RIDGE

CONTENTS

ACKNOWLEDGMENTS

Once again I am pleased to acknowledge my debt to Mary Robertson, William A. Moffett Curator of Manuscripts at the Huntington Library, for access to the original manuscript of the autobiography in the archives there. For help with the science and art of word processing, I am also indebted to my old friends Frederick Kuri and Warren Johnson, and for unfailing encouragement to Martin Ridge, former Director of Research and sometime Acting-Director of the Huntington Library, Art Galleries, and Botanical Gardens. Thanks.

A NOTE ON THE TEXT

Not just another edition of Franklin's autobiography, this version represents his first draft so far as that is recoverable from the original manuscript. To fill in the period not covered by the original, I have selected passages from his journals and letters that talk frankly about his private life and opinions of his public life. This has meant omitting some delightful nonfiction writing such as his bagatelles or his serious writing about electricity or charting the Gulf Stream. But my aim has been to provide a unique perspective generally available only to specialists in such technical works as the genetic text of the Autobiography edited by Leo Lemay and me in 1981.

The first twenty-three chapters represent the first draft interspersed with revisions (in italics) made close to the time of composition rather than, in many cases, five or ten years later, as discussed in the Introduction. The genetic text showed all the revisions with estimates of when, where and how Franklin made them. My *Franklin's Autobiography: a Model Life* (1989) speculated on his reasons for making them. The Norton Critical Edition of the autobiography by Lemay and me (1986) provided fully annotated factual and textual information about the final work.

I have tried to follow Franklin's style even with respect to spelling and typography such as capitalizing proper nouns, with inconsistencies resulting from copyists of journals or correspondence. I have omitted some passages not focused on Franklin himself and rearranged the sequence of others for a more direct story, but otherwise I have tried to represent the words faithfully as the language Franklin would speak as well as write. Sources of passages from the draft as well as from supplementary sources are indicated with reference to the Selected Bibliography.

My own notes, intended to clarify the context, are no substitute for the exhaustive annotation of the Norton Critical Edition or in the magisterial edition of the *Papers of Benjamin Franklin* in process of publication since 1959 or in the detailed chronology in process by Leo Lemay on line at www.english.udel.edu/lemay/Franklin.

Introduction

BEN FRANKLIN REVISING

Editor Mathew Carey of the *Columbian Magazine* asked eighty-year-old Benjamin Franklin for permission to publish a biographical sketch of him. Franklin declined, insisting that he would do it himself. "I have in hand a full Account of my life,"[1] he said, adding that it would be published after his death. Who more capable of presenting himself to posterity than an expert writer who had practiced the art from childhood? Nevertheless, it would be another three years before death cut off the story at 1757, forty-three years short of being "a full account."

The autobiography remained in manuscript for many more years after that before the public would see Franklin's story the way he wrote it in his own words. The way he revised the manuscript over eighteen years would reveal Franklin himself in a different way, not so self-possessed and self-controlled as he would like others to believe. His was not Rousseau's confession, displaying his heart upon his sleeve, but as covert a composition as any of his promotional or diplomatic productions. Some would call the autobiography duplicitous, for the revisions sometimes deceive in the way he deceived the legislature into funding the Pennsylvania Hospital, a charitable act for which, he said, "I more easily excus'd myself for having made some use of Cunning."[2]

The classical example for comparison would be his most

popular writing, "The Way to Wealth," originally composed for the last edition Franklin prepared of *Poor Richard's Almanac*. It is a sketch of old Father Abraham preaching industry and thrift to a crowd waiting for an auction. His text is not the Bible but proverbs from Poor Richard—who is so impressed that he postpones buying clothes for another year. Readers who miss the mockery aimed at Poor Richard find that they mistake Franklin the ventriloquist for his comical dummy.

From age fifteen, Franklin had masqueraded in a succession of humorous characters, such as Silence Dogood, Anthony Afterwit, Alice Addertongue, and Polly Baker. The latter appeared so lifelike as to be taken for years as an actual case of an overbearing woman persecuted by the Puritans.[3] The fine line between art and illusion dissolves in an incident from the memoir, when the leading antagonist in battling over electricity insists that "Franklin of Philadelphia" is a figment of imagination.[4] Just as relevant is the way Franklin began the text of his will: "I, Benjamin Franklin, of Philadelphia, printer."[5] As printer, he doubled as writer.

His almanac and newspaper enabled early retirement at age forty-two and allowed him to spend another forty-two years pursuing the science and public service that would prove to be dual paths to honors and recognition. Writing offered a third path. The proverbs of "The Way to Wealth," published in broadside and pamphlet, went through 145 editions in his lifetime, in such different languages as Hebrew and Icelandic.[6] In hearts and minds of generations, they formed the bedrock of the work ethic and the cult of success now identified with the industrial middle class, but with firm support from Franklin's autobiography. For if the proverbs told people to work hard and save wisely and be good, the autobiography showed them how.

Introduction

As precept and practice the two works shaped the sentimental center binding an entire people to a common heritage. A century of America's youth believed in poor boys making good as the American way of life. During the Great Depression, Franklin Roosevelt urged Americans to read the autobiography for hope,[7] and at the nation's bicentennial, *Reader's Digest* toasted Franklin for qualities its three million readers like best about themselves.[8] Yet the story so celebrated had up to that time not been read as Franklin had written it, a bizarre circumstance understandable by recourse to its printing history and then the history of its composition.

Many are still surprised that Franklin's autobiography was printed first in French. This was another result of his working covertly. He composed in five distinct phases. The first segment of eighty-seven pages (part one) was done on vacation in rural England during summer 1771 but revised extensively on his voyage home in May 1775. The second portion (part two) was written in France while he waited for Congress's permission to go home. This part shows few revisions and in some instances seems merely copied from other material. Parts three and four, both composed in America from August 1788 to December 1789, show different batches of ink. One batch was used to make revisions to part one, suggesting that even on his deathbed Franklin continued revising. The first printed text was surely based on Franklin's manuscript as revised in 1775 and consisted entirely of part one.[9]

The second edition was an English translation of the French edition, the third another English translation of the same text. In 1818, grandson William Temple Franklin's printing from what he thought the original manuscript resulted in only parts one, two, and three—for reasons related to its history. Sailing for France in 1776, Franklin left the manuscript with protege Joseph Galloway. Galloway turned Tory and went into exile, leaving it with his wife, Grace Galloway, in whose effects it was found after her death by her lawyer Abel James. James sent Franklin the outline found with the manuscript, urging him to continue writing while James held the document pending Franklin's return. The clerks in James's office thus had ample time to take at least one copy which surfaced in the first edition in French.

This circumstance also explains the nature of part two. Written without access to the autobiography so far composed, it seems less memoir than meditation on behavior modification. The whole segment amounts to seventeen pages compared to the 112 pages of part three composed under pressure of public service and pain of kidney stones and enlarged prostate, which halted progress. A respite during October through May 1789 enabled him to write five more pages. Unsure of his judgment, he had grandson Benny Bache make a copy for friends in France and another for friends in England. After sending off those copies, however, he was able somehow to complete part four, seven and three-quarters pages more.

After Franklin died of pleurisy in April 1790, the rights to the manuscript passed to grandson William Temple Franklin, who, because the original looked like a mere rough draft, exchanged it for the copy made in France. (Both copies, for France and for England, have apparently disappeared.) The rough draft is the text in this edition. To make the case more bizarre still, he used material from earlier editions to complete his grandfather's life story, sometimes in preference to manuscript readings.

These events explain why readers had to wait until 1868

to have an edition of the entire manuscript made by former Ambassador to France John Bigelow, who had purchased it while there. He modernized Franklin's style and the revisions appearing on almost every one of the manuscript's 134 pages. I have included those revisions that transformed the structure and theme of the story, particularly in part one where parallel and contrasting characters are made to play off one another as in an eighteenth-century novel.[10] The young Franklin finds himself contrasted with a succession of youths ruining themselves by compulsion or willfulness, drinking, gambling, shucking responsibility, or succumbing to animal spirits.

Interpolated passages subtly refocus the theme from the good-humored celebration of being a reasonable creature (because it enables one to find a reason for doing anything one has a mind to do). Later interpolations redirect the focus to amending our feckless behavior. Five statements are added to part one at strategic points to explain that Franklin had "corrected" such "errata" as breaking his indentures or his promise to Deborah Read. (Poignantly, these additions were made after Deborah Read Franklin's death in 1774.)

Such interpolations also enhance the narrative technique, as in the celebrated depiction of Franklin entering Philadelphia munching on a roll, carrying two others, one under each arm. The first draft had him merely passing by the door of his future father-in-law. The interpolation had him seen by Deborah Read, who thought he made a ridiculous figure, an image later recalled in contrasting his early poverty with his increasing prosperity. Here it also established the characteristic tone of an amiable, self-effacing old man amused by the antics of his feckless youth, always with an overlay of assurance that the lad will turn out all right.

Some revisions undercut that tone. In explaining why he left his brother James despite the indenture that bound him, Franklin later added a marginal comment: "I fancy his harsh & tyrannical Treatment of me, might be a means of impressing me with that Aversion to arbitrary Power that has stuck to me thro' my whole life."[11] This coloring of vindictiveness appeared at the close of his outline: "Costs me nothing to be civil to inferiors, a good deal to be submissive to superiors."[12] It reappears repeatedly in part three, when interpolated passages refer to the British Army's cowardice and meanness, and in the last part when accusing opposing lawyer Fernando John Paris of an unfair practice but one in fact occurring after Paris' death, a decided loss of Franklin's sweet reasonableness.

The dominant theme, however, remains the one explained to close friend Benjamin Vaughan, 24 October 1788: "I omit all facts and transactions that may not have a tendency to benefit the young reader, by showing him from my example, and my success in emerging from poverty, and acquiring some degree of wealth, power, and reputation, the advantages of certain modes of conduct which I observed, and of avoiding the errors which were prejudicial to me."[13] In effect, this passage summarizes one of the longest interpolations, the preamble to the genealogical introduction. That material bears a correction in the ink Franklin was using on his deathbed, leaving little doubt about it being his final intention for the work. The statement appears to have been added in the segments, indicated by my paragraphing below.

> Having emerged from the Poverty and Obscurity in which I was born & bred, to a State of Affluence & some Degree of Reputation in the World, and having gone so far thro' Life with a considerable Share of

Introduction

Felicity, the conducing Means I made use of, which, with the Blessing of God, so well succeeded, my Posterity may like to know, as they may find some of them suitable to their own Situations, & therefore fit to be imitated.

That Felicity, when I reflected on it, has induc'd me sometimes to say, that were it offer'd to my Choice, I should have no Objection to a Repetition of the same Life from its Beginning, only asking the Advantage Authors have in a second Edition to correct some Faults of the first. So would I if I might, besides correcting the Faults, change some sinister Accidents & Events of it for others more favourable, but tho' this were deny'd, I should still accept the Offer. However, since such a Repetition is not to be expected, the Thing most like living one's Life over again, seems to be a Recollection of that Life, and to make that *Recollection* as durable as possible, the putting it down in Writing.

Hereby, too, I shall indulge the inclination so natural in old Men, to be talking of themselves and their own past Actions, and I shall indulge it, without being troublesome to others who thro' respect to Age might think themselves oblig'd to give me a Hearing, since this may be read or not as any one pleases. And lastly, (I may as well confess it, since my Denial of it will be believ'd by no body) perhaps I shall a good deal gratify my own *Vanity*. Indeed I scarce ever heard or saw the introductory Words, *Without Vanity I may say, &c.* but some vain thing immediately follow'd. Most People dislike Vanity in others whatever Share they have of it themselves, but I give it fair Quarter wherever I meet with it, being persuaded that it is often productive of Good to the Possessor & to others that are within his Sphere of Action: And therefore in many Cases it would not be quite absurd if a Man were to thank God for his Vanity among the other Comforts of Life.

And now I speak of thanking God, I desire with all Humility to acknowledge, that I owe the mention'd Happiness of my past Life to his kind Providence, which led me to the Means I us'd & gave them Success. My Belief of This, induces me to *hope*, tho' I must not *presume*, that the same Goodness will still be exercis'd towards me in continuing that Happiness, or in enabling me to bear a fatal Reverso, which I may experience as others have done, the Complexion of my future Fortune being known to him only, and in whose Power it is to bless to us even our Afflictions.[14]

The basic function of the revisions was to improve the story's style, either clarifying the meaning or improving the sound of a text meant to be read aloud. Still, in being interpolated over a period of eighteen years they are bound to reflect the private feelings Franklin artfully hid from public view. If the vindictive tone of some later insertions seems inconsistent with the intention to be "entertaining, interesting, and useful," it is consistent with that of private correspondence or journals talking about relations with the Penn family of proprietors and the British ministry or later Congress for disrespecting his petition to be relieved or his request to be reimbursed for services rendered. Their treatment would justify his bitterness, but the overflow of powerful feelings seems out of place in the otherwise amiable autobiography, suggesting a sign that Franklin lost self-control even in writing for posterity.

Introduction

Thus seen through layers of revision, along with personal correspondence, Franklin emerges as different from the common perception of a cool, crafty, cunning "Man of Reason" always in control of self or circumstances. Instead he may be seen as an authentic human being susceptible to fallibility, frustration, and foibles of his own as well as others. But he remains an uncommon common man. Despite behavior modification and attempts to imitate Socrates and Jesus, he suffers a sense of injured merit, a sense that self-sacrificing public service ought to have brought respect and honor at least as easily as he earned fame for science.

A closing episode in Thomas Jefferson's own autobiography offers a clue to Franklin's motives in working over what he had written the previous eighteen years. Jefferson visited a month before Franklin died in April 1790. After Jefferson mentioned hearing about the autobiography, Franklin confessed he had not reached very far in his "life" but offered a ream or so of a manuscript to his old colleague. The manuscript was probably the journal he kept detailing his negotiations with British officials in hopes of preventing the Revolution. Jefferson misunderstood him. He promised to read the manuscript and return it. "He said, 'No, keep it.' Not certain of his meaning, I again looked into it, and said again, I would certainly return it. 'No,' said he, 'keep it.'"[16] This insistence seems odd for one who only a couple of years earlier had refused the public even a biographical sketch. But Jefferson, like his mentor, was another Great Communicator and would know how to publicize British villainy, for—as Franklin said in his preface—"putting it down in Writing" makes it as durable as possible. People would know the truth, and the truth would make them furious.

Alas, Jefferson missed Franklin's meaning and gave the

manuscript of the negotiations to William Temple Franklin as residuary legatee. William Temple Franklin delayed its publication until a generation surviving the War of 1812 needed no reminder of that truth or its consequences. Had Jefferson known how hard his old mentor had worked over his other manuscript, the autobiography, he would have recognized from Franklin's model that it is not enough to be understood; one must be careful of being misunderstood.

1

GROWING UP BOSTONIAN

JANUARY 1706–APRIL 1722

One January morning in 1706, Franklin's mother went to church and at intermission went home to birth him, then took him back to church for the rest of the day. Thus he could assure friends that he had attended church all day the first day of his life.[1]

Josiah, my Father, married young, and brought his Wife with three Children unto New England about 1682. . . . where they expected to enjoy their Mode of Religion with Freedom. By the same Wife he had 4 Children more born there, and by a second Wife ten more, in all 17, of which I remember 13 sitting at one time at my Father's Table, who all grew up to be Men & Women, and married. I was the youngest Son & was born in Boston, N. England.[2]

Josiah Franklin had left England because the state outlawed worship in churches other than the official Church of England. He and second wife Abiah Folger, Franklin's mother, lived behind his shop just across from the Old South Church. Her father, Peter Folger, a Nantucket pioneer, had paid twenty pounds for the remaining service of her mother, Mary Morrill, an indentured servant.[3]

Finding no work in his trade as a dyer, Josiah Franklin made candles and soap for a living.

Perhaps you may like to know something of his Character. He had an excellent Constitution of Body, was of middle Stature, but well set and very strong. He was ingenious, could draw prettily, was skill'd a little in Music and had a clear pleasing Voice, so that when he play'd Psalm Tunes on his Violin & sung withal as he often did in an Evening after his Business was over, it was extreamly agreable to hear. But his great Excellence lay in a sound Understanding, and solid Judgment in prudential Matters, both in private & publick Affairs. In the latter indeed he was never employ'd, the numerous Family he had to educate keeping him close to his Trade, but I remember well his being frequently visited by leading People, who consulted him for his Opinion in Affairs of the Town & show'd him a good deal of Respect for his Judgment and Advice. *He was also much consulted by private Persons about their Affairs & frequently an Arbitrator between contending Parties.*

At his Table he lik'd to have as often as he could, some sensible Friend or Neighbour to converse and always took care to start some ingenious or useful Topic for Discourse, which might tend to improve the Minds of his Children. By this means he turn'd our Attention to what was good, just, prudent in the Conduct of Life; and no Notice was ever taken of what related to the Victuals or Dish on the Table, whether it was well or ill drest, in or out of Season, of good or bad flavour, preferable to this or that other; so that I was bro't up in so perfect an Inattention to those Matters as to be quite indifferent what kind of Food was set before me; and so unobservant of it, that to this Day, if I am ask'd I can scarce tell a few Hours after Dinner, what I din'd upon. This has been a Convenience to me in travelling, where my Companions have been very unhappy for want of a suitable Gratification of their more delicate because better instructed Tastes and Appetites.

My Mother had likewise an excellent Constitution. She suckled all her Children. I never knew either my Father or Mother to have any Sickness but that of which they dy'd, he at 89 & she at 85 Years of age. They lie buried together at Boston.[4] . . .

My elder Brothers were all put Apprentices to different Trades. I was put to the Grammar School at Eight Years of Age, my Father intending to devote me as the Tithe of his Sons to the Service of the Church.

> The Old South Church would today be closest to Congregationalist, so to have become a minister Franklin would likely have attended Boston's Free Latin School and Harvard. His sister said he could read at age five and that as a boy he was "addicted to all kinds of reading" and would study "incessantly a nights."[5] This could account for his rapid pace in a time when the school required facility in both writing and reading Latin.[6]

My early Readiness in learning to read (which must have been very early, as I do not remember when I could not read) and the Opinion of all his Friends that I should certainly make a good Scholar, encourag'd him to this Purpose of his. My Uncle Benjamin too approv'd of it, and intended to give all his Shorthand Volumes of Sermons if I would learn his Character [orthography]. I continu'd however at the Grammar School only one Year, tho' in that time I had risen gradually from the Middle of the Class of that Year to be the Head of it, and farther was remov'd into the next Class above it, in order to go with that into the third at the End of the Year. But my Father in the mean time, from a View of the Expence of a College Education which, having so large a Family, he could not well afford, and the mean Living many so educated were afterwards able to obtain, Reasons that he gave to his Friends in my Hearing, altered his first Intention, took me from the Grammar School, and sent me to a School for Writing & Arithmetic kept by a then famous Man, Mr Geo. Brownell, very successful in his Profession generally. Under him I acquired fair Writing pretty soon, but I fail'd in Arithmetic, & made no Hand of it.[7]

> Writing schools taught both girls and boys basic arithmetic through rote memory and penmanship by copying from models repeatedly, with no thought to composition.[8]

At Ten Years old, I was taken home to assist my Father in his Business, which was that of a Tallow Chandler and Sope-Boiler. A Business he was not bred to, but had assumed on his Arrival in New England & finding his Dying Trade would not maintain his Family, being in little Request. Accordingly I was employed in cutting Wick for the Candles, filling the Dipping Mold, & the Molds for cast Candles, attending the Shop, going of Errands, &c.

I dislik'd the Trade and had an Inclination for the Sea; but my Father declar'd against it, and so it seem'd that I was destin'd for a Tallow Chandler; however, living near the Water, I learnt early to swim well.[9] *I made two oval Palettes, each about ten inches long and six broad, with Holes for the Thumbs to hold them tightly in each hand, like Painter's Palettes. In swimming I would hold them edgewise for forward and on the flat Side to draw them back. . . . They helped me swim much faster but fatigued my Wrist. I also fitted a sort of Sandals to the Soles of my Feet but found them unsatisfactory, observing that Motion required the inside of Feet and Ankles as well as Soles.[10]*

I amused myself one Day flying a Kite when I came to the

Side of a Pond about a mile broad. As it was very warm, I tied the Kite String to a Stake while I went swimming, allowing the Kite to fly on high. In a while, wishing to play with the Kite and swim at the same time, I returned, untied the Kite, held the Stick in my Hands, lay on my Back to be drawn across the Water very nicely. Then having another Boy carry my Clothes to the other Side, I had my Kite carry me all the way across with the least Fatigue and most Pleasure imagineable. I had to slow occasionally, since it seemed that following too swiftly would raise it once more. I have not practiced this Method since that Time but imagine it would be possible to cross from Dover to Calais in this way—though crossing by Boat would be better yet.[11]

And when with other Boys I was generally allow'd to govern, especially in any case of Difficulty; and upon other Occasions I was generally a Leader among the Boys, and sometimes led them into Scrapes, of which I will mention one Instance, as it shows an early projecting public Spirit, tho' not honestly conducted.

There was a Marsh that bounded part of the Mill Pond, on the Edge of which at Highwater, we us'd to stand to fish for Minews. By much Trampling there, we had made it a mere Quagmire. My Proposal was to build a Wharf there fit for us to stand upon, and I show'd my Comrades a large Heap of Stones which were intended for a new House near the Marsh, and which would very well suit our Purpose. Accordingly in the Evening when the Workmen were gone, I assembled a Number of my Playfellows, and working with them diligently like so many Emmets, sometimes two or three to a Stone, we brought them all away and built our Wharff.

The next Morning the Workmen were surpriz'd at Missing the Stones; they were found in our Wharff; Enquiry was made after the Removers; we were discovered & complain'd of; several of us were corrected by our Fathers; and tho' I pleaded the Usefulness of the Work, mine convinc'd me that nothing was useful which was not honest.[12]

When I was a Child of seven Years old, my Friends on a Holiday fill'd my little Pocket with Halfpence. I went directly to a Shop where they sold Toys for Children; and being charm'd with the Sound of a Whistle that I met by the way, in the Hands of another Boy, I voluntarily offer'd and gave all my Money for it. When I came home, whistling all over the House, much pleas'd with my Whistle, but disturbing all the Family, my Brothers, Sisters & Cousins, understanding the Bargain I had made, told me I had given four times as much for it as it was worth, put me in mind what good Things I might have bought with the rest of the Money, & laught at me so much for my Folly that I cry'd with Vexation; and the Reflection gave me more Chagrin than the Whistle gave me Pleasure. This however was afterwards of use to me, the Impression continuing on my Mind; so that often when I was tempted to buy some unnecessary thing, I said to my self, "Do not give too much for the Whistle;" and I sav'd my Money.[13]

When Boston numbered only about two thousand families, even a poor boy like Franklin would have known venerable pioneers and illustrious citizens as part of everyday life.

Cotton and Increase Mather I remember. The Father, Increase, I once when a Boy, heard preach at the Old South and . . . was some years afterwards at his House at the Northend, on some Errand to him, and remember his sitting in an easy Chair apparently very old and feeble. But Cotton I remember in the vigour of his Preaching and Usefulness. And apparently in [1724] I had reason to remember, as I still do a Piece of Advice he gave me. I had been some time with him in his Study,

*where he condescended to entertain me, a very Youth, with
some pleasant and instructive Conversation. As I was taking
my Leave he accompany'd me thro' a narrow Passage at which
I did not enter, and which had a Beam across it lower than
my Head. He continued Talking which occasion'd me to keep
my Face partly towards him as I retired, when he suddenly
cry'd out, "Stoop! Stoop!" Not immediately understanding
what he meant, I hit my Head against the Beam. He then
added, "Let this be a Caution to you not always to hold your
Head so high. Stoop, young Man, stoop —as you go through
the World—and you'll miss many hard Thumps." This was a
way of hammering Instruction into one's Head: And it was so
far effectual, that I have ever since remember'd it, tho' I have
not always been able to practise it.*[14]

By my rambling Digressions I perceive my self to be
grown old. I us'd to write more methodically. But one does
not dress for private Company as for a publick Ball. 'Tis
perhaps only Negligence.

To return. I continu'd thus employ'd by my Father's
Business for two Years, that is till I was 12 Years old, and my
Brother John, who was bred to that Business having left
my Father, married and set up for himself at Rhodeisland,
there was all Appearance that I was destin'd to supply his
Place and be a Tallow Chandler. But my Dislike to the Trade
continuing, my Father was under Apprehension that if he
did not find one for me that was more agreable, I should
break away and get to Sea, as his Son Josiah to his great
Vexation had done. He therefore sometimes took me to
walk with him, and see Joiners, Bricklayers, Turners, Bra-
ziers, &c at their Work, that he might observe my Inclination, & endeavour to fix it on some Trade or other on Land.

It has ever since been a Pleasure to me to see Workmen
handle their Tools; and it has been useful to me, having

learnt so much by it, as to be able to do little Jobs my self in my House, when a Workman could not readily be got; & to construct little Machines for my Experiments while the Intention of making them was fresh & warm in my Mind.

My Father at last fix'd upon a Cutler's as Trade, and my Uncle Benjamin's Son Samuel being about that time establish'd in Boston, I was sent to be with him some days on liking. But his Expectations of a Fee with me displeasing my Father, I was taken home again.

From a Child I was fond of Reading, and all the little Money that came into my Hands was ever laid out in Books. Pleas'd with the Pilgrim's Progress, my first Collection was of John Bunyan's Works. I afterwards sold them to enable me to buy R. Burton's Collections: they were little Chapmen's Books and cheap, 40 or 50 in all.

> Popular John Bunyan's works cost a shilling a volume (about $2.50 in today's money), the price of an almanac. Books by prolific "R. Burton" (Nathaniel Crouch) at the same cost were small enough (about 8 cm by 4 cm) to be carried by itinerant chapmen (peddlers) yet these badly printed compilations of myth, fantasy, and history averaged over two hundred pages of tiny type.

My Father's Library was small & consisted chiefly of Books in Divinity, Sermons, &c. most of which I read, and have since regretted, that at a time when I had such a Thirst for Knowledge, more proper Books had not fallen in my Way, nor any judicial *Director*, since it was now resolv'd I should not be a Clergyman. Plutarch's Lives there was, in which I read abundantly, and I still think that time spent to Advantage. *There was also a book of Defoe's called an Essay on Projects and another of Dr Mather's call'd Essays to do Good, which perhaps gave me a Turn of Thinking as to have an Influence on my Conduct through Life.*[15]

This Bookish Turn at length determin'd my Father to make me a Printer, tho' he had already one Son (James) of that Profession. In 1717 he return'd from England with a Press & Letters to set up his Business in Boston. I lik'd it much better than that of my Father, but still had a hankering for the Sea. To prevent that, my Father was impatient to have me bound to my Brother. I stood out for some time, but at last was persuaded and signed the Indentures, when I was yet but 12 Years old. I was to serve as an Apprentice till I was 21 Years of Age, only to be allow'd Journeyman's Wages during the last year. In a little time I made great Proficiency in the Business, and became a useful Hand to my Brother.

> The indenture, or contract, bound Franklin to his brother for a nine-year term rather than the more common seven-year term, but the provision for journeyman's wages was standard.

I now had better Access to better Books. An Acquaintance with the Apprentices of Booksellers, enabled me sometimes to borrow a small one, which I was careful to return soon & clean. Often I sat up in my Room reading the greatest Part of the Night, when the Book was borrow'd in the Evening & to be return'd early in the Morning lest it should be miss'd or wanted. And after some time an ingenious Tradesman who had a pretty Collection of Books, & who frequented our Printing House, took Notice of me, invited me to his Library, & very kindly lent me such as I chose to read.

I now took a Fancy to Poetry, and made some little Pieces. My Brother, thinking it would turn to account encourag'd me, & put me on composing two of them. One was called the Light House Tragedy & contain'd an Account of the drowning of Capt. Worthilake & his Two Daughters;

the other was a Sailor Song on the Taking of Teach the Pirate. They were wretched Stuff, in the Grubstreet Ballad Stile, and when they were printed he sent me about the Town to sell them. The first sold wonderfully, the Event being recent, having made a great Noise. This flatter'd my Vanity.

> Both ballads were timely. George Worthylake drowned in Boston Harbor with his wife and one daughter on 3 November 1718. Teach, alias Blackbeard, slain off Carolina, 22 November, was subject of a 1719 broadside ballad conceivably written by Franklin. It opened:
>
>> Will you hear of a bloody Battle,
>> Lately fought upon the Seas,
>> It will make your Ears to rattle,
>> And your Admiration cease.[16]

But my Father discourag'd me, by ridiculing my Performances, and telling me Versemakers were always Beggars; so I escap'd being a Poet, probably a bad one. But as Prose Writing has been of great Use to me in the Course of my Life, and was a principal Means of my Advancement, I shall tell you how in such a Situation I acquir'd what little Ability I have in that way.

There was another Bookish Lad in the Town, with whom I was intimately acquainted. We sometimes disputed, and very desirous we were of confuting one another: Which disputacious Turn, by the way, is a very bad Habit, making People often extreamly disagreable in Company, by Contradiction that is necessary to bring it into Practice, & thence productive of Disgusts & Enmities where perhaps you have occasion for Friendship. *I had caught it by reading my Father's Books of Dispute about Religion.* Men of good Sense, I have since observ'd, seldom fall into it, except Lawyers,

University Men, and Men of all Sorts that have been bred at Edinborough.

> During Franklin's visits to Edinburgh in 1757 and 1771, the favorite indoor sport of clubs was disputation. Franklin and his chum, John Collins, in debating education for women, engaged a timely topic ignited by a pamphlet by schoolmistress Bathusa Makin, fanned by Defoe's *Essay upon Projects*, and exploded in a firestorm of pamphlet and periodical satire.

A question was some how or other started between us of the Propriety of educating the Female Sex in Learning, & their Abilities for Study. He was of Opinion that it was improper, & that they were naturally unequal to it. I took the contrary Side, perhaps for Dispute sake. He was more eloquent, had a ready Plenty of Words, and sometimes as I thought bore me down more by that than by the Strength of his Reasons. As we parted without settling the Point, & were not to see one another again for some time, I sat down to reduce my Arguments in Writing, which I copied fair & sent to him. Three or four Letters of a Side had pass'd, when my Father happened to find the Papers, and read them. I lodg'd then at his House. Without entring into the Discussion, he took occasion to talk to me about the Manner of Writing, observ'd that tho' I had the Advantage of my Antagonist in correct Spelling & pointing (which I ow'd to the Printing House) I fell far short in elegance of Expression, in Method and in Perspicuity, of which he convinc'd me by several Instances. I saw the Justice of his Remarks, & thence grew more attentive to the *Manner* and determin'd by some Means to endeavour an Improvement.

> Franklin's model for self-improvement, a random volume about the same size as Burton's chapbooks, reprinted tales and essays on ambition, fame, and disputation from

Addison and Steele's *Spectator* (1711–12), would later be
imitated for his own essay series by "Silence Dogood."

About this time I met with an odd Volume of the Spectator. It was the third. I had never before seen any of them. I
bought it, and was much delighted with it. I thought the
Writing excellent, & I wish'd to imitate it. With that View, I
took some of the Papers, & making short Hints of the Sentiment in each Sentence, laid them by a few Days, and then
without looking at the Book, try'd to compleat the Papers
again, by expressing each Sentiment fully & at length as it
had been before, but in any Words that should come to
hand. Then I compar'd my Spectator with the Original,
discover'd some of my Deficiencies & corrected them. But
I found I wanted a Copia Verborum, *a Stock of Words or a
Readiness in finding & using what I had,* which I thought I
should have acquir'd before that time, if I had gone on
making Verses, since the continual Occasion for Words of
the same Import but of different Length, to suit the Measure, or of different Sound for the Rhyme, would have laid
me under a constant Necessity of searching for Variety and
so have tended to fix that Variety in my Mind, & by that
Means make me Master of it. Therefore I took some of the
Tales & turn'd them into Verse. And after a time, when I
had pretty well forgotten the Words of the Prose, turn'd
them back again.

I also sometimes jumbled my Collection of Hints into
Confusion, and after some Weeks, endeavour'd to reduce
them into the best Order, before I began to form the full
Sentences & compleat the Paper. This was to teach me
Method in the Arrangement of Thoughts. By comparing
afterwards with the original, I discover'd many faults and
amended them; but I sometimes had the Pleasure of Fancying that in certain places I had been lucky enough to

improve the Method or the Language and this encourag'd me to think I might possibly in time come to be a tolerable English Writer, of which I was extreamly ambitious.

Franklin would propose a similar program for teaching composition in a 1751 essay, "Idea of the English School."

My Time for these Exercises was after Work at Night, or before it began in the Morning; or on Sundays, when I contrived to be in the Printing House alone, evading as much as I could the usual Attendance on publick Worship, which my Father used to exact of me when I was under his Care: And which indeed I still thought a Duty; tho' I could not, it seemed, afford the Time to practise it.

Thomas Tryon's posthumous *Memoirs* (1705) offered a model for this work ethic. After a fifteen-hour workday, Tryon would read or study two or more hours, subsisting only on water, bread, and a little fruit. Franklin was a follower of Tryon's *Wisdom's Dictates* (1691), which listed on pages 139–153, "A Bill of Fare of 75 Noble Dishes of Excellent Food, far exceeding those made of Fish or Flesh." When a neighbor asked Franklin's mother what she thought of his following Tryon's vegetarian diet, she is supposed to have said, "It's not so bad; it teaches him self-control," and, in effect, "He'll grow out of it."

When about 16 Years of Age, I happen'd to meet with a Book written by one Tryon, recommending a Vegetable Diet. I determined to practise it. My Brother being yet unmarried, did not keep House, but boarded himself & his Apprentices in another Family. My refusing to eat Flesh occasioned an Inconveniency, and I was frequently chid for my singularity. I made my self acquainted with Tryon's Manner of preparing some of his Dishes, such as Boiling Potatoes or Eggs, making Hasty Pudding, & some others, and propos'd to my Brother, that if he would give me Weekly half the Money he paid for my Board, I would board my self. He instantly agreed to it, and I presently found that I could save half what he paid me. This was an additional Fund for buying Books.

But I had another Advantage in it. My Brother and the rest going from the Printing House to their Meals, I remain'd there alone, and dispatching presently my light Repast *(which often was no more than a Slice of Bread, a Handful of Raisins & a Glass of Water)* had the rest of the Time for Reading & my Study, in which I made the greater Progress from that Clearness of Head & quicker Apprehension which usually attend Temperance in Eating & Drinking. And now it was that being on some Occasion made asham'd of my Ignorance in Arithmetick, which I had twice failed in learning when at School, I took [Edward] Cocker's Book of Arithmetick, & went thro' the whole by my self with great Ease. I also read [John] Seller's & [Samuel] Sturmy's Books of Navigation, & became acquainted with the little Geometry they contain *but never proceeded far in that Science.* And I read Locke on Human Understanding *and the Art of Thinking by Messrs du Port Royal.*

> Franklin remembers two influential classics: Locke on empiricism and Antoine Arnauld and Pierre Nicole's *Logic; or the Art of Thinking (1662)*, which applied Cartesian inductive method to teaching and also followed DesCartes in preferring vernacular to classical languages. Among other books mentioned are Earl Shaftesbury's *Characteristics of Men, Manners, Opinions, Times (1711)* on benevolence and Anthony Collins's books on deism. In trying to recall the inspiration for his Socratic method, Franklin mentions James Greenwood's *Essay towards a Practical English Grammar*(1711) and Edward Bysshe's translation

of Xenophon (1712) but neglects the more influential
Provincial Letters by Blaise Pascal, which, even in a very
bad translation (1657), taught the art of Socratic irony
Franklin would employ for fun and profit.

While I was intent on improving my Language, I met with
an English Grammar (I think it was Greenwood's) at the
End of which there were two little Sketches of the Arts of
Rhetoric and Logic, the Latter finishing with a Specimen
of a Dispute in the Socratic Method. And soon after I
procur'd Xenophon's Account of Memorable Things of
Socrates, wherein there are many Instances of the same
Method. I was charm'd with it, adopted it, dropt my Contradiction, and put on the humble Enquirer & Doubter.
And being then a real Doubter in many Points of our Religious Doctrine from reading Shaftsbury & Collins, I found
this Method safest for my self & very embarassing to those
against whom I used it, therefore I practis'd it continually
& grew very expert in drawing People *even of superior
Knowledge* into Concessions of which they did not foresee,
& entangling them in Difficulties out of which they could
not extricate them selves, and so obtaining Victories that
neither my self nor my Cause always deserved.

I continu'd this Method some Years, but gradually left
it, retaining only the Habit of expressing my self in Terms
of modest Diffidence, never using in any thing that may
possibly be disputed, the Words, "Certainly, undoubtedly,"
or any others that give the Air of Positiveness to an Opinion; but rather say, "I conceive," or "I apprehend a Thing to
be so or so," "It appears to me," or "I should think it so or
so," or "I imagine it to be so, if I am not mistaken." And this
Habit I believe has been of great Advantage to me, in in-
culcating my Opinions & persuading Men into Measures
that I have been from time to time engag'd in promoting.[17]

2

BECOMING A JOURNALIST

APRIL 1722–SEPTEMBER 1723

Franklin entered the history of American journalism very early, first as a newsboy for the *Boston Gazette*, for which his brother James was only the printer, and then for the *New England Courant*, which James Franklin owned, printed, and published. The *Courant* was the fourth rather than "the second that appear'd in America," having been preceded by the *Boston News-Letter, Boston Gazette*, and *Philadelphia Weekly Mercury*. But among them, the *Courant* was uniquely literary. Along with staple local and reprinted items, its columns carried essays and poems. Its writers offered a good school for Franklin, who between 12 April and 8 October 1722 published the earliest essays series. The fourteen "Dogood Letters" heralded a distinctively American voice—colloquial, dramatic, and irreverent. His success seemed to merit more than mere apprenticeship.

My Brother had in 1720 or 21, begun to print a Newspaper. It was the second that appear'd in America, & was called *The New England Courant*. The only one before it was the *Boston News Letter*. I remember his being dissuaded by some of his Friends from the Undertaking, as not likely to succeed, one Newspaper being enough for America. [Now,] there are not less than five & twenty. He went on however with the Undertaking, and I was employ'd to carry the Papers thro' the Streets to the Customers, after having work'd in composing the Types & printing off the Sheets.

He had some ingenious Men among his Friends who amus'd themselves by writing little Pieces for this Paper, which gain'd it Credit, and made it more in Demand; and these Gentlemen often visited us. Hearing their Conversations, and their Accounts of the Approbation their Papers were receiv'd with, I resolv'd to try my Hand among them. But suspecting that my Brother would object to printing any Thing of mine in his Paper if he knew it to be such, I contriv'd to disguise my Hand, & writing a Paper under a feigned Name, had it deliver'd to him, put it at Night under the Door of the Printing House. It was found in the Morning & communicated to his Intimates, when they call'd in as Usual. They read it, commented on it in my Hearing, and I had the exquisite Pleasure, of finding it had their Approbation, and that by their different Guesses at the Author none were named but Men of some Character among us for Learning & Ingenuity.

I suppose now that I was rather lucky in my Judges: And that perhaps they were not so very good ones as I then esteem'd them.

Encourag'd by this, I wrote and convey'd in the same Way to the Press several more Papers, which were equally approv'd, and I kept my Secret till my small Fund of Sense for such Performances was pretty well exhausted, & then I discover'd it; when I began to be considered a little more by my Brother's Acquaintance, and in a manner that did not quite please him, as he thought, probably with reason, that it tended to make me too vain. And perhaps this might be one Occasion of the Differences that we frequently had about thisTime. Tho' a Brother, he considered himself as my Master, & me as his Apprentice; and accordingly expected the same Services from me as he would from another; while I thought he demean'd me too much in some he requir'd of me, who from a Brother expected more Indulgence.

Our Disputes were often brought before our Father, and I fancy I was either generally in the right, or else a better Pleader, because the Judgment was generally in my favour: But my Brother was passionate & had often beaten me, which I took extreamly amiss; *(I fancy his harsh & tyrannical Treatment of me, might be a means of impressing me with that Aversion to arbitrary Power that has stuck to me thro' my whole Life.)* and thinking my Apprenticeship extreamly tedious,I was continually wishing for some Opportunity of shortening it, which at length offered in a Manner unexpected.

> In the next episode, Franklin compresses events. His brother was jailed from 12 June until 7 July 1722 for hinting that local authorities cooperated with pirates. Then in mid-January the next year, after the *Courant* alluded to hypocrisy in local government, James Franklin had to submit to censorship or cease publishing.

One of the Pieces in our News-Paper gave Offence to the Assembly. He was taken up, censur'd and imprison'd for a Month by the Speaker's Warrant, I suppose because he would not discover his Author. I too was taken up & examin'd before the Council; but tho' I did not give them any Satisfaction, they contented themselves with admonishing me, and dismiss'd me, considering me perhaps as an Apprentice who was bound to keep his Master's Secrets. During my Brother's Confinement, which I resented a good deal, notwithstanding our private Differences, I had the Management of the Paper, and I took care to give our Rulers some Rubs, which my Brother took very kindly, while others began to consider me in unfavourable Light, as a young Genius that had a Turn for Libelling & Satyr.

My Brother's Discharge was accompany'd with an Order of the House (a very odd one) "that James Franklin should no longer print the Paper called the *New England Courant.*" There was a consultation among his Friends what he should do in this Case. Some propos'd to evade the Order by changing the Name of the Paper; but Inconveniences being seen in that, it was finally concluded on as a better Way, to let it be printed for the future under the Name of "Benjamin Franklin." And to avoid the Censure of the Assembly that might fall on him as still printing it by his Apprentice, the Contrivance was, that my Indenture should be return'd to me with a full Discharge on the Back of it, to be shown on Occasion; but to secure him the Benefits of my Service I was to sign new Indentures for the Remainder of the Term which were to be kept private. A very flimsy Scheme it was, but however it was immediately executed, and the Paper went on accordingly under my name for several months.

At length a fresh Difference arising between my Brother and me, I took upon me to assert my Freedom, presuming that he would not venture to produce the new Indentures. It was not fair in me to take this Advantage, *and this I therefore reckon one of the first Errata of my Life*: But the Unfairness of it weigh'd little with me, when under the Impressions of Resentment, for the blows his Passions often urg'd him to bestow upon me when I offended. He was otherwise not an ill-natur'd Man: Perhaps I was too saucy & provoking.

When he found I would leave him, he took care to prevent my getting Employment in any other Printing-House of the Town, by going round & speaking to every Master, who accordingly refus'd to give me Work. I then thought of going to New York as the nearest Place where there was a Printer; *and I was the rather inclin'd to leave Boston, when I reflected that I had made my self a little obnoxious, & from the arbitrary Proceedings of the Assembly in my Brother's Case it was likely I might bring my self into Scrapes, and my indiscrete Disputations about Religion began to make me pointed at with Horror by good People, as an Infidel or Atheist. I determin'd on the Point.*

But my Father in this Affair now siding with my Brother, I was sensible that if I attempted to go openly, Means would be used to prevent me. My Friend Collins therefore undertook to manage a little for me. He agreed with the Captain of a New York Sloop for my Passage, under the Notion of my having got a naughty Girl with Child, whose Friends would compel me to marry her, and therefore I could not appear or come away publickly. So I sold some of my Books to raise a little Money, was taken on board privately, and in three Days found my self in New York near 300 Miles from home, without the least Recommendation to or Knowledge of any Person in the Place, and with very little Money in my Pocket.[1]

3

ON THE ROAD TO PHILADELPHIA

25 SEPTEMBER-1 OCTOBER 1723

Although he was without friends in New York, Franklin
was known, since the Courant listed him as a printer
(from 11 February 1723 until it failed in 1724), and his
brother James had become a hero in the printing trade as
defender of a free press. Outsiders, however, would look
upon him as just another runaway apprentice who, if
caught, would serve double the time he spent absent.
Whoever entertained him would be fined five pounds.
Thus an immanent cloud of suspicion hovered over
Franklin on the rough, two-day walk across New Jersey, still
in his working clothes, and on a boat ride to Philadelphia.[1]

My Inclinations for the Sea, were by this time worn out, or
I might now have gratify'd them. But having a Trade, &
supposing my self a pretty good Workman, I offer'd my
Service to the Printer of the Place, old Mr Wm. Bradford,
who had been the first Printer in Pensilvania, but remov'd
from thence upon the quarrel of Geo. Keith.[2] He could give
me no Employment, having little to do, and help enough
already. But, says he, my Son at Philadelphia has lately lost
his principal Hand, Aquila Rose, by Death. If you go thither
I believe he may employ you. Philadelphia was 100 miles

———

farther. I set out, however, in a Boat for Amboy, *leaving my chest and Things to follow me round by sea.*

> Franklin would sail on two types of vessels. The boat of choice on both Long Island Sound and Chesapeake Bay was the two-masted sloop with "leg of mutton" sails, but rivermen preferred the canoe-like bateau built of planking, which could be handled by two or three persons.[3]

In crossing the Bay we met with a Squall that tore our rotten Sails to pieces, prevented our getting into the Kill, and drove us upon Long Island. In our Way a drunken Dutchman, who was a Passenger too, fell overboard; when he was sinking I reach'd thro' the Water to his Shock Pate & drew up so that we got him in again.

I sober'd him a little, & he went to sleep, taking first out of his Pocket a Book which he desir'd I would dry for him. It prov'd to be my old Favourite Author Bunyan's *Pilgrim's Progress* translated into Dutch, finely printed with copper Cuts, a Dress better than I had ever seen it wear in its own Language, and I have since found that it has been translated into most of the Languages of Europe, and suppose it has been more generally read than any other Book except perhaps the Bible. He was the first that mix'd Narration & Dialogue, a Method of Writing that has been since found very engaging to the Reader, as in the most interesting Parts he is as it were brought into the Company, & present at the Discourse. Defoe in his Cruso, his Moll Flanders, Religious Courtship, Family Instructor, & other Pieces, has practis'd it with Success. And Richardson the same in his Pamela, &c.

> Alluding to influences on his own style, Franklin lists the best-selling books (besides the Bible) of the era. Surprising, he does not mention Jonathan Swift, his favorite

model for his satires. Later, his reprint of the psychological romance *Pamela* was the first novel published in America.[4]

When we drew near the Island we found it was at a place where there could be no Landing, being a great Surff on the stony Beach. So we dropt Anchor & swung round towards the Shore. Some People came down to the Water Edge & hallow'd to us, as we did to them. But the Wind was so high & the Surff so loud, that we could not hear each other. There were Canoes on the Shore & we made Signs & hallow'd that they should fetch us, but they either did not understand us, or thought it impracticable. So they went away, and Night coming on, we had no Remedy but to wait till the Wind should abate, and in the mean time the Boatmen & I concluded to sleep if we could, and so crouded into the Scuttle with the drunken Dutchman who was still wet, and the Spray beating over the Head of our Boat, leak'd thro' to us, so that we arose soon almost as wet as he. In this Manner we lay all Night with very little Rest. But the Wind abating the next Day, we made a Shift to reach Amboy before Night, having been 30 Hours on the Water without Victuals, or any Drink but a Bottle of filthy Rum: the Water we sail'd on being Salt.

In the Evening I found my self very feverish, & went in to Bed. But having read that cold Water drank plentifully was good for a Fever,[5] I followed the Prescription, sweat plentifully most of the Night, my Fever left me, and proceeded on my Journey, having 50 Miles to walk to Burlington where I was told I should find Boats that would carry me the rest of the Way to Philadelphia.

It rain'd very hard all the Day, I was thoroughly soak'd, and by Noon a good deal tir'd so I slept at a miserable Inn, where I staid all Night, beginning now to wish I had never left home. I cut so miserable a Figure too, that I found I was suspected to be some runaway Servant, and in danger of being taken up on that Suspicion. However I proceeded the next Day, and got in the Evening to an Inn within 8 or 10 Miles of Burlington, kept by one Dr. Brown.

> In a 1737 obituary, Franklin would celebrate Dr. John Brown as a skilled surgeon. Browne, who had most likely traveled in Europe for medical training, owned 230 acres near Burlington when he died.[6]

He had been, I imagine, an itinerant Doctor, for there was no Town in England, or Country in Europe of which he could not give a very particular Account. He had some Letters, & was ingenious,but much of an Unbeliever, & wickedly undertook to travesty the Bible in doggerel Verse as Cotton had done Virgil. By this means he set many of the Facts in a very ridiculous Light, & might have hurt weak minds if his Work had been publish'd: but it never was.

At his House I lay that Night, and the next Morning reach'd Burlington. But had the Mortification to find that the regular Boats were gone, and no other expected to go till Tuesday, this being Saturday. *Wherefore I agreed with an old Woman that sold Gingerbread to lodge at her House till a Passage by Water should offer, being tir'd with my foot Travelling. She understanding I was a Printer would have had me stay at that Town & follow my Business, being ignorant of the Stock necessary to begin with. She was very hospitable, gave me a Dinner of Ox Cheek with great Goodwill, accepting only of a Pint of Ale in return. And I tho't my self fix'd till Tuesday should come.* However walking in the Evening by the Side of the River a Boat came by that seem'd going towards Philadelphia. They took me in, and as there was no Wind, we row'd all the Way; in which I bore a Share and about Midnight not having yet seen the City, some of the Company were confident we must have pass'd it, and would row no farther, the others knew not where we were, so we put to the Shore, got into a Creek, landed near an old Fence with the Rails of which we made a Fire, *the Night being cold, in October,* and remain'd there till Morning. Then one of the Company knew it to be Cooper's Creek a little above Phila-delphia, where we arriv'd about 8 a Clock, on the Sunday morning, and landed at the Market street Wharff.[7]

4

SETTLING AT PHILADELPHIA

OCTOBER 1723–MAY 1724

Then said to be the second largest city in the British
Empire, Philadelphia was described as a prosperous place
by thirty-year-old German immigrant Christopher Sauer,
who arrived just a year after Franklin, pleased to find that
with one year's wages an artisan could purchase a farm of
his own. Franklin's fortune, however, consisted of a mere
few shillings when a bushel of wheat sold for eight shillings. A journeyman printer could hardly expect more
than 1½ shillings for an eight to nine hour day.[1]

I shall be the more particular in a Description of my first
Entry into that City, that you may in your Mind compare
such unlikely Beginning with the Figure I have since made
there. I was in my working Dress, my best Cloaths being to
come round by Sea. I was dirty by tumbling about from
my Journey; my Pockets were stuff'd out with Shirts &
Stockings; I knew no Soul, nor where to look for Lodging,
and I was very hungry, and my whole Stock of cash consisted of a Dutch Dollar and about a Shilling in Copper.
The latter I insisted on the Boatman's taking for my Passage who at first refus'd it on Account of my Rowing; but a
Man is sometimes more generous when he has but a little

Money than when he has plenty, perhaps thro' Fear of being thought to have but little. Then I walk'd up the Street, gazing about, till near the Market House I met a Boy with Bread as from the Baker's. I had many a Meal on Bread, & inquiring where he got it, I went immediately to the Baker's in second Street; and ask'd for Biskit, intending such as we had in Boston, but they were not made in Philadelphia, then not considering the Difference of Money & the Cheapness nor the Names of his Bread, I had him give me three pennyworth. He gave me accordingly three great Puffy Rolls. I was surpriz'd at the Quantity, but took it, and having no Room in my Pockets, walk'd off, with a Roll under each Arm, & eating the other. Thus I went up Market Street as far as fourth Street, *passing by the Door of Mr Read, my future Wife's Father, when she standing at the Door saw me, and thought I made as I certainly did a most awkward ridiculous Appearance.*

Then I turn'd and went down Chestnut Street and part of Walnut Street, eating my Roll all the Way, and coming round found my self again at Market Street Wharff, near the Boat I came in, to which I went for a Draught of the River Water, and being fill'd with one of my Rolls, gave the other two to a Woman & her Child that came down the River in the Boat with us and were waiting to go farther.

Thus refresh'd I walk'd again up the Street, which by this time had many People in it who were all walking the same Way; I join'd them, and thereby was led into the great Meeting House of the Quakers near the Market. I sat down among them, and after looking round a while & hearing nothing said; being very drowzy thro' Labour & want of Rest the preceding Night, I fell fast asleep, and continu'd so till the Meeting broke up, when one was kind enough to rouse me. This was the first House I was in or slept in, in Philadelphia.

Walking again down towards the River, & looking in the Faces of People, I met a young Quaker Gentleman whose Countenance I lik'd, and accosting him requested he would tell me where a Stranger could get a Lodging. We were then near the Three Mariners. There, says he, is one Place that entertains Strangers, but it is not a reputable House; if thee wilt walk with me, I'll show thee a better. He brought me to the Crooked Billet in Water-Street. Here I got Dinner. And while I was eating it, several sly Questions were ask'd me as it seem'd to be suspected from my Appearance, that I might be some Runaway. After Dinner my Sleepiness return'd: and being shown to a Bed, I lay down without undressing, and slept till Six in the Evening; rose to Supper; went to Bed again very early and slept soundly to the next Morning. Then I made my self as tidy as I could, and went to look for the Printer's. I found the old Man his Father, whom I had seen at New York, and who coming on horse back had got to Philadelphia before me. He introduc'd me to his Son, who gave me a Breakfast, but told me he did not at present want a Hand, being lately supply'd with one. But there was another Printer in town lately set up, who perhaps might employ me; if not, I should be welcome to lodge at his House, & he would give me a little Work to do till fuller Business should offer.

The old Gentleman then said, he would go with me to the new Printer. And when we found him, Neighbour, says Bradford, I have brought to see you a young Man of your Business, perhaps you may want such a One. He ask'd me a few Questions, put a Composing Stick in my Hand to see how I work'd, and then said he would employ me. And taking Bradford for one of the Towns People who had a

Good Will for him, enter'd into a Conversation with him on his present Undertaking & Prospects, while Bradford not discovering that he was the other Printer's Father; *on Keimer's Saying he expected soon to get the greatest Part of the Business into his own Hands,* drew him on by artful Questions and starting little Doubts, to explain all his Views, what Interest he rely'd on, what manner he intended to proceed. I saw immediately that one of them was a crafty old Sophister, and the other a mere Novice. Bradford left me with Keimer, who was greatly surpriz'd when I told him who the old Man was.

Keimer's Printing House I found, consisted of an old Shackling shatter'd Press, and one small worn-out Fount of English, which he was then using himself, composing in it an Elegy on Aquila Rose before-mentioned, a young Man of excellent Character, much respected in the Town, & himself a pretty Poet. Keimer made Verses, too, but very indifferently. He could not be said to write them, for his Manner was to compose them in the Types directly out of his Head; so there being no Copy, but one Pair of Cases, and the Work requiring all the Letter, no one could help him. I endeavour'd to put his Press (of which he understood nothing) into a little Order fit to be work'd with; & promising to come & print off his Elegy as soon as he should have got it ready, I return'd to Bradford's who gave me a little Job to do for the present, & there I lodged & dieted. A few Days after Keimer sent for me to print off the Elegy. And now he had got another Pair of Cases, and a Pamphlet to reprint, on which he set me to work.

These two Printers I found poorly qualified for their Business, Bradford very illiterate; and Keimer tho' something of a Scholar, was a mere Compositor, knowing nothing of Press work. He had been one of the French Prophets and could act their enthusiastic Agitations. At this time he did not profess any particular Religion, but had something of all at times; was very ignorant of the World, & had, as I afterwards found, a good deal of the Knave in his Composition. He did not like my Lodging at Bradford's while I work'd with him. He had a House indeed, but without Furniture, so he could not lodge me: But he got me a Lodging at Mr Read's before-mentioned who was the Owner of his House. And my Chest & Clothes being come by this time, I made a more respectable Appearance in the Eyes of Miss Read, than I had done when she first happen'd to see me eating my Roll in the Street.

I began now to have some Acquaintance among the young People of the Town that were Lovers of Reading, and gaining Money by my Industry & Frugality, I lived very agreably.[2]

5

A PRODIGAL'S RETURN
TO BOSTON

APRIL 25–JUNE 1724

I had a Brother-in-Law, Robert Holmes, Master of a Sloop that traded between Boston and Delaware. He being at New Castle, 40 Miles below Philadelphia, heard there of me, and wrote me a Letter, mentioning the Concern of my Friends in Boston at my abrupt Departure, assuring me of their Goodwill to me, and that every thing would be accommodated to my Mind if I would return, which he exhorted me to very earnestly. I wrote an Answer to his Letter, thank'd him for his Advice, but stated my Reasons for quitting Boston fully, & in such a Light as to convince him I was not so much in the Wrong as he had apprehended. Governor Keith was then at New Castle, and my Brother Capt. Holmes happening to be in Company with him when my Letter came to hand, spoke to him of me, and show'd him the Letter. The Governor read it, and seem'd surpriz'd when he was told my Age. He said I was a young Man of promising Parts, and ought to be encouraged. The Printers at Philadelphia were wretched ones, and if I would set up there, he made no doubt I should succeed; for his Part, he would procure me the publick Business, & do me every other Service in his Power. This my Brother-in-Law afterwards told me. But I knew as yet nothing of it; when one Day Keimer and I being at Work together near the Window, we saw the Governor and another Gentleman finely dress'd, come directly across the Street to our House, & heard them at the Door. Keimer ran down directly, thinking it a Visit to him. But the Governor enquir'd for me, came up, & with a Politeness I had been quite unus'd to, made me many Compliments, desired to be acquainted with me, blam'd me kindly for not having made myself known to him when I first came to the Place, and would have me away with him to the Tavern where he was going with Col. French to taste as he said some excellent Madeira. Keimer star'd like a Pig poison'd. I went with the Governor & Col. French, to a Tavern the Corner of Third Street, and over the Madeira he propos'd my Setting up my Business, laid beforre me the Probabilities of Success, & both he & Col French, promising me their Interest & Influence in procuring me the Public Business of both Governments. On my doubting whether my Father would assist me in it, Sir William said he would give me a Letter to him, in which he would state the Advantages, and he did not doubt of prevailing with him. So it was concluded I should return to Boston in the first Vessel with the Governor's Letter recommending me to my Father. In the mean time the Intention was to be kept a secret, and I went on working with Keimer as usual, the Governor sending for me now & then to dine with him, a very great Honour I thought it, and conversing with me in the most familiar, friendly manner imaginable.

About the End of April 1724 a little Vessel offer'd for Boston. I took Leave of Keimer as going to see my Friends. The Governor gave me an ample Letter, saying many flattering things of me to my Father, and which I read before it was sealed. We struck on a Shoal in going down the Bay & sprung a Leak, we had a blustring time at Sea, and were oblig'd to pump almost continually, at which I took my Turn. We arriv'd safe however at Boston in about a Fortnight. I had been absent Seven Months only and my Friends had heard nothing of me; for my Brother Holmes was not yet return'd; my unexpected Appearance surpriz'd the Family; all were however very glad to see me and made me Welcome, except my Brother. I went to see him at his Printing-House: I was better dress'd than ever while in his Service, having a genteel new Suit from Head to foot, a Watch, and my Pockets lin'd with near Five Pounds Sterling in Silver. He receiv'd me not very frankly, look'd me all over, and turn'd to his Work again. The Men were inquisitive where I had been, what sort of a Country it was, and how I lik'd it? I prais'd it much, & the happy Life I led in it; and one asking what kind of Money we had there, I took out a handful of Silver to show them, which was a kind of Show they had not been us'd to, Paper being the Money of Boston. Then I took an Opportunity of letting them see my Watch: and lastly, (my Brother still grum & sullen) I gave them a Piece of Eight to drink & took my Leave.

This Visit of mine offended him extreamly. For when my Mother sometime after spoke to him of a Reconciliation & her Wishes to see us on good Terms together, & that we might live for the future as Brothers, he said, I had insulted him in such a Manner before his People that he could never forget or forgive it. In this however he was mistaken.

My Father receiv'd the Governor's Letter with some Surprize; but said little of it to me for some Days; when Capt. Homes returning, he show'd it to him, ask'd if he knew Keith, and what kind of a Man he was: Adding that he must be of small Discretion, to think of setting a Boy up in Business that wanted yet 3 Years of being at Man's Estate. Homes said what he could in favor of the Project; but my Father was clear in the Impropriety of it; and he had advanc'd too much already to my Brother James and gave me a flat Denial to it. Soon after, he wrote a civil Letter to Sir William thanking him for Patronage he had so kindly offered me, but declining to assist me as yet in Setting up, I being in his Opinion too young to be trusted with the Management of a Business so important, & for which the Preparation must be so expensive.

My Friend Collins, who was a Clerk at the Post Office, pleas'd with the Account I gave him of my new Country, determin'd to go thither also: And while I waited for my Fathers Determination, he set out before me by Land to Rhodeisland, leaving his Books which were a pretty Collection of Mathematicks & Natural Philosophy, to come with mine to New York where he props'd to wait for me. My Father, tho' he did not approve Sir William's Proposition was yet pleas'd that I had been able to obtain so advantageous a Character from a Person of such Note where I had resided, and that I had been so industrious & careful as to equip my self so handsomely in so short a time: therefore no Prospect of an Accommodation between my Brother & me, he gave his Consent to my Returning again to Philadelphia, advis'd me to behave respectfully to the People there, endeavour to obtain the general Esteem, avoid lampooning & libelling to which he thought I had too much Inclination; and telling me, that by steady Industry and a prudent Parsimony, I might save enough by the time I was One and Twenty to set me up, & that if I came near the Matter he would help me out with the Rest. This was all I could obtain *except some small Gifts as Tokens of his & my*

Mother's Love, when I embark'd again for New-York, now with their Approbation & their Blessing.

> He had left Philadelphia about 16 April 1724 and departed Boston about 13 May. Laying over a few days at Newport, he arrived at New York about 20 May and at Philadelphia a week later.

The Sloop putting in at Newport Rhodeisland, I visited there my Brother John, who had been married & settled there some Years. He received me very affectionately, for he always lov'd me. *A Friend of his, One Vernon, having some Money due to him in Pensilvania, about 35 Pounds Currency, desired I would receive it for him, and keep it till I had his Directions what to remit it in. Accordingly he gave me an Order. This afterwards occasion'd me a good deal of Uneasiness.*

At Newport we took in a Number of Passengers for New York: Among which were two young Women, Companions, and a Matron-like Quaker-Woman with her Attendants. I had shown a Readiness to do her some little Services which impress'd her I suppose with some Good-will towards me. Therefore when she saw a growing Familiarity between me & the two Young Women, which they appear'd to encourage, she took me aside & said, Young Man, I am concern'd for thee, as thou has no Friend with thee, and seems not to know much of the World, or of the Snares Youth is expos'd to; depend upon it these are very bad Women, I can see it in all their Actions, and if thee art not upon thy Guard, they will draw thee into some Danger: I advise thee in a friendly Concern for thy Welfare, to have no Acquaintance with them. As I seem'd at first not to think so ill of them as she did, she mention'd some Things she had observ'd & heard that had escap'd my Notice; but now convinc'd me she was right. I thank'd her for her kind Advice, and promis'd to follow it.

When we arriv'd at New York they told me where they liv'd, & invited me to come and see them: but I avoided it. And it was well I did: For the next Day, the Captain miss'd a Silver Spoon that had been taken out of his Cabbin, and knowing that these were a Couple of Strumpets, he got a Warrant to search their Lodgings, found the stolen Goods, and had the Thieves punish'd. So tho' we had escap'd a sunken Rock which we scrap'd upon the Passage, I thought this Escape of still more Importance to me.

At New York I found my Intimate Collins, who had arriv'd there some Time before me. We had been intimate from Children, and had read the same Books together. But he had the Advantage of more time for Reading, and a Genius for Mathematical Learning in which he far outstript me. While I liv'd in Boston most of my Hours of Leisure for Conversation were spent with him, & he continu'd a sober as well as industrious Lad; *was much respected for his Learning by several of the Clergy & other Gentlemen, and seem'd to promise making a good Figure in Life*: but during my Absence he had acquir'd a habit of Sotting with Brandy; and I found by his own Account & what I heard from others, that he had been drunk every day since his Arrival at New York, & behav'd very oddly. He had gam'd too and lost his Money, so that I was oblig'd to discharge his Lodgings, & defray his Expences to and at Philadelphia. Which prov'd extreamly inconvenient to me. The then Governor of N York, William Burnet, Son of Bishop Burnet, hearing from the Captain that a young Man, one of his Passengers, had a great many Books, desired he would bring me to see him. I waited upon him accordingly. The Governor treated me with great Civility, show'd me his Library, & we had a good deal of Conversation about Books & Authors. This was the second Governor who had done me the Honour to take Notice of me, which to a poor Boy like me was very pleasing. Collins was too drunk to go with me on this Visit.

We proceeded to Philadelphia. I received on the Way Vernon's Money, without which we could hardly have finish'd our Journey. Collins wish'd to be employ'd in some Counting House; but whether they discover'd his Dramming by his Breath, or by his Behaviour, tho' he had some Recommendations, he met with no Success in any Application, and continu'd Lodging & Boarding at the same House with me & at my Expence. Knowing I had that Money of Vernon's he was continually borrowing of me, still promising Repayment as soon as he should be in Business. At length he had got so much of it, that I was distress'd to think what I should do, in case of being call'd on to remit it.

His Drinking continu'd, about which we sometimes quarrel'd for when a little intoxicated he was very fractious. Once in a Boat on the Delaware with some other young Men, he refus'd to row in his Turn: I will be row'd home, says he. We will not row you, says I. You must row, says he, or stay all Night on the Water, just as you please. The others said, Let us row, what signifies it? But my Mind being soured with his other Conduct, I continu'd to refuse. So he swore he would make me row, or throw me overboard; and coming along stepping on the Thwarts towards me, when he came up & struck at me, I clapt my Hand under his Crutch, and rising pitch'd him head-foremost into the River. I knew he was a good Swimmer, and so was under little Concern about him; but before he could get round to lay hold of the Boat, we had with a few Strokes pull'd her out of his Reach. And ever when he drew near the Boat, we ask'd if he would row, striking a few Strokes to slide her away from him. He was ready to die with Vexation, & would not promise to row; however seeing him at last beginning to tire, we lifted him in; and brought him home dripping wet in the Evening. We hardly exchang'd a civil Word afterwards.

> Franklin's problems with Collins represented a clinical case of alcoholism described by Benjamin Rush's *Effects of Spiritous Liquors* (? 1784): the afflicted become "peevish and quarrelsome; after a while they lose by degrees their moral sense. They violate promises and engagements without shame or remorse."[1]

At Length a West India Captain who had a Commission to procure a Tutor for the Sons of a Gentleman at Barbadoes, happening to meet with Collins, agreed to carry him thither. He left me then, promising to remit me the first Money he should receive in order to discharge the Debt. But I never heard of him after. *The Breaking into this Money of Vernon's was one of the first great Errata of my Life. And this Affair show'd that my Father was not much out in his Judgment when he suppos'd me too young to manage Business of Importance.*[2]

6

PLOTTING TO DECEIVE
& BEING DECEIVED

JUNE-NOVEMBER 1724

With no regularly scheduled transatlantic ships to London,
Franklin waited for Captain Thomas Annis's *London Hope*
as the first available packet boat, playing practical jokes
and being beguiled by Governor Keith's gratuitous false
promises.

Sir William, on reading my Father's Letter, said he was too
prudent. There was great Difference in Persons, and Discretion did not always accompany Years, nor was Youth always without. And since he will not set you up, says he, I
will do it my self. Give me an Inventory of the Things necessary to be had from England, and I will send for them.
You shall repay me when you are able. I am resolv'd to have
a good Printer here, and I am sure you must succeed. This
was spoken with such an Appearance of Cordiality, that I
had not the least doubt of his meaning what he said. I had
hitherto kept the Proposition a Secret in Philadelphia, & I
still kept it. Had it been known that I depended on the
Governor probably some Friend would have advis'd me not
to rely on him, as I afterwards heard it as his known Char-

acter to be liberal of Promises which he never meant to keep. Yet unsolicited as he was by me, how could I think his generous Offers insincere? I believed him one of the best Men in the World.

I presented him with an Inventory of a little Printing House, amounting by my Computation to about 100 £ Sterling. He lik'd it, but ask'd me if my being on the Spot in England to chuse the Types & see that every thing was good of the kind, might not be of some Advantage. Then, says he, when there, you may make Acquaintances & establish Correspondencies in the Stationary Way. I agreed that this might be advantageous. Then says he, get your self ready to go with Annis; which was the annual Boat, and the only one at that Time between London and Philadelphia. But it would be some Months before Annis sail'd so I continu'd working with Keimer, fretting about the Money Collins had of me, and in daily Apprehensions of being call'd upon by Vernon, which however did not happen for some Years after.

I believe I have omitted mentioning that in my first Voyage from Boston, being becalm'd off Block Island, our People set about catching Cod & hawl'd up a great many. Hitherto I had stuck to my Resolution of not eating animal Food; and on this Occasion, I consider'd with my Master Tryon, the taking every Fish as a kind of Murder, since none of them had or ever could do us any Injury *that might justify the Slaughter.*[1] All this was very reasonable. But I had formerly been a great Lover of Fish, & when this came out of the Frying Pan, it smelt admirably well. I balanc'd some time between Principle & Inclination: At length I recollected, that when the Fish were opened, I saw smaller Fish taken out of their Stomachs: Then, thought I, if you eat one another, I don't see why we may n't eat you. So I din'd upon Cod very heartily and continu'd to eat with other People, returning only now & then to a vegetable Diet. So convenient a thing it is to be a *reasonable Creature*, since it enables one to find or make a Reason for every thing one has a mind to do.

Keimer & I lived on a pretty good Footing & agreed tolerably well: for he suspected nothing of my Setting up. *He retain'd a good deal of his old Enthusiasms, and lov'd a Dispute. We therefore had many. I work'd him so with my Socratic Method and had trapann'd him so often by Questions apparently so distant from any Point we had in hand, and yet by degrees led to the Point, that at last he grew ridiculouly cautious, and would hardly answer me the most common Question, without asking first, "What do you intend to infer from that?" However it gave him so high an Opinion of my Abilities in the Confuting Way, that he seriously propos'd my being his Colleague in a Project he had of setting up a new Sect. He was to preach the Doctrines, and I was to confound all Opponents. When he came to explain with me upon the Doctrines, I found several Conundrums which I objected to, unless I might have my Way a little too, and introduced some of mine. Keimer wore his Beard at full Length, because somewhere in the Mosaic Law it is said, "thou shalt not mar the Corners of thy Beard." He likewise kept the seventh day Sabbath; and these two Points were Essentials with him. I dislik'd both, but agreed to admit them upon Condition of his adopting the Doctrine of using no animal Food. I doubt, says he, my Constitution will not bear that. I assur'd him it would, & that he would be the better for it. He was usually a great Gourmandizer, and I promis'd myself some Diversion in half-starving him.* Hearing me talk of that Mode of Living, he said he would try it if I would keep him Company. I did so for three Months.

We had our Vegetables dress'd and brought to us regularly by a Woman in the Neighbourhood, who had from me a list of 40 Dishes to be prepar'd for us at different times, in which there was neither Fish Flesh nor Fowl, and the Whim suited me the better at this time from the Cheapness of it, not costing above 18 pence Sterling each, per Week.... I went on pleasantly, but poor Keimer tir'd of the Project, long'd for the Flesh Pots of Egypt, and order'd a roast Pig, invited me & two Women Friends to dine with him, but it being brought too soon upon the Table, he could not resist the Temptation and ate it all up before we came.

I have since kept several Lents most strictly, leaving the full common Diet for that and that for the common, abruptly, without the least Inconvenience: So that I think there is little in the Advice of doing those Changes by easy gradations.

I had made some Courtship during this time to Miss Read, *I had a great Respect and Affection for her, and had some Reason to believe she had the same for me*: but as I was about to take a long Voyage, and we were both very young, *only a little above 18*, it was thought most prudent by her Mother to prevent our going too far at present, as a Marriage if it was to take place would be more convenient after my Return, when I should be as I expected set up in my Business. Perhaps too she thought my Expectations not so well founded as I imagined them to be.

My chief Acquaintances at this time were, Charles Osborne, Joseph Watson & James Ralph; all Lovers of Reading. The two first were Clerks to a Scrivener in the Town, Charles Brogden; the other was Clerk to a Merchant. Watson was a pious sensible young Man, of great Integrity: The others rather more lax in their Principles of Religion, particularly Ralph, who as well as Collins had been a little unsettled by me, for which they both afterwards made me suffer. Osborne was candid, frank, sincere, and affectionate to his Friends; Ralph was ingenious, genteel in his Manners, & extreamly eloquent; I think I never knew a prettier Talker. Both of them great Admirers of Poetry, and began to try their Hands in little Pieces. Many pleasant Walks we four had together into the Woods near Skuylkill, where we read to one another & conferr'd on what we read. Ralph was inclin'd to pursue the Study of Poetry, not doubting but he might become eminent in it and make his Fortune by it, alledging that the best Poets must when they first began to write, make as many Faults as he did. Osborne dissuaded him, assur'd him he had no Genius for Poetry, & advis'd him to think of nothing beyond the Business he was bred to; that in the mercantile way tho' he had no Stock, he might by his Diligence & Punctuality recommend himself to Employment as a Factor, and in time acquire wherewith to trade on his own Account. I allow'd the amusing one's self with Poetry now & then, so far as to improve one's Language, but no farther. On this it was propos'd that we should each of us at our next Meeting produce a Piece of our own Composing in order to improve by our mutual Observations, Criticisms & Corrections. As Language & Expression was what we had in View, we excluded all Considerations of Invention, by agreeing that the Task should be a Version of the 18th Psalm, which describes the Descent of a Deity. When the Time of our Meeting drew nigh, Ralph call'd on me first, & let me know his Piece was ready. I told him I had been busy, & having little Inclination had done nothing. He then show'd me his Piece for my Opinion; and I much approv'd it, as it appear'd to me to have great Merit. Now, says he, Osborne never will allow any Merit in any thing of mine, but makes 1000 Criticisms out of mere Malice & Envy. I wish therefore you would take this Piece of mine, & produce it as yours. I will pretend not to have had time, & so produce nothing: We shall then see what he will say to it. It was agreed, and I immediately transcrib'd it that it might appear in my own Hand. We met. Watson's was read: there were some Beauties in it: but many Defects. Osborne's was read: It was much better. Ralph did it Justice, remark'd some Faults, but applauded the Beauties. He had nothing to produce. I was backward seem'd desirous of being excus'd, had not had sufficient Time to correct, &c. but no Excuse could be admitted, produce I must. It was read and repeated; Watson and Osborne gave up the Contest; and join'd in applauding it immoderately. Ralph only made some Criticisms & propos'd some Amendments. Osborne was against him, & said he was no better a Critic than Poet; so he dropt the Argument. As they two went home together, Osborne express'd himself still more strongly in favour of what he thought my Production, having restrain'd himself before as he said, lest I should think it Flattery. But who would have imagin'd says he, that Franklin had been capable of such a Performance; such Painting, such Force! such Fire! he has even improv'd the Original! In his common Conversation, he seems to have no Choice of Words; he hesitates and blunders; and yet, good God, how he writes!

When we next met, Ralph discover'd the Trick, and Osborne was laught at. This fix'd Ralph in his Resolution of becoming a Poet. I did all I could to dissuade him from it, but He continu'd scribbling Verses, till Pope cur'd him. He became however a pretty good Prose Writer. More of him hereafter.

In 1728 Alexander Pope's *Dunciad* ridiculed Ralph's poem "Night" by picturing him as a wolf howling at the moon. [2]

As I may not have occasion to mention the other two, I shall just remark here, that Watson died in my Arms a few Years after, much lamented, being the best of our Set. Osborne went to the West Indies, where he became an eminent Lawyer & made Money, but died young. He and I made a serious Ageement, that the one who happen'd first to die, should make a friendly Visit to the other, and acquaint him how he found things in that separate State. But he never fulfilled his Promise.

The Governor, seeming to like my Company, had me frequently to his House; & his Setting me up was always mention'd as a fix'd thing. I was to take with me Letters recommendatory to a Number of his Friends, besides the Letter of Credit whereby I was to obtain the necessary Money for purchasing the Press & Types, Paper, &c. *For these Letters I was appointed to call at different times, when they were to be ready, but a future time was still named.* Thus we went on till the Ship *whose Departure too had been several times postponed* was on the Point of Sailing. Then when I call'd to take my Leave & receive the Letters, his Secretary, Dr Bard, came out to me and said the Governor was extreamly busy, in writing, but should be down at Newcastle before the Ship, & there the Letters would be delivered to me.

Ralph, tho' married & having one Child, had determined to accompany me in this Voyage. It was thought he intended to obtain Goods to sell on Commission. But I found afterwards, that thro' some Discontent with his Wife's Friends, he purposed to leave her on their Hands, & never return again.

Having taken leave of my Friends, & interchang'd some Promises with Miss Read, I left Philadelphia in the Ship, which anchor'd at Newcastle. The Governor was there. But when I went to his Lodging, the Secretary came to me from him with the civillest Message in the World, that he could not then see me being engag'd in Business of the utmost Importance, but should send the Letters to me on board, wish'd me heartily a good Voyage and a speedy Return, &c. I return'd on board, a little puzzled, but still not doubting.

Mr. [Andrew] Hamilton, a famous Lawyer of Philadelphia, had taken Passage in the same Ship for himself and Son: and with Mr Denham a Merchant, & Messers Onion & Russell Masters of an Iron Work in Maryland, had engag'd the Great Cabin; so that Ralph and I were forc'd to take up with a Birth in the Steerage: And none on board knowing us, were considered as ordinary Persons. But Mr. Hamilton & his Son (it was James, since Governor) return'd from New Castle to Philadelphia, the Father being recall'd by a great Fee to plead for a seized Ship. And just before we sail'd Col. French coming on board, & showing me great Respect, I was more taken Notice of, and with my Friend Ralph invited to come into the Cabin, there being now Room. Accordingly we remov'd thither.

Understanding that Col. French had brought on board the Governor's Dispatches, I ask'd the Captain for those that were to be under my Care. He said all were put into the Bag together; and he could not then come at them; but before we came to England, I should have an Opportunity of picking them out. So I was satisfy'd for the present, and we proceeded on our Voyage. We had a sociable Company in the Cabin, and lived well, having the Addition of all Mr Hamilton's Stores, who had laid in plentifully. In this Passage Mr [Thomas] Denham contracted a Friendship for me that continued during his Life. The Voyage was otherwise not a pleasant one, as we had bad weather.

Packets normally crossed in five weeks, but the *London*

Hope took six or seven weeks. In contrast, Franklin would cross in only three weeks in 1757 (but at higher fare) thanks to improved vessels and regular schedules. [3]

When we came into the Channel, the Captain kept his Word with me, & gave me an Opportunity of examining the Bag for the Governor's Letters. *I found none upon which my Name was put, as under my Care.* I picked out 4 or 5 that by the Hand I thought might be the promis'd Letters, especially as one of them was directed to Basket the King's Printer, and another to some Stationer.

We arriv'd in London the 24th of December 1724. I waited upon the Stationer who came first in my Way, delivering the Letter as from Gov. Keith. I don't know such a Person, says he: but opening the Letter, O, this is from Riddlesden; I have lately found him to be a compleat Rascal, and I will have nothing to do with him, nor receive any Letters from him. So putting the Letter into my Hand, he turn'd on his Heel & left me to serve some Customer. I was surprized to find these were not the Governor's Letters. And after recollecting and comparing Circumstances, I began to doubt his Sincerity.

I found my Friend Denham, and opened the whole Affair to him. He let me into Keith's Character, *told me there was not the least Probability that he had written any such Letters for me,* that no one who knew him had the least Dependance on him, and laught at the Notion of his giving me a Letter of Credit, having as he said no Credit to give. On my expressing some Concern about what I should do: He advis'd me to endeavour getting some Employment in the Way of my Business. Among the Printers here, says he, you will improve yourself; and when you return to America, you will set up to greater Advantage.[4]

We both of us happen'd to know, as well as the Stationer,

that Riddlesden the Attorney was a very Knave. He had half ruin'd Miss Read's Father by drawing him in to be bound for him. By his Letter it appear'd, there was a Scheme to the Prejudice of Hamilton (Suppos'd to be then coming over in our Ship) and that Keith was concern'd in it with Riddlesden. Denham, who was a Friend of Hamilton's, thought he should be acquainted with it. So when he arriv'd in England, which was soon after, partly from Resentment & Ill-Will to Keith & Riddlesden, and partly from Good Will to him; I waited on him, and gave him the Letter. He thank'd me cordially, the Information being of Importance to him. And from that time he became my Friend, greatly to my Advantage afterwards on many Occasions.

But what shall we think of a Governor's playing such pitiful Tricks, & imposing so grossly on a poor Boy! It was a Habit he had acquired. He wish'd to please every body; and having little to give, he gave Expectations. He was otherwise an ingenious sensible Man, a pretty good Writer, & a good Governor for the People, tho' not for his Constituents the Proprietaries, whose Instructions he sometimes disregarded. Several of our best Laws were of his Planning, and pass'd during his Administration.

Appointed their deputy governor (1717–26) by the proprietary Penn family, Sir William was heir to a baronetcy in Nova Scotia. With an M.A. from secular Marischal College, he would have been familiar with Newtonian science and liberal politics. Preferring to follow the latter, as governor he promoted debtor relief and paper money and protested proprietors' arbitrary power and instructions to him, for which they dismissed him.[5]

7

LIVING IN LONDON

25 DECEMBER 1724–21 JULY 1726

Daniel Defoe described London in 1724 as driven by trade,
commerce, and the stock market. Once country villages
and noble country houses, booming construction began
producing one continued building now "crouded with
people." [1]

Ralph and I were inseparable Companions. He led me about
& show'd me the City. We took Lodgings together *at a Fan
Shop in Little Britain* at 3/6 per Week, as much as we could
then afford. He found some Relations, but they were poor &
unable to assist him. He now let me know his Intentions of
remaining in London, and that he never meant to return to
Philadelphia. He had brought no Money with him, the whole
he could muster having been expended in paying for his
Passage. I had about 15 Pistoles: So he borrowed occasionally of me, while he was looking out for Business. He first
endeavoured to get into the Playhouse, believing himself
qualify'd for an Actor; but Wilkes, to whom he apply'd,
advis'd him candidly not to think of that Employment, as
it was impossible he should succeed in it. Then he propos'd
to Roberts, a Publisher in Paternoster Row, to write for him
a Weekly Paper like the Spectator, on certain Conditions,

which Roberts did not approve. Then he endeavour'd to get Employment as a Hackney Writer for the Stationers & Lawyers about the Temple, but could find no Vacancy.

I immediately got into Work at Palmer's then a Famous Printing House in Bartholomew Close, and here I continu'd near a Year. I was pretty diligent; but spent with Ralph a good deal of my Earnings in going to Plays & other Places of Amusement. We had together consum'd all my Pistoles, and now just rubb'd on from hand to mouth. He seem'd quite to forget his Wife & Child, and I by degrees my Engagements with Miss Read to whom I never wrote more than one Letter, & that was to let her know I was not likely soon to return. In fact, I was unable to pay my Passage.

This was one of the great Errata of my Life, which I should wish to correct if Living a second Edition.

At Palmer's I was employ'd in Composing for the second Edition of Woollaston's Religion of Nature. Some of his Reasonings not appearing to me to be well-founded, I wrote a little Piece, in which I made Remarks on them. It was entitled, A Dissertation on Liberty & Necessity, Pleasure and Pain.[2] *... The purport of it was to prove the Doctrine of Fate, from the suppos'd Attributes of God; in some such Manner as this: That in creating & governing the World, as he was infinitely wise he knew what would be best; infinitely good, he must be dispos'd; and infinitely powerful, he must be able to execute it. Consequently* all is right *...[3] I inscribed it to my Friend Ralph. I printed a small Number.[4] ... a hundred Copies, of which I gave a few to Friends, and afterwards disliking the Piece, as conceiving it might have an ill Tendency, I burnt the Rest, except one Copy the Margin of which was fill'd with manuscript Notes by Lyons, Author of the* Infallibility of Human Judgement, *who was at that time another of my Acquaintances in London.[5]*

He took great Notice of me, call'd on me often, to converse on these Subjects, carried me to the Horns a pale Ale-House in Lane, Cheapside, and introduc'd me to Dr Mandevile, Author of the Fable of the Bees who had a Club there, of which he was the Soul, being a most facetious Companion. Lyons introduced me, too, to Dr Pemberton, at Batson's Coffee House, who promis'd to give me an Opportunity some time or other of seeing Sir Isaac Newton, of which I was extreamly desirous; but this never happened.

[My Pamphlet] occasion'd my being more consider'd by Mr Palmer, as a Person of some Ingenuity, tho' the Principles ... were abominable, and he seriously expostulated with me about them. The printing this Pamphlet was another Erratum [6] *... (I was not 19 Years of Age when it was written.)* [7]

I had brought over a few Curiosities among which the principal was a Purse made of the Asbestos, which purifies by Fire. Sir Hans Sloane heard of it, came to see me, and invited me to his House in Bloomsbury Square, where he show'd me all his Curiosities, and persuaded me to let him add that to the Number, for which he paid me handsomely. [8] *...*

It was Franklin himself who made the overture to Sloane, offering to sell three pieces of asbestos, including a purse, in a letter dated 2 June 1725 from "the Golden Fan in Little Britain." [9]

While I lodg'd in Little Britain I made an Acquaintance with one Wilcox a Bookseller, whose Shop was the next Door. He had an immense Collection of second-hand Books. Circulating Libraries were not then in Use; but we agreed that on certain reasonable Terms which I have now forgotten, I might take, read & return any of his Books. This I esteem'd a great Advantage, & I made as much Use of it as I could. [10]

In the House with us there lodg'd two single Women; one a Mantua-maker, another who was a Millener, who I think had a shop in the Cloisters. She was a genteel Person, was sensible & lively, and of most pleasant Conversation. Ralph read Plays to her of an Evening, they grew Intimate, and at length she took another Lodging, and he follow'd her. They liv'd together some time, but he being still out of Business, & her Income not sufficient to maintain them both, he took a Resolution of going from London and endeavouring to get into a Country School, which he thought himself well qualify'd to undertake, as he wrote an excellent Hand, & was a Master of Arithmetic & Accounts. This however he thought a Business below him, & confident of future better Fortune when he should be unwilling to have it known that he once was so meanly employ'd, he chang'd his Name, & did me the Honour to assume mine. For I soon after had a Letter from him, acquainting me, that he was settled in a small Village in Berkshire, I think it was, where he taught reading & writing to 10 or a dozen Boys at 6 pence each per Week, and desiring me to write to him directing for Mr. Franklin, Schoolmaster at such a Place.

> An entry in Franklin's outline suggests that the village was
> Redmayne, three miles east of Cockermouth, Cumberland.

I continu'd to receive Letters from him very frequently, sending me large Specimens of an Epic Poem, which he was then writing, and desiring my Remarks & Corrections. These I gave him from time to time, but endeavour'd rather to discourage his Proceeding. One of Young's Satires was then just publish'd. I copy'd

> "Is thy ambition sweating for a rhyme,
> Thou unambitious fool, at this late time?"
> —Edward Young,
> *The Universal Passion, Satire II* (1725)

& sent him a great Part, which set in a strong Light the

Folly of pursuing the Muses. All was in vain. Sheets of the Poem continu'd to come by every Post, so that the Postage was a Bother.

In the mean time Mrs. T. having on his Account lost her Friends & Business, was often in Distresses, & us'd to send for me, and borrow what I could spare to help her out of them. I grew fond of her Company, and being at this time under no Religious Restraints, & presuming on my Importance to her, attempted Familiarities (*another Erratum*), which she repuls'd with a proper Resentment, and acquainted him with my Behaviour. This made a Breach between us, & when he return'd again to London, he let me know he thought I had cancel'd all the Obligations he had been under to me. So I found I was never to expect his Repaying me what I lent to him or advanc'd for him. It was not then of much Consequence, as he was totally unable. And I found my self reliev'd from a Burthen, in the Loss of his Friendship.

I now began to think of getting a little Money beforehand; and expecting better Work, I left Palmer's to work at Watts's near Lincoln's Inn Fields, a still greater Printing House. Here I continu'd all the rest of my Stay in London.

At my first Admission into the Printing House, I took to working at Press, imagining I felt a Want of the Bodily Exercise I had been us'd to in America, where Presswork is mix'd with Composing. I drank only Water; the other Workmen, near 50 in Number, were great Guzzlers of Beer. They wonder'd to see from several Instances that the American was *stronger* than themselves who drank *strong* Beer. My Companion at the Press, drank every Day a Pint before Breakfast, a Pint at Breakfast with his Bread and Cheese; a Pint between Breakfast and Dinner; a Pint at Dinner; a Pint in the Afternoon about Six o'Clock, and another when he had done his Day's-Work. I thought it a detestable Custom. But it was necessary, he suppos'd to drink *strong* Beer that he might be *strong* to labour. I endeavour'd to convince him that the Strength afforded by Beer could only be in proportion to the Grain dissolved in it, and that there was more Flour in a Penny-worth of Bread, and therefore if he would eat that with a Pint of Water, it would give him more Strength than a Quart of Beer. He drank on however, & had 4 or 5 Shillings to pay out of his Wages every Saturday Night for that muddling Liquor; an Expence I was free from. And thus these poor Devils keep themselves always under.

Watts after some Weeks desiring to have me in the Composing Room, I left the Pressmen. A new *Bienvenu* or Sum for Drink, was demanded of me by the Compostors. I thought it an Imposition, as I had paid below. The Master thought so too, and forbad my Paying it. I stood out two or three Weeks, was accordingly considered as an Excommunicate, and had so many little Pieces of private Mischief done me, by mixing my Sorts, transposing my Pages, breaking my Matter, &c. &c. all in the Night and ascrib'd to the Chapel Ghost, which they said haunted all those not regularly admited, that notwithstanding the Master's Protection, I found myself oblig'd to comply and pay the Money; convinc'd of the Folly of being on ill Terms with those one is to live with continually. I was now on a fair Footing with them, and soon acquir'd considerable Influence. I propos'd some reasonable Alterations in their Laws, and carried them against all Opposition. From my Example, the great Part of them, left their muddling Breakfast of Beer & Bread & Cheese, finding they could be supply'd from a neighbouring House with a large Porringer of hot Watergruel, crumb'd with Bread , & a Bit of Butter in it, for the Price of a Pint of

Beer, viz, three halfpence. This was a more comfortable as well as cheaper Breakfast, & kept their Heads clearer. Those who continu'd sotting with Beer all day, were often out of Credit at the Alehouse, and us'd to make Interest with me to get a Pint of Beer, *their Light*, as they phras'd it, *being out*. I watch'd the Paytable on Saturday Night, & collected what I stood engag'd for them, paying sometimes some Thirty Shillings a Week for them. This, and my being then a pretty good Riggite, that is a jocular verbal Satyrist, supported my Consequence in the Society. My constant Attendance, (never making a St. Monday), recommended me to the Master; and my Quickness at Composing, occasion'd my being put upon all Work of Dispatch which was generally better paid. So I went on now very agreably.

My Lodging in Little Britain being too remote, I found another in Duke-street opposite to the Romish Chapel. It was at an Italian Warehouse, two pair of Stairs backwards for 3/6 per Week. A Widow Lady kept the House, and she had a Daughter & a Maid Servant, and a Journey-man who kept the Warehouse, but lodg'd abroad. After enquiring my Character at the House I last lodg'd at, she agreed to take me in at the same Rate, 3/6 per Week, cheaper as she said from the Protection in having a Man Lodge in the House. She had been bred among People of Quality, & knew a 1000 Anecdotes of them. She was lame in her Knees with the Gout, and therefore seldom stirr'd out of her Room, so sometimes wanted Company, and hers was highly entertaining to me; and therefore I was sure to spend an Evening with her whenever she desired it. Our Supper was half an Anchovy each, on a mighty little Strip of Bread & Butter, and half a Pint of Ale between us. But the Entertainment was in her Conversation. My always keeping good Hours, and giving little Trouble in the Family, made her unwilling to part with me; so that when I talk'd of a Lodging I had heard of, nearer my Business, for 2 Shillings a Week, which, intent as I now was on saving Money, made some Difference; she bid me not think of it, for she would abate me two Shillings a Week for the Future; so I remain'd with her at 1/6 as long as I staid in London.[11]

At Watt's Printing house I contracted an Acquaintance with an ingenious young man, one Wygate, *who having wealthy Relations, had been better educated in Learning than most Printers, was a tolerable Latinist, and spoke French. I taught him, & a young Gentleman, a Friend of his, to swim, at twice going into the River, & they soon became good Swimmers. They introduc'd me to a genteel Company who went to Chelsea by Water to see the College and Don Saltero's Curiosities.*

> Chelsea Hospital, an old soldiers' home, had lovely gardens
> on the site of a former college. Don Saltero's curios
> included "Pontius Pilate's wife's chambermaid's sister's
> hat."[12]

In our Return, at the Request of the Company, whose Curiosity Wygate had excited, I stript & leapt into the River, & swam from near Chelsea to Blackfryars, performing on the Way a Number of Feats of Activity that surpriz'd & pleas'd those to whom they were Novelties. I had ever been delighted with this Exercise, had studied & practis'd all Thevenot's Motions & Positions, added several of my own, aiming at the graceful & easy, as well as the Useful.

> Melchisedech Thevenot's book, a French version of
> Everard Digby's *De Arte Natandi* (1587) appeared in
> English as the *Art of Swimming* (1699) with woodcuts
> showing forty individual strokes or positions.[13]

All these I took this Occasion of exhibiting to the Company,

& was much flatter'd by their Admiration. And Wygate, who was desirous of becoming a Master, grew more & more attach'd to me, on that account, as well as from the Similarity of our Studies. He at length propos'd to me travelling all over Europe together, supporting ourselves every where by working at our Business. I agreed to it. But mentioning it to my good Friend Mr Denham, with whom I often spent an Hour, as he lik'd my Company when I had Leisure. He dissuaded me from it, advising me to think only of returning to Pensilvania, which he was now about to do.

I must record one Trait of this good Man's Character. He had formerly been in Business at Bristol, but fail'd in Debt to a Number of People, and went to America. There, by a close Application to Business, he acquir'd a plentiful Fortune in a few Years. Returning to England in the Ship with me, He invited his old Creditors to an Entertainment, at which he thank'd them for the Easy Composition they had favour'd him with, & when they expected nothing but the Treat, every Man at the first Remove, found under his Plate an Order on a Banker for the full Amount of the Remainder with Interest.

He now told me he was about to return to Philadelphia, and should carry over a great Quantity of Goods in order to open a Store there: He propos'd to take me over as his Clerk to keep his Books (in which he would instruct me) copy his Letters, and attend the Store. He added, that as soon as I should be acquainted with mercantile Business he would promote me by sending me with a Cargo of Flour & Bread to the West Indies, and procure me Commissions from others; which Business would be profitable, & if I manag'd well, would establish me handsomely. The Thing pleas'd me, for I was grown tired of London, remember'd with Pleasure the happy Months I had spent in Pennsylva-

nia, and had wish'd to see it once more. Therefore I immediately clos'd with him, agreed on the Terms of Fifty Pounds
a Year; less indeed than my present Gettings as a Compostor,
but affording a better Prospect.

I now took Leave of the Printing-House and was daily
employ'd in my new Business, going about with Mr
Denham to purchase various Articles, & seeing them pack'd
up, calling upon Workmen to dispatch, &c. and when all
was on board, I had a few Days Leisure. On one of these
Days I was sent for and waited upon Sir William Wyndham.
He had heard of my Swimming from Chelsey to Blackfryars
and of my teaching Wygate and another young Man to swim
in a few Hours. He had two Sons about to set out on their
Travels; & he wish'd to have them first taught Swimming;
and propos'd to gratify me handsomely if I would teach
them. They were not yet come to Town and I expected my
Stay was uncertain, so I could not undertake it. But I then
thought it likely, that if I were to remain in England and
open a Swimming School, I might get some Money. And it
struck me so strongly, that had the Overture been sooner
made me, probably I should not so soon have returned to
America.

Thus I spent about 18 Months in London. For the Most
Part of the Time, I work'd hard at my Business, & spent but
little except in seeing Plays, & in Books. My Friend Ralph
had kept me poor. He owed me now about 27 Pounds; a
great Sum out of my small Earnings. I lov'd him notwithstanding, for he had many amiable Qualities. I had improv'd
my Knowledge, however, by Reading & Conversation, tho'
I had by no means improv'd my Fortune. By one Means or
other, I had pick'd up some very ingenious & learned Acquaintance, and I had read considerably.[14]

8

SAILING HOME

23 JULY-11 OCTOBER 1726

We sail'd from Gravesend on the 23d of July 1726. For the Incidents of the Voyage, I refer you to my Journal, where you will find them all minutely related. *Perhaps the most important Part of that Journal is the* Plan *to be found in it which I formed at Sea, for regulating my future Conduct in Life. It is the more remarkable, as being form'd when I was so young, and yet being pretty faithfully adhered to quite thro' to old Age:*[1]

> *Those who write of the Art of Poetry teach us that if we would write what may be worth the Reading, we ought always, before we begin, to form a regular Plan and Design of our Piece: otherwise, we shall be in danger of Incongruity. I am apt to think it is the same as to Life. I have never fixed a regular Design in Life; by which means it has been a confused Variety of different Scenes. I am now entering upon a new One: Let me, therefore, make some Resolutions, and form some Scheme of Action, that, henceforth, I may live in all respects like a rational Creature:*

> 1. It is necessary for me to be extremely frugal for some time, till I have paid what I owe.

2. To endeavour to speak Truth in every instance; to give nobody Expectations that are not likely to be answered, but aim at Sincerity in every Word and Action—the most amiable Excellence in a rational Being.

3. To apply my self industriously to whatever Business I take in hand, and not divert my Mind from my Business by any foolish Project of growing suddenly Rich; for Industry and Patience are the surest Means of Plenty.

4. *I resolve to speak Ill of no Man whatever, not even in a matter of Truth, but rather by some Means excuse the Faults I hear charged upon Others, and upon proper Occasions speak all the Good I know of every body.* [2]

From: "Occurrences in my Voyage to Philadelphia on board the Berkshire, Henry Clark Master, from London."

Friday 22 July 1726. Yesterday in the afternoon we left London, and came to an anchor off Gravesend about 11 at night. I lay ashore all night, and this morning took a walk up to the Windmill Hill, whence I had an agreeable prospect of the country for above 20 miles round, and two or three reaches of the river with ships and boats sailing both up and down, and Tilbury Fort on the other side, which commands the river and passage to London. This Gravesend is a cursed biting place; the chief dependence of the people being the advantage they make of imposing upon strangers. If you buy any thing of them, and give half what they ask, you pay twice as much as the thing is worth. Thank God, we shall leave it tomorrow. [3]

Ships from London going to sea stopped at Gravesend for inspection by customs agents "who forget not to take a compliment for their civility" in finding no contraband. [4]

Saturday 30 July. [At Yarmouth] Having taken a view of the church, town, and fort (on which there is seven large guns mounted), three of us took a walk up further into the island, and having gone about two miles, we headed a creek that runs up one end of the town, and then went to Freshwater church, about a mile nearer the town, but on the other side of the creek. Having stayed here some time it grew dark, and my companions were desirous to be gone, lest those whom we had left drinking where we dined in the town, should go on board and leave us. We were told that it was our best way to go straight down to the mouth of the creek, and that there was a ferry boy that would carry us over to the town. But when we came to the house the lazy whelp was in bed, and refused to rise and put us over; upon which we went down to the waterside, with a design to take his boat, and go over by ourselves.

We found it very difficult to get the boat, it being fastened to a stake and the tide risen near 50 yards beyond it: I stripped all to my shirt to wade up to it; but missing the causeway, which was under water, I got up to my middle in mud. At last I came to the stake; but to my great disappointment found she was locked and chained. I endeavoured to draw the staple with one of the thole-pins, but in vain; I tried to pull up the stake, but to no purpose: so that after an hour's fatigue and trouble in the wet and mud, I was forced to return without the boat.

We had no money in our pockets, and therefore began to conclude to pass the night in some hay-stack, though the wind blew very cold and very hard. In the midst of these troubles one of us recollected that he had a horseshoe in his pocket which he found in his walk, and asked me if I could not wrench the staple out with that. I took it, went, tried and succeeded, and brought the boat ashore to them.

Now we rejoiced and all got in, and when I had dressed my self we put off. But the worst of our troubles was to come yet; for, it being high water and the tide over all the banks, though it was moonlight we could not discern the channel of the creek, but rowing heedlessly straight forward, when we got about half way over, we found ourselves aground on a mud bank, and striving to row her off by putting our oars in the mud, we broke one and there stuck fast, not having four inches water.

We were now in the utmost perplexity, not knowing what in the world to do; we could not tell whether the tide was rising or falling; but at length we plainly perceived it was ebb, and we could feel no deeper water within the reach of our oar. It was hard to lie in an open boat all night exposed to the wind and weather; but it was worse to think how foolish we should look in the morning, when the owner of the boat should catch us in that condition, where we must be exposed to the view of all the town.

After we had strove and struggled for half an hour and more, we gave all over, and sat down with our hands before us, despairing to get off; for if the tide had left us we had been never the nearer, we must have sat in the boat, as the mud was too deep for us to walk ashore through it, being up to our necks.

At last we bethought ourselves of some means of escaping, and two of us stripped and got out, and thereby lightening the boat, we drew her upon our knees near 50 yards into deeper water, and then with much ado, having but one oar, we got safe ashore under the fort; and having dressed ourselves and tied the man's boat, we went with great joy to the Queen's Head [tavern] where we left our companions, whom we found waiting for us, though it was very late. [5]

Thursday, 25 August. *Man is a sociable being, and it is*

for aught I know one of the worst punishments to be excluded from society. I have read abundance of fine things on the subject of solitude, and I know 'tis a common boast in the mouths of those that affect to be thought wise, that they are never less alone than when alone. I acknowledge solitude an agreeable refreshment to a busy mind; but were these thinking people obliged to be always alone, I am apt to think they would quickly find their very being insupportable to them. I have heard of a gentleman who underwent seven years close confinement, in the Bastile at Paris. He was a man of sense, he was a thinking man; but being deprived of all conversation, to what purpose should he think? For he was denied even the instruments of expressing his thoughts in writing. There is no burden so grievous to man as time that he knows not how to dispose of. He was forced at last to have recourse to this invention: he daily scattered pieces of paper about the floor of his little room, and then employed himself in picking them up and sticking them in rows and figures on the arm of his elbow-chair; and he used to tell his friends, after his release, that he verily believed if he had not taken this method he should have lost his senses. One of the philosophers, I think it was Plato, used to say, that he had rather be the veriest stupid block in nature, than the possessor of all knowledge without some intelligent being to communicate it to.

What I have said may in a measure account for some particulars in my present way of living here on board. Our company is in general very unsuitably mixed, to keep up the pleasure and spirit of conversation: and if there are one or two pairs of us that can sometimes entertain one another for half an hour agreeably, yet perhaps we are seldom in the humour for it together. I rise in the morning and read for an hour or two perhaps, and then reading grows tiresome. Want of exercise occasions want of appetite, so that eating and drink-

ing affords but little pleasure. I tire myself with playing at draughts [checkers], then I go to cards; nay there is no play so trifling or childish, but we fly to it for entertainment. A contrary wind, I know not how, puts us all out of good humour; we grow sullen, silent and reserved, and fret at each other upon every little occasion. 'Tis a common opinion among the ladies, that if a man is ill-natured he infallibly discovers it when he is in liquor. But I, who have known many instances to the contrary, will teach them a more effectual method to discover the natural temper and disposition of their humble servants. Let the ladies make one long sea voyage with them, and if they have the least spark of ill nature in them and conceal it to the end of the voyage, I will forfeit all my pretensions to their favour. [6]

Friday 23 September. This morning we spied a sail to windward of us about two leagues. We shewed our jack upon the ensign-staff and shortened sail for them till about noon, when she came up with us. She was a snow from Dublin, bound to New York, having upwards of fifty servants on board, of both sexes; they all

These indentured servants bound themselves to a sea captain who, upon arrival, sold them for the passage money. Franklin's paternal grandmother was an indentured servant and so was Franklin on this return voyage having owed ten pounds for his passage to Denham.

appeared upon deck, and seemed very much pleased at the sight of us. There is really something strangely cheering to the spirits in the meeting of a ship at sea, containing a society of creatures of the same species and in the same circumstances with ourselves, after we had been long separated and excommunicated as it were from the rest of mankind. My heart fluttered in my breast with joy when I saw so many human countenances, and I could scarce refrain from that kind of laughter which proceeds from some degree of inward pleasure. When we have been for a considerable time tossing on the vast waters, far from the sight of any land or ships, or any mortal creature but ourselves (except a few fish and sea birds) the whole world, for aught we know, may be under a second deluge, and we (like Noah and his company in the Ark) the only surviving remnant of the human race. The two Captains have mutually promised to keep each other company; but this I look upon to be only matter of course, for if ships are unequal in their sailing they seldom stay for one another, especially strangers. This afternoon the wind that has been so long contrary to us, came about to the eastward (and looks as if it would hold), to our no small satisfaction. I find our messmates in a better humour, and more pleased with their present condition than they have been since we came out; which I take to proceed from the contemplation of the miserable circumstances of the passengers on board our neighbour, and making the comparison. We reckon ourselves in a kind of paradise, when we consider how they live, confined and stifled up with such a lousy stinking rabble in this sultry latitude.[7]

Saturday 1 October. *Last night our consort, who goes incomparably better upon a wind than our vessel, got so far to windward and ahead of us, that this morning we could see nothing of him, and 'tis like shall see him no more.*

Sunday 2 October. Last night we prepared our line with a design to sound this morning at 4 o'clock, but the wind coming about again to the North West, we let it alone. I cannot help fancying the water is changed a little, as is usual when a ship comes within soundings, but 'tis probable I am mistaken; for there is but one besides myself of my opinion, and we are very apt to believe what we wish to be true.

Monday 3 October. *The water is now very visibly changed to the eyes of all except the Captain and Mate, and they will by no means allow it; I suppose because they did not see it first.*[8]

Tuesday night 4 October. *Since 11 o'clock we have struck three fine dolphins, which are a great refreshment to us. This afternoon we have seen abundance of grampuses, which are seldom far from land, but towards evening we had a more evident token, to wit, a little tired bird, something like a lark, came on board us, who certainly is an American, and 'tis likely was ashore this day. It is now calm. We hope for a fair wind next.*[9]

Friday 7 October. Last night, about 9 o'clock, sprung up a fine gale at North East, which run us in our course at the rate of 7 miles an hour all night. We were in hopes of seeing land this morning, but cannot. The water, which we thought was changed, is now as blue as the sky; so that unless at that time we were running over some unknown shoal our eyes strangely deceived us. All the reckonings have been out these several days; though the Captain says tis his opinion we are yet an hundred leagues from land: for my part I know not what to think of it, we have run all this day at a great rate; and now night is come on we have no soundings. Sure the American continent is not all sunk under water since we left it.

Sunday 9 October. *We have had the wind fair all the morning: at 12 o'clock we sounded, perceiving the water visibly changed, and struck ground at 25 fathoms, to our universal joy. After dinner one of our mess went up aloft to look out, and presently pronounced the long-wished for sound, LAND! LAND! In less than an hour we could descry it from the deck, appearing like tufts of trees. I could not discern it so soon as the rest; my eyes were dimmed with the suffusion of two small drops of joy. By 3 o'clock we were run in within two leagues of the land, and spied a small sail standing along shore.*

We would gladly have spoken with her, for our captain was unacquainted with the coast, and knew not what land it was that we saw. We made all the sail we could to speak with her. We made a signal of distress; but all would not do, the ill natured dog would not come near us. Then we stood off again till morning, not caring to venture too near.

Monday 10 October. This morning we stood in again for land; and we that had been here before, all agreed that it was Cape Henlopen: about noon we were come very near, and to our great joy saw the pilot-boat come off to us, which was exceeding welcome. He brought on board about a peck of apples with him; they seemed the most delicious I ever tasted in my life: the salt provisions we had been used to, gave them a relish. We had an extraordinary fair wind all the afternoon and ran above an hundred miles up the Delaware before 10 at night. The country appears very pleasant to the eye, being covered with woods, except here and there a house and plantation. We cast anchor when the tide turned, about two miles before Newcastle, and there lay till the morning tide.

Tuesday 11 October. *This morning we weighed anchor with a gentle breeze, and passed by Newcastle, whence they hailed us and bade us welcome. 'Tis extreme fine weather. The sun enlivens our stiff limbs with his glorious rays of warmth and brightness. The sky looks gay, with here and there a silver cloud. The fresh breezes from the woods refresh us, the immediate prospect of liberty after so long and irksome confinement ravishes us. In short all things conspire to make this the most joyful day I ever knew. As we passed by Chester some of the company went on shore, impatient once more to tread on terra firma, and designing for Philadelphia by land. Four of us remained on board, not caring for the fatigue of travel when we knew the voyage had much weakened us. About eight at night, the wind failing us, we cast anchor at Redbank, six miles from Philadelphia, and thought we must be obliged to lie on board that night: but some young Philadelphians happening to be out upon their pleasure in a boat, they came on board and offered to take us up with them: we accepted of their kind proposal, and about 10 o'clock landed at Philadelphia, heartily congratulating each other upon our having happily completed so tedious and dangerous a voyage. Thank God!* [10]

9

FACING UNCERTAIN FUTURE IN PHILADELPHIA

1726–1727

Clerking for Thomas Denham would prove an excellent
school of business ethics, for his mentor exemplified the
Quaker virtues of honesty, hard work, thrift, prudence,
and others now associated with liberal capitalism—
especially the notion that honesty is good for business and
good business positions one to do good works for human-
ity, an idea underpinning Franklin's career. However,
1726–27 found him more concerned with paying off his
passage along with the liability of Vernon's money hanging
over an uncertain future.

We landed in Philadelphia the 11th of October, where I
found sundry Alterations. Keith was no longer Governor,
being superceded by Major [Patrick] Gordon; I met him
walking the Streets as a common Citizen. He seem'd a little
asham'd to see me, but pass'd without saying any thing. I
should have been as much asham'd at seeing Miss Read,
had not her Friends, despairing of my Return, persuaded
her to marry another, one Rogers, a Potter—which was
done in my Absence. With him however she was never

---

happy. He was a worthless Fellow tho' an excellent Workman. He spent what he got with her, got into Debt, and left her. It was said he had another Wife. He went to the West Indies, and died there. Keimer had got a better House, plenty of new Types, and a number of Hands, none very good, and seem'd to have a great deal of Business.

Mr. Denham took a Store in Water Street, where we open'd our Goods. I attended the Business diligently, studied Accounts, and grew in a little Time expert at selling. We lodg'd and boarded together, he counsell'd me as a Father, & having a sincere Regard for me; I respected & lov'd him; and we might have gone on together very happily; But in February 1726/7 when I had just pass'd my 21st Year, we both were taken ill. My Distemper was a Pleurisy, which very nearly carried me off. I suffered a good deal, gave up the Point in my own mind, & was rather disappointed when I found my self recovering; regretting in some degree that I must now have all that disagreable Work to do over again. I forget what his Distemper was. It held him a long time, and at length carried him off.

He left me a small Legacy in a nuncupative Will, as a Token of his Kindness for me, and he left me once more to the wide World. For the Store was shut up by his Executors, and my Employment under him ended.

Apparently Franklin worked for Denham from October 1726 until February 1727 when he fell ill with pleurisy (from which he would suffer again in 1735 and fatally in 1790), which must have lasted till sometime in March when Denham hired a new clerk and Franklin returned to Keimer. Denham died July 1728, but his oral will forgiving Franklin's debt did little to remove Franklin's burden until approved a year later.

My Brother-in-law Homes, being now at Philadelphia, advis'd my Return to my Business. And Keimer tempted me with an Offer of large Wages to come & take the Management of his Printing-House that he might better attend his Stationer's Shop. I had heard a bad Character of him in London, & was not fond of having any more to do with him. I try'd for farther Employment as a Merchant's Clerk, but not readily meeting with any, I clos'd again with Keimer.

A few years earlier, Keimer had abandoned his wife and child in London, but his publishing record wasn't as bad as Franklin's sketch implies. He introduced to America such authors as Steele and Defoe.

I found in *his* House these Hands: Hugh Meredith a Welsh-Pennsilvanian, 30 Years of Age, bred to Country Work; Stephen Potts, a young Country Man bred to the Same. These he had agreed with at extream low Wages, per Week, to be rais'd a Shilling every 3 Months. One of them was to work at Press, the other Potts at Bookbinding, which he was to teach them, tho' he knew neither one nor t'other. John—a wild Irishman brought up to no Business, whose Service for 4 Years Keimer had purchas'd from the Captain of a Ship. He too was to be made a Pressman. George Webb, an Oxford Scholar, whose Time for 4 Years he had likewise bought, intending him for a Compositor; and David Harry, a Country Boy, whom he had taken Apprentice. I soon perceiv'd that the Intention of engaging me at 80 Pounds a Year, Wages so much higher than he had been us'd to give, was to have these raw cheap Hands form'd thro' me, and as soon as I had instructed them, then, they being all articled to him, he should be able to do without me. I went on however, very chearfully; put his Printing House in Order, which had been in great Confusion, and brought his Hands by degrees to mind their Business, and to do it better.[1] John the Irishman soon ran away. With the rest I began to live very agreably; for they all respected me; the more as they found Keimer incapable of instructing them as he had promis'd and that from me they learnt something daily. Keimer himself treated me with great Civility & apparent Regard; and nothing made me uneasy but my Debt to Vernon, which I was yet unable to pay. He however kindly made no Demand on me.

Our Printing-House often wanted Sorts, and there was no Letter Founder in America. I had seen Types cast at James's in London, but without much Attention to the Manner. But I now contriv'd a Mould, made use of the Letters we had, as Puncheons, struck the Matrices in Lead, and this supply'd in a pretty tolerable way all Deficiencies.

I also engrav'd several Things on occasion; I made [Keimer's] Ink and was quite a Factotum. But however serviceable I might be, I found that my Services became every Day of less Importance, as the other Hands improv'd in the Business. And when Keimer paid my second Quarter's Wages, he let me know that he felt them too heavy, and that he thought I should make an Abatement. He grew by degrees less civil, put on more of the Master, frequently found Fault, was captious and seem'd ready for an Outbreaking. I went on however with a good deal of Patience, thinking that his incumber'd Circumstances were partly the Cause. At length on the Day of the County Election, a great Noise happening at the Courthouse, I put my Head out of the Window to see what was the Matter. Keimer being in the Street look'd up & saw me, call'd out to me in a loud and angry Tone to mind my Business, adding some reproachful Words, that nettled me the more for their Publicity, all the Neighbours who were out at their Doors looking out on the same Occasion being Witnesses how I was treated. He came up immediately into the Printing-House, continu'd the Quarrel, high Words pass'd on both Sides, he gave me the Quarter's Warning we had stipulated, I told him it was unnecessary for I would leave him that Instant; and so taking my Hat walk'd out of Doors; desiring Meredith whom I saw below to take care of some Things I left, & bring them to my Lodging.

> The noise that brought Franklin to the street on the rainy
> Monday (2 October) of the county elections probably
> came from followers of Sir William Keith, whose machine
> still controlled Philadelphia politics. The ensuing break
> with Keimer lasted only a couple of weeks thanks to the
> need for printing New Jersey bills with cuts only Franklin
> could make.

Meredith came accordingly in the Evening, when we talk'd my Affair over. He had conceiv'd a great Regard for me, & was very unwilling that I should leave the House while he remain'd in it. He dissuaded me from returning to my native Country which I began to think of. He reminded me that Keimer was in debt for all he possess'd, that his Creditors began to be uneasy, that he kept his Shop miserably, sold often without Profit for ready Money, and often trusted without Accounts. That he must therefore fail; and that would make a Vacancy I might profit of. I objected my Want of Money. He then let me know, that his Father had a high Opinion of me, and from some Discourse that had pass'd between them, he was sure would advance Money to set us up, if I would enter into Partnership with him. My Time, says he, will be out with Keimer in the Spring. By that time we may have our Types in from London: Your Skill in the Business shall be set against the Money I furnish; and we will share the Profits equally. The Proposal was agreable, and I consented. His Father was in Town, and approv'd of it, the more as he saw I had great Influence with his Son, had prevail'd on him to abstain long from Spirituous Liquors, and he hop'd might break him of that wretched Habit entirely, when we came to be so closely connected. I gave an Inventory to the Father, who apply'd to a Merchant; the Things were sent for; the Secret was to be kept till they should arrive, and in the mean time I was to get work if I could at the other Printing House. But I found no Vacancy there, and so remain'd idle a few Days, when Keimer, on a Prospect of being employ'd to print the Paper-money in New Jersey, which as it would need Cuts & various Types that I only could supply, and apprehending Bradford might engage me & get the Work from him, sent me the civillest Message, that we should not part for a few Words that were the Effect of sudden Passion, and wishing me to return. Meredith persuaded me to comply, as it gave more Opportunity for his Improvement under my daily Instructions. So I return'd, and we went on more smoothly than for some time before.

The New Jersey Jobb was obtained. I contriv'd a Copper-Plate Press for it, the first that had been seen in the Country. I cut several Ornaments and Checks for the Bills. We went together to Burlington, where I executed the Whole to Satisfaction, & he received so large a Sum for the Work that he was enabled thereby to keep his Head much longer above Water.

At Burlington I made an Acquaintance with most of the principal People of the Province. They had been appointed by the Assembly a Committee to attend the Press, and take Care that no more were printed than the Law directed. One or other of them was therefore constantly with us, and generally he who attended brought with him a

Friend or two for Company. My Mind having been much more improv'd by Reading than Keimer's, I suppose it was for that Reason my Conversation seem'd to be more valu'd. They had me to their Houses, and show'd me much Civility, while he, tho' the Master, seem'd to be neglected. In truth he was an odd Fish, ignorant of common Life, slovenly and a little Knavish withal. We continu'd there near 3 Months, and by that time I could reckon among my acquired Friends, Judge Allen, Samuel Bustill, the Secretary of the Province, Isaac Pearson, & several of the Smiths, Members of Assembly, and Isaac Decow the Surveyor General. The latter was a shrewd sensible old Man, who told me that he began for himself when a young Man by wheeling Clay for the Brickmakers, learnt to write and to survey after he was of Age, and had now by his Industry acquir'd a good Estate; and says he, I foresee, that you will turn this Man out of his Business & make a Fortune at Philadelphia. He had not then the least Intimation of my Intention to set up there at Philadelphia, there or any where. These Friends were afterwards of great Use to me, as I occasionally was to some of them. They all continued their Regard for me as long as they lived.[2]

[In the autumn I] form'd most of my ingenious Acquaintance into a Club, which we call'd the Junto. We met every Friday Evening. The Rules I drew up, requir'd that every Member in his Turn should produce one or more Queries on any Point of Morals, Politics or Natural Philosophy, to be discuss'd by the Company, and that every once in three Months produce and read an Essay of his own Writing on any Subject he pleas'd. Our Debates were to be under the Direction of a President, and to be conducted in the sincere Spirit of Enquiry after Truth, without fondness for Dispute, or Desire of Victory; and all Expressions of Positiveness in Opinion, or of direct Contradiction, were contraband & prohibited under pecuniary Penalties. The Members were, Joseph Brientnal, a Copyer of Deeds for the Scriveners, a good-natur'd friendly middleag'd Man, a great Lover of Poetry, reading all he could meet with, & writing some that was tolerable; very ingenious in many little Nicknackeries, & of sensible Conversation. He was much my Favourite. Thomas Godfrey, a self-taught Mathematician, great in his Way, & afterwards Inventor of what is now call'd Hadley's Quadrant. Nicholas Scull, a Surveyor, afterwards Surveyor-General, who lov'd Books, & sometimes made a few Verses. William Parsons, bred a Shoemaker, but loving Reading, had acquir'd a considerable Share of Mathematics, which he first studied with a View to Astrology that he afterwards laught at. He also became afterwards Surveyor-General. Hugh Meredith, Stephen Potts, & George Webb, I have Characteris'd before. Robert Grace, a young Gentleman of some Fortune, lively & witty, a Lover of Punning and of his Friends. And William Coleman, then a Merchant's Clerk, about my Age, who had the coolest, clearest Head, the best Heart, and the exactest Morals, of almost any Man I ever met with. He became afterwards a Merchant of great Note, and one of the Provincial Judges. Our Friendship continued without interruption to his Death, upwards of 40 Years. And the Club continu'd almost as long.[3]

Before I enter upon my Appearance in Business for my self, it may be well to let you know the then State of my Mind, with regard to my Principles and Morals, that you may see how far they influenc'd the future Events of my Life. My Parents had early given me religious Impressions, and brought me through my Childhood piously in the Dissenting Way. But I was scarce 15 when, after doubting by turns of several Points as I found them disputed in the different Books I read, I began to doubt of Revelation, & in a little Time Some Books against Deism fell into my hands; they were the Substance of Sermons preached at Boyle's Lectures. It happened that they wrought an Effect on me quite contrary to what was intended by them: For the Arguments of the Deists which were quoted to be refuted, appeared to me much stronger than the Refutations. In short I soon became a thorough Deist. My Arguments perverted some others, particularly Collins & Ralph: but each of them having afterwards wrong'd me without Compunction, *and recollecting Keith's Conduct towards me, (who was another Freethinker) and my own towards Vernon and Miss Read which at Times gave me great Trouble,* I began to suspect that this Doctrine tho' it might be true, was not very useful.

My London Pamphlet, which had for its Motto these Lines of [Pope and] Dryden

"Whatever is, is right—
Tho' purblind Man
Sees but a Part of the Chain, the nearest Link,
His Eyes not carrying to the equal Beam
That poizes all above,"

And from the Attributes of God, his Wisdom, his Goodness & Power concluded that nothing could possibly be wrong in the World, & that Vice & Virtue were empty Distinctions, no such Things existing, appear'd now not so clever a Performance as I once thought it; and I doubted whether some unperceiv'd Error had not insinuated itself unperceiv'd *into my Argument so as to infect all that follow'd, in the Train of my Reasoning, as is common in metaphysical Reasonings.*

I grew convinc'd that *Truth, Sincerity & Integrity* in

Dealings between Man & Man, were of the utmost Importance to the Felicity of Life, and I form'd written Resolutions (which still remain in my Journal Book) to practise them ever while I lived. Reveal'd Religion had indeed no weight with me as a Revelation but I entertain'd an Opinion, that tho' certain Actions might not be bad *because* they were forbidden by it, or good *because* it commanded them; yet probably these Actions might be forbidden *because* they were bad for us, or commanded *because* they were beneficial to us, in their own Natures, all the Circumstances of things considered. And this Persuasion, with the kind hand of Providence, or some guardian Angel, or favourable Circumstances & Situations, or all together, preserved me thro' this dangerous Time of Youth & the hazardous Situations I was sometimes in among Strangers, remote from the Eye of my Father, without any *wilful* gross Immorality that might have been expected from my Want of Religion, some foolish Intrigues with low Women excepted, which from the Expence were rather more prejudicial to me than to them. *I say "wilful," because the Instances I have mentioned, had something of Necessity in them, from my Youth, Inexperience, & the Knavery of others.* I had therefore a tolerable Character to begin the World with, I valued it properly, & determin'd to preserve it.[4]

10

VENTURING INTO BUSINESS

MAY 1728–SEPTEMBER 1730

When Franklin ventured into business in May 1728, Philadelphia was emerging from a severe depression. Citizens bartered to pay debts, interest rates fell from 8 to 6 per cent, and paper currency was devalued so that 100 pounds of sterling that had cost in Pennsylvania money 133 pounds now cost 150 pounds.[1]

We had not been long return'd to Philadelphia, before the Printing-House arriv'd from London. I found a House to hire near the Market, and took it. To lessen the Rent (which was then about 24£ a Year tho' I have since known it let for 70), I took in Thomas Godfrey & his Family, who were to pay a considerable Part of it to me, and we to board with them. We settled with Keimer & left him by his Consent. We had scarce opened our Letters & put our Press in Order, before George House, an Acquaintance of mine, brought a Countryman to us; whom he had met in the Street enquiring for a Printer. All our Cash was now expended in the Variety of Particulars we had been obliged to procure, & this Countryman's Five Shillings, being our First Fruits & coming so seasonably, gave me more Pleasure than any Crown I have since earn'd; and has made me often more ready than perhaps I should otherwise have been to assist young Beginners.[2]

Every one [of the Junto] exerted themselves in recommending Business to us. Brientnal particularly procur'd us from the Quakers, the Printing 40 Sheets of their History, the rest being to be done by Keimer: and upon this we work'd exceeding hard, for the Price was low. It was a Folio, Pro Patria Size, in Pica with Long Primer Notes. I compos'd of it a Sheet a Day, and Meredith work'd it off at Press. It was often 11 at Night before I had finish'd my Distribution [of type] for the next days Work. For the little Jobbs sent in by our other Friends sometimes put us back. But so determin'd I was to continue doing a Sheet a Day of the Folio, that one Night when I thought my Days Work over, had impos'd my Forms, one of them by accident was broken and two Pages reduc'd to Pie, I immediately distributed & compos'd it over again before I went to bed.[3]

> Composing a sheet of four pages meant averaging about 675 words per 30.5–centimeter page, about 20 per cent faster than the normal rate. For the edition of 500 copies, Franklin and Meredith completed the final 178 pages plus the index and title page in October 1728.[4]

And this Industry began to give us Character and Credit; particularly I was told, that mention being made of the new Printing Office at the Merchants every-night-Club, the general Opinion was that it must fail, there being already two Printers in the Place, Keimer & Bradford; but Doctor [Patrick] Baird . . . gave a contrary Opinion; the Industry of that Franklin, says he is superior to any thing I ever saw of the kind: I see him still at work when I go home from Club; and he is at Work again before his Neighbours are out of bed. This struck the rest, and we soon after had Offers from one of them to supply us with Stationary.

I mention this Industry the more freely, tho' it seems to be talking in my own Praise, that those of my Posterity who shall read it, may see the Use of that Virtue, when they see its Effects in my Favour throughout this Relation.

George Webb was lucky enough to be taken care of by a Female Friend that lent him wherewith to purchase his Time of Keimer, now came to offer himself as a Journeyman to us. We could not then imploy him, but I let him know that I soon intended to begin a Newspaper, & might then have Work for him. I requested him not to mention it, but he told it immediately to Keimer, who immediately to be beforehand with me, published Proposals for Printing one himself, of which Webb was to be employd. I resented this, and to counteract them, as I could not yet begin my Paper, I wrote several Papers for Bradford's Paper which Brientnal continu'd some time.[5]

> Keimer's newspaper, *Universal Instructor in All Arts &*
> *Sciences: and Pennsylvania Gazette*, appeared in December
> 1728, but the "Busy-Body" essays did not appear in
> Bradford's *American Weekly Mercury* until the following
> February. Franklin composed the first four and parts of
> the fifth and eighth of the weekly series running until
> September 1729 when Franklin bought Keimer's paper,
> shortening the title to *Pennsylvania Gazette*.

Keimer's Proposals were disregarded. He began his Paper however, and after carrying it on three Quarters of a Year, with at most only 90 subscribers, he offer'd it to me for a Trifle, & I being then ready took it in hand directly.

I perceive that I am apt to speak in the singular Number though our Partnership still continu'd. The Reason may be, that in fact the whole Management of the Business lay upon me. Meredith was no Compostor, a poor Pressman,

& seldom sober. My Friends lamented my Connection with him, but I was to make the best of it.

> Meredith's name paired with Franklin's until 1732;
> Franklin's stood alone until 1748 when joined by David
> Hall's name. "It gradually became the most widely read
> newspaper in the colonies" [Lemay, Chronology].
> Franklin's paper was off to a good start with a column on
> the Massachusetts legislature objecting to paying their
> governor's salary, an issue of interest to Pennsylvanians.

Our first Papers made a quite different Appearance from any before in the Province, better Type & better printed; but some spirited Remarks of my Writing on the Dispute then going on between Governor Burnet and the Massachusetts Assembly [9 October], struck the principal People, occasion'd the Paper & the Manager of it to be much talk'd of, & in a few Weeks brought them all to be Subscribers. Their Example was follow'd by many, and our Number went on growing continually. This was one of the first good Effects of my having learnt to scribble. Another was, that the leading Men, seeing a News Paper now in the hands of one who could also handle a Pen, thought it convenient to oblige & encourage me. Bradford still printed the Votes & Laws & other Business. He had printed an Address of the House to the Governor [29 March 1729] in a coarse blundering manner: We reprinted it elegantly & correctly, and sent one to every Member. They were sensible of the Difference, *it strengthen'd the Hands of our Friends in the House,* and they voted us their Printer for the Year ensuing [the following January].

Among my Friends in the House I must not forget Mr Hamilton before mentioned, who was now returned from England & had a Seat in it. He interested himself for me strongly in that Instance, as he did in many others afterwards, continuing his Friendship & Patronage to his Death [1741]. I too was at times of some small Service to him; and after his Death in grateful remembrance of his Friendship *I got his Son once 500£.*

Mr Vernon about this time put me in mind of the Debt I ow'd him; but did not press me. I wrote him an ingenuous Letter of Acknowledgments, crav'd his Forbearance a little longer which he allow'd me, & as soon as I was able I paid the Principal with Interest & many Thanks. *So that Erratum was in some degree corrected.*

But now another Difficulty came upon me, which I had never the least Reason to expect. Mr Meredith's Father, who was to have paid for our Printing House according to the Expectations given me, was able to advance only one Hundred Pounds, which had been paid, & a Hundred more was due to the Merchant; who grew impatient & su'd us all. We gave Bail, but saw that if the Money could not be rais'd in time, the Suit must come to a Judgment & Execution, & our hopeful Prospects must be ruined, & the Press & Letters sold for Payment, perhaps at half Price. In this Distress two true Friends whose Kindness I have never forgotten nor ever shall forget while I can remember any thing, came to me separately unknown to each other, and without any Application from me, offering each of them to advance me all that should be necessary to take the whole Business upon my self if that should be practicable, but they did not like my continuing the Partnership with Meredith, who was often seen drunk in the Streets, & playing at low Games in the Alehouses, much to our Discredit. These two Friends were *William Coleman & Robert Grace.* I told them I could not propose such a thing while any Prospect remain'd of the Merediths fulfilling Part of our Agreement. *Because I thought my self under great Obligations to them for what they had done & would do if they could.* But if they finally fail'd in their Performance, I should then think my self at Liberty to accept the Assistance of my Friends. Thus the matter rested for some time. When I said to my Partner, perhaps your Father is dissatisfied at the Part you have undertaken in this Affair of ours, and is unwilling to advance for you & me what he would for you alone: If that is the Case, tell me, and I will resign the whole to you & go about my Business. No, says he, my Father has been disappointed and is really unable; and I am unwilling to distress him farther. I see this is a Business I am not fit for. I was bred a Farmer, and it was a Folly in me to come to Town & put my self at 30 Years of Age an Apprentice to learn a new Trade. Many of our Welsh People are going to settle in North Carolina where Land is cheap: I am inclin'd to go with them, & follow my old Employment. *You may find Friends to assist you* . . . If you will take the Debts of the Company upon you, return to my Father the hundred Pound he has advanc'd, pay my little personal Debts, and give me Thirty Pounds & a new Saddle, I will relinquish the Partnership & put the whole into your Hands. I agreed to this Proposal. It was drawn up in Writing, sign'd & seal'd immediately. I gave him what he demanded & he went soon after to Carolina; from whence he sent me next Year two long Letters, containing the best Account that had been given of that Country, the Climate, Soil, Husbandry, &c. for in those Matters he was very judicious. I printed them in the Papers, and they gave grate Satisfaction to the Publick.

As soon as he was gone, I recurr'd to my two kind Friends; and because I would not give an unkind Preference to either, I took half what I wanted of one, & half of the other, paid off the Company Debts, and went on with the Business alone in my own Name, advertising that the Partnership was dissolved. I think this was in or about the year 1729.[6]

11

ENTERING BUSINESS
FOR HIMSELF

1729–1730

Once again, Franklin seized an opportunity to write about an immediate controversy, this time involving a bill passed by the legislature to reissue paper currency. Arguing for the legislature's position, his pamphlet, dated 3 April 1729, attracted favorable attention in circles of Pennsylvania political power, a great boost for a 24–year-old printer about to enter business for himself.

About this time there was a Cry for more Paper-Money, there being but 15,000£ extant in the Province & that soon to be sunk. The wealthy Inhabitants oppos'd any Addition, fearing it would depreciate as it had done in New England to the Prejudice of all Creditors. We had discuss'd this Point in our Junto, where I was on the Side of an Addition, being persuaded that the first small Sum struck in 1723 had done much good, by increasing the Trade & Number of Inhabitants in the Province, since I now saw all the Houses inhabited, & many new ones building, where as I remember'd well that when I first walk'd about the Streets of Philadelphia, eating my Roll, I saw most of the Houses *in Walnut*

Street between Second & Front streets, with Bills on their Doors, to be let; and many in Chestnut Street, & other Streets; which made me think the Inhabitants of the City were deserting it one after another. Our Debates possess'd me so fully of the Subject, that I wrote and printed an anonymous Pamphlet on it, entituled, *The Nature & Necessity of a Paper Currency*. It was well receiv'd by the People in general but the Rich Men dislik'd it; for it increas'd and strengthen'd the Clamour for more Money; and they happening to have no Writers among them that were able to answer it, their Opposition slacken'd, & the Point was carried by a Majority in the House. My Friends there, who thought I had been of some Service, thought fit to reward me, by employing me in printing the Money, a very profitable Jobb, and a great Help to me.

> Bradford printed the 1729 currency, but Franklin and Meredith were awarded the reissue in 1731.

This was another Advantage gain'd by my being able to write.

The Utility of this Currency grew by Time and Experience so evident, as never afterwards to be much disputed, so that it grew soon to 55000£ and in 1739 to 80000£ since which it arose during War to upwards of 350,000£. Trade, Building & Inhabitants all the while increasing. Tho' I now think there are Limits beyond which the Quantity may be hurtful.

I soon after obtain'd, thro' my Friend Hamilton, the Printing of the New-Castle Paper Money, another profitable Jobb, as I then thought it; and small Gains appearing great to those in small Circumstances. And these to me were really great Advantages, as they were great Encouragements. He procured me also the Printing

From 1729 through 1735, Andrew Hamilton served as
speaker in both the Pennsylvania and Lower Counties
assemblies.

of the New Laws and Votes of that Government which
continu'd in my Hands as long as I follow'd the Business.

I now open'd a little Stationer's Shop. I had in it Blanks
of all Sorts the correctest that had ever appear'd among us,
being assisted in that by my Friend Brientnal; Paper, Parch-
ment, Chapmen's Books, &c. One Whitemarsh a Compositor I had known in London, an excellent Workman now
came to me & work'd with me constantly & diligently, and
I began gradually to pay off the Debts I was under for the
Printing-House. In order to secure my Credit and Character

The advertisement in his newspaper (2 October) listed,
"Accompt-Books, Bills of Lading bound and unbound,
Common Blank Bonds for Money, Bonds with Judgment,
Counterbonds ... Powers of Attorney, Writs, Summons,
Apprentice Indentures, Promissory Notes, etc."

[i.e., Reputation] as a Tradesman, I took care not only to
be in *Reality* Industrious & frugal, but to avoid all *Appear-
ances* to the Contrary. I drest plainly; I was seen at no Places
of idle Diversion; I never went out afishing or Shooting; a
Book, indeed, sometimes debauch'd me from from my
Work; but that was snug & gave no Scandal: and to show
that I was not above my Business, I sometimes brought
home the Paper I purchas'd at the Stores, thro' the Streets
on a Wheelbarrow. Thus being esteem'd an industrious
thriving young Man, the Merchants who imported Stationary solicited my Custom, others propos'd supplying me with
Books, & we went on swimmingly.

In the mean time Keimer's Credit & Business declining

daily, he was at last forc'd to sell his Printing-house to sat-isfy his Creditors. He went to Barbadoes, & there lived some Years, *in very poor Circumstances.*

His Apprentice David Harry, whom I had instructed while I work'd with him, set up in his Place having bought his Materials. I was at first apprehensive of a powerful Ri-val in him, as his Friends were very able, & had a good deal of Interest. I therefore propos'd a Partnership to him, which he, fortunately for me, rejected with Scorn. He was very proud, dress'd like a Gentleman, liv'd expensively, took much Diversion & Pleasure abroad, & neglected his Busi-ness, upon which all Business left him; and finding noth-ing to do, he follow'd Keimer to Barbadoes; *taking the Printing-house with him.* There this Apprentice employ'd his former Master as a Journeyman. They quarrel'd often. Harry went continually behind-hand, and at length was forc'd to sell his Types *and return to his Country Work in Pensilvania.* The person that bought them, employ'd Keimer to use them, and there he continu'd but in a few Years he died.[1]

> Keimer's *Barbadoes Gazette* in 1731–38 was the first newspaper in America to regularly appear twice a week. Franklin tried to print the *Pennsylvania Gazette* twice a week in October-December 1729 but failed.

There remain'd then no Competitor with me at Phila-delphia but the old one, Bradford, who was rich & easy, did a little now & then by straggling Hands, but was not very anxious about the Business. However, as he kept the Post Office his Paper was thought a better Distributor of Adver-tisements than mine, & therefore had many more, which was a profitable thing to him & a Disadvantage to me. For tho' I did indeed send Papers by the Post, yet the publick Opinion was otherwise; and what I did send was by Bribing the Riders who took them privately: Bradford being unkind enough to forbid them: which occasion'd some Resentment on my Part; and I thought so meanly of him for it, that when I afterwards came into his Situation, I took care never to imitate it.

I had hitherto continu'd to board with Godfrey who took Part of the House with his Wife & Children, & had one Side of the Shop for his Glazier's Business; tho' he work'd little, being always absorb'd in his Mathematics. Mrs Godfrey projected a Match for me with a Relation's Daughter, took Opportunities of bringing us often together, till a Courtship on my Part ensu'd. The old Folks encourag'd me by continual Invitations to Supper, & leaving us together, till at length it was time to explain. Mrs Godfrey manag'd the Treaty. I let her know that I expected as much Money with their Daughter as would pay off the Remaining Debt for the Printing-house, which I believe was not then above a Hundred Pounds. She brought me Word they had no such Sum to spare. Then says I they may mortgage their House in the Loan Office. The Answer to this after some Days was that they did not approve the Match; that on Enquiry of Bradford they had been inform'd the Business was not a profitable one, the Types would soon be worn out & more wanted, that Keimer & D. Harry had fail'd one after the other, and I should probably soon follow them; and therefore I was forbidden the House, & the Daughter shut up. Whether this was real or only Artifice, on a Supposition of our being too far engag'd in Affection to retract, & therefore that we should steal a Marriage, which would leave them at Liberty to give or withold what they pleas'd, I know not: But I suspected the latter, & resented it, and went no more. Mrs Godfrey brought me afterwards some more favourable Accounts of their Disposition; & would have drawn me on again: But I declar'd absolutely my Resolution to have nothing more to do with that Family. This was resented by Godfrey, we differ'd, and they removed, leaving me the whole House, and I resolved to take no more Inmates. But this Affair having turn'd my Thoughts to Marriage, I made Overtures in other places, tho' without Success, and I found that the Business of a Printer being generally thought a poor one, I was not to expect Money with a Wife unless with such a one, as I should not otherwise think agreable. In the mean time, that hard-to-be-govern'd Passion of Youth, hurried me frequently into Intrigues with such low Women as fell in my Way, which were attended with some Expence & Inconvenience, besides a continual Risque to my Health by a Distemper which of all Things I dreaded, tho' by great good Luck I escaped it.

A friendly Correspondence as Neighbours & old Acquaintances, had continued between me & Mrs Read's Family. Her youngest Daughter had married my Friend Watson (early mentioned in this Account) and had some Regard for me on his Account.

. . . I was often invited there and consulted in their Affairs, wherein I sometimes was of Service. I pity'd poor Miss Read's unfortunate Situation, *who was generally dejected, seldom chearful, and avoided Company* I consider'd my Inconsiderateness when in London as in a great degree the Cause of it; tho' the Mother was good enough to think the Fault more hers than mine, as she had prevented our Marrying before I went thither, and persuaded the other Match in my Absence *on receiving my foolish Letter. Our mutual Affection was revived, but* there were now great Objections to our Union. That Match was indeed look'd upon as invalid as another preceding Wife was said to be living in

England; but could not easily be prov'd, because of the Distance. And tho' there was a Report of his Death, it was not certain. Then, he had left many Debts which his Successor might be call'd to pay. But we ventur'd over all these Difficulties, and I took her to Wife Sept. 1, 1730. None of the

> She had wed John Rogers, a potter, 5 August 1725 but apparently left him before Franklin's return from London. Rogers ran off with a fugitive slave in December 1727, so his whereabouts remained unknown. If Rogers had died and they married, Franklin would be responsible for his debts; if he lived, they would be guilty of bigamy and subject to thirty-nine lashes and hard labor.

Inconveniencies happened that we had apprehended, she prov'd a good Wife, help'd me much by attending the Shop, we throve together and have ever mutually endeavour'd to make each other happy. *Thus I corrected that great Erratum as well as I could.*[2]

We have an English Proverb that says,

> He that would thrive
> Must ask his Wife;

It was lucky for me that I had one as much dispos'd to Industry & Frugality as my self. She assisted me chearfully in my Business, folding and stitching Pamphlets, tending Shop, purchasing Linen for the Paper-makers, &c &c. We kept no idle Servants, our Table was plain & simple, our Furniture of the cheapest. For instance my Breakfast was a long time Bread & Milk (no Tea), and I ate it out of a twopenny earthen Porringer with a Pewter Spoon. But mark how Luxury will enter *Families* and make a Progress, in spite of Principle. Call'd one Morning to Breakfast, I found it in a China Bowl with a Spoon of Silver. They had been bought for me without my Knowledge by my Wife, and had cost her the enormous Sum of three-and-twenty Shillings, for which she had no other Excuse or Apology to make, but that she thought *her* Husband deserv'd a Silver Spoon & China Bowl as well as any of his Neighbours. This was the first Appearance of Plate & China in our House, which afterwards in a Course of Years as our Wealth encreas'd, amounted gradually to several Hundred Pounds in Value.[3]

12

FINDING FELICITY
IN PHILADELPHIA

1731–1732

With new wife and small son born of an earlier affair with
an unnamed woman whom he would continue to support,
Franklin's life assumed a productive routine of printing for
the government, publishing the *Pennsylvania Gazette*, and
meeting with Junto on Friday nights, Masons on first
Mondays, and members of a new Library Company on
second Mondays. By the end of 1731 he could install
Thomas Whitmarsh in a South Carolina partnership, the
first of many eventually extending along the Atlantic
seaboard, an early version of the system now known as
"vertical integration." By the close of 1732, the Franklins
had added baby Francis to the household and *Poor
Richard's Almanac* to the stock-in-trade.

At the time I establish'd my self in Pensylvania, there
was not a good Bookseller's Shop to the Southward of Boston. In New-York & Philadelphia the Printers were indeed
Stationers, they sold Paper, &c. Almanacks, and Ballads, and
a few common School Books. Those who lov'd Reading
were oblig'd to send for their Books to England. The Mem-

bers of the Junto had each a few. We had left the Tavern where we first met, and hired a Room to hold our Club in. I propos'd that we should all of us bring our Books to that Room, where they could not only be ready to consult in our Conferences, but become a common Benefit, each of us being at Liberty to borrow such as he wish'd to read at home. This was accordingly done, and for some time contented us. Finding the Advantage of this Little Collection, I propos'd to render the Benefit from Books more common by commencing a Public Library.[1] ... I set on foot my first Project of a public Nature, that for a Subscription Library. I drew up the Proposals, got them put into Form by our great Scrivener Brockden, and *by the help of my Friends in the Junto,* procur'd Fifty Subscribers of 40 shillings each to begin with & 10 shillings a Year for 50 Years, the Term our Company was to continue. This Agreement was afterwards abolish'd when we obtain'd a Charter, the Company being increas'd to 100. *This was the Mother of all the N. American Subscription Libraries now so numerous.* It is become a great thing itself & continually increasing. These Libraries have improv'd the general Conversation of the Americans; made the common Tradesmen & Farmers as intelligent as most Gentlemen from other Countries; and contributed to the Stand so generally made in the Colonies in Defence of their Privileges.[2] ... Reading became fashionable, and our People having no publick Amusements became better acquainted with Books, and in a few Years were observ'd to be better instructed & more intelligent than People of the same Rank generally are in most other Countries.

When we were about to sign the above-mentioned Articles, which were to be binding on us, our Heirs, &c for fifty Years, Mr. Brockden, the Scrivener, said to us, "You are young Men, but it is scarce possible that any of you will live

to see the Expiration of the Term fix'd in this Instrument."
A Number of us, however, are yet living: But the Instrument was after a few Years rendered null by a Charter that gave Perpetuity to the Company.

The Difficulties, Objections, & Reluctances I met with in Soliciting the Subscriptions, made me feel the Impropriety of presenting one's self as the Proposer of any useful Project that might raise one's Reputation in the smallest degree above that of one's Neighbours, when one has need of Assistance to accomplish that Project. I therefore put my self as much as I could out of sight, and propos'd it as a Scheme of a Number of Friends, who had requested me to go about and propose it to such as they thought were Lovers of Reading. In this way my Affair went on more smoothly, and I ever after practis'd it on fresh Occasions; and from my Successes, can recommend it. The present Sacrifice of your Vanity will afterwards be amply repaid. If it remains a while uncertain to whom the Merit belongs, some one more vain than yourself will be encourag'd to claim it, and then even Envy will be dispos'd to do you Justice, by plucking those assum'd Feathers & restoring them to their right Owner.

This Library afforded me the Means of Improvement by constant Study, for which I set apart an Hour or two each Day; and *thus repair'd in some Degree the Loss of the Learned Education my Father once intended for me.* Reading was my only Amusement I allow'd my self. I spent no time in Taverns, or Frolicks of any kind. And my Industry in my Business continu'd indefatigable as it was necessary. I had a young Family coming on to be educated, and I had two Printers who were establish'd in the Place before me to contend with for Business. My Circumstances however grew daily easier, my original Frugality continuing. My Father had among his Instructions to me when a Boy, frequently repeated to me a Proverb of Solomon, "Seest thou a Man diligent in his Calling, he shall stand before Kings, he shall not stand before mean Men." I from thence consider'd Industry as a Means of obtaining Wealth and Distinction, which encourag'd me, tho' I did not think that I should ever literally stand before Kings which however has since happen'd....

> He stood before both George II and George III of England as well as Louis XV and Louis XVI of France, besides sitting to dinner with Christian XVI of Denmark in 1768.

I had been religiously educated as a Presbyterian; but some of the Dogmas of that Persuasion, such as the Eternal Decrees of God, Election, Reprobation, &c. appearing to me unintelligible, I early absented myself from the Public Assemblies of the Sect, *Sunday being my Studying Day.*

I never was without Principles; I never doubted, for instance, the Existence of the Deity, that he made the World, & govern'd it by his Providence; that the Service of God most acceptable to him was the doing Good to Man; that our Souls are immortal; and that all Crimes will be punished & Virtue rewarded either here or hereafter; these I esteem'd the Essentials of every Religion, and being to be found in all, I respected all, tho' with different degrees of Respect as I found them more or less mix'd with other Articles which without any Tendency to inspire, promote or confirm our Morals, Virtue, serv'd principally to divide us & make us unfriendly to one another. This Respect, with an Opinion that the worst was better than none had some good Effects, induc'd me to avoid all Conversation that might tend to lessen the good Opinion another might have for his own Religion; and as our Province increas'd in People and new

Places of worship were continually created and generally erected by Contribution, my Mite for that purpose, whatever might be the Sect, was never refused.[3]

> By 1748, Swedish traveller Peter Kalm found a dozen churches, including two Quaker meeting houses as well as others, churches of the Anglican, Lutheran, Swedish, Old and New Presbyterians, Calvinist, Anabaptist, Moravian, and Roman Catholic faiths.[4]

Tho' I seldom attended any Public Worship, I had still an Opinion of its Propriety, and Utility and I regularly paid my Subscription for the Support of the Presbyterian Minister in Philadelphia. He us'd to visit me sometimes as a Friend, and admonish me to attend his Administrations, and I was now and then prevail'd on to do so, once for five Sundays successively. Had he been a good Preacher perhaps I might have continued, notwithstanding the occasion I had for the Sunday's Leisure in my Course of Study: But his Discourses were chiefly either on polemic Points, or Explications of the peculiar Doctrines of our Sect, all to me very very dry, uninteresting and unedifying, since not a single moral Principle was inculcated or enforc'd, and their Aim seeming to be rather to make us Presbyterians than good Citizens. At length he took for his Text that Verse of the 4th Chapter of Philippians, *Finally, Brethren, Whatsoever Things are honest, just, pure, lovely, or of good report, if there be any virtue, and if there be any praise, think on these Things;* & I imagin'd in a Sermon on such a Text, we could not miss of having some Morality: But he confin'd himself to five Points only as meant by the Apostle, viz. l. Keeping holy the Sabbath Day. 2. Being diligent in Reading the Holy Scriptures. 3. Attending duly the Publick Worship. 4. Partaking of the Sacrament. 5. Paying a due Respect to God's

Ministers. These might be all good Things, but they were not the kind of good Things that I expected from the Text. I was disgusted, and went no more.[5]

About the Year 1734 there arrived among us from Ireland a young Presbyterian Preacher named Hemphill, who delivered with a good Voice, & apparently extempore, most excellent Discourses, which drew together considerable Numbers of different Persuasions, who join'd in admiring them. Among the rest I became one of his constant Hearers, his Sermons pleasing me as they had little of the dogmatical kind, but inculcated strongly the Practice of Virtue, or what in the religious Stile is called Good Works. Those however who considered themselves as orthodox, disapprov'd his Doctrine, and were join'd by most of the old Clergy, who arraign'd him of Heterodoxy before the Synod, in order to have him silenc'd. I became his zealous Partisan, and contributed all I could to raise a Party in his Favour; and we combated for him a while with some Hopes of Success. There was much Scribbling pro & con upon the Occasion; and finding that tho' an elegant Preacher he was but a poor Writer, I lent him my Pen and wrote for him two or three Pamphlets, and one Piece in the Gazette of April [10] 1735. These Pamphlets, as is generally the Case with controversial Writings, tho' eagerly read at the time, were soon out of Vogue, and I question whether a Copy of them now exists.[6]

> Franklin's three pamphlets responded intemperately to the Synod's charges, calling his antagonists asses for institutionalizing "the hellish Fires of Furious Zeal and Party Bigotry," dividing them into three classes: First "Men of Honesty who wanted Sense; secondly the Men of Sense, who wanted Honesty; and, lastly, those who had neither Sense, nor Honesty."[7]

During the Contest an unlucky Occurrence hurt his Cause exceedingly. One of our Adversaries having heard him preach a Sermon that was much admired, thought he had somewhere read that Sermon before, or at least a part of it. On Search he found that Part quoted at length in one of the British Reviews, from a Discourse of Dr [James] Foster's. This Detection gave many of his Hearers Disgust, who accordingly abandoned his Cause, and occasion'd our more speedy Discomfiture in the Synod. I stuck by him indeed to the last, as I rather approv'd of his giving us good Sermons made by others, than bad ones of his own Manufacture; the Practice of our common Teachers. He afterwards own'd to me that none of those he preach'd were his own; adding that his Memory was such as enabled him to retain and repeat any Sermon after one Reading only. On our Defeat he left us, in search elsewhere of better Fortune, and I quitted the Congregation; never joining it after, tho' I always continu'd my Subscription for the Support of its Ministers.[8] ... I had some Years before [1728] compos'd a little Liturgy or Form of Prayer for my own private Use, entitled *Articles of Belief & Acts of Religion.* I return'd to the Use of this, and went no more to the Public Assemblies. My Conduct might be blameable, but I leave it without attempting farther to excuse it, my present purpose being to relate Facts, and not to make Apologies for them.

It was about this time that I conceiv'd the bold and difficult Project of arriving at Perfection. I wish'd to live without committing any Fault at any time; I would conquer all that either Natural Inclination, Custom, or Company might lead me into. As I knew what was right and wrong, I did not see why I might not *always* do the one and avoid the other. But I soon found I had undertaken a Task of more difficulty than I had imagined. While my *Attention was taken up* in guarding against one Fault, I was surpriz'd by another. Habit took the Advantage of Inattention. Inclination was sometimes too strong for Reason. I concluded at length, that the mere speculative Conviction that it was my Interest to be compleatly virtuous, was not sufficient to prevent my Slipping, and that the contrary Habits must be broken and good Ones acquired and established, before we can have any Dependance on a steady uniform Rectitude of Conduct. For this purpose I therefore contriv'd the following Method.

In the various Enumerations of the moral Virtues I had met with in my Reading, I found the Catalogue more or less numerous as different Writers included more or less Ideas under the same Name. Temperance, for example, was by some extended to moderate every Pleasure, Appetite, Inclination or Passion, bodily or mental, even to our Avarice & Ambition. I therefore propos'd to my self, for the sake of Clearness, to use rather more Names than fewer Ideas annex'd to each, than a few Names with more Ideas; and I included under Thirteen Names of Virtues all that at that time occurr'd to me as desirable, and annex'd to each a short Precept, which fully express'd the Extent of its Meaning.

These Virtues were

1. Temperance.

Eat not to Dullness

Drink not to elevation.

2. Silence.

Speak not but what may benefit others or your self. Avoid trifling Conversation.

3. Order.

Let all your Things have their Places.

Let each Part of your Business have its Time.

4. Resolution.
   Resolve to Perform what you ought.
   Perform without fail what you resolve.
5. Frugality.
   Make no Expence but to do good to
   others or your self: i.e. Waste nothing.
6. Industry.
   Lose No Time. — Be always employ'd in
   something useful. — Cut off all unnecessary
   Actions.
7. Sincerity.
   Use no hurtful Deceit.
   Think innocently and justly; and, if you
   speak, speak accordingly.
8. Justice.
   Wrong none, by doing Injuries or omitting
   the Benefits that are your Duty.
9. Moderation.
   Avoid Extreams. Forebear resenting Injuries
   so much as you think they deserve.
10. Cleanliness.
   Tolerate no Uncleanness in Body, Cloaths
   or Habitation.
11. Tranquility.
   Be not disturbed at Trifles. or at
   Accidents common and unavoidable.
12. Chastity.
   Rarely use Venery but for Health or
   Offspring; Never to Dulness, Weakness, or
   the Injury of your own or another's Reputation.
13. Humility.
   Imitate Jesus and Socrates.

My Intention being to acquire the *Habitude* of all these

111

Virtues, I judg'd it would be well not to distract my Attention by attempting the whole at once, but to fix it on one of them at a time, and when I should be Master of that, then to proceed to another, and so on till I had gone thro' the thirteen. And as the previous Acquisition of some might facilitate the Acquisition of certain others, I arrang'd them with that View as they stand above. *Temperance* first, as it tends to procure that Coolness & Clearness of Head, which is necessary where constant Vigilance was to be kept up against the Attraction of ancient Habits, and perpetual Temptations. This being establish'd, it would be more easy, and my Desire being to improve in Knowledge at the same time that I improv'd in Virtue, and considering that in Conversation it was obtain'd rather by the Use of the Ears than of the Tongue, & therefore wishing to break a Habit I was getting into of Prattling, Punning & Joking, which made me acceptable to trifling Company, I gave *Silence* the second Place. This, and the next, *Order*, I expected would procure me more Time for attending to my Project and my Studies; *Resolution* once become habitual, would keep me firm in my Endeavours to obtain the subsequent Virtues; *Frugality* & *Industry*, by making my Circumstances easy, producing Affluence & Independence would make more easy the Practice of *Sincerity* and *Justice*, &c &c. Conceiving then that agreeable to the Advice of Pythagoras in his Golden Verses, daily Examination would be necessary, I contrived the following Method for conducting the Examination.

I made a little Book in which I allotted a Page for each of the Virtues. I rul'd each Page with red Ink so as to have seven Columns, one for each Day of the Week, marking each Column with a Letter for the Day. I cross'd these Columns with thirteen red Lines, marking the Beginning of each Line with the first Letter of one of the Virtues, on which Line I might mark by a little black Spot every Fault I had committed respecting that Virtue, and in the Column of the Day.

I determined to give a Week's strict Attention to each of the Virtues successively. Thus in the first Week my great Guard was against every the least Act of Intemperance, leaving the other Virtues to their ordinary Chance, only marking every Evening the Faults of the Day. Thus if in the first Week I could keep my first Line marked T clear of Spots, I suppos'd the Habit of that Virtue so much strengthen'd that I might venture to extend my Attention to the next, and for the following Week keep both Lines clear of Spots. Proceeding thus to the last, I could go thro' a Course compleat in Thirteen Weeks, and four Courses in a Year. And like him who having a Garden to weed, does not attempt to eradicate all the bad Herbs at once, which would exceed his Reach and his Strength, but works on one of the Beds at a time, & having accomplish'd the first proceeds to a second; so I should have, (I hoped) the Pleasure of seeing on my Pages the Progress I made in Virtue, by clearing successively my Lines of their Spots, till in the End by a Number of Courses, I should be happy in viewing a clean Book after a thirteen Weeks daily Examination.

This little book had for its Motto these Lines of Addison's *Cato*:

Here will I hold: If there is a Pow'r above us
(And that there is, all Nature cries aloud
Thro' all her Works) he must delight in Virtue,
And that which he delights in must be happy.

Another from Cicero:
O Vitae Philosophia Dux! O Virtutum indagatrix,

*expultrixque vitiorum! Unus dies bene, & ex preceptis
tuis actus, peccanti immortalitati est anteponendus.*

Another from the Proverbs of Solomon speaking of Wisdom or Virtue:

> Length of Days is in her right hand, and in her Left
> Hand Riches and Honours; All her Ways are Ways of
> Pleasantness, and all her Paths are Peace. III, 16, 17.

And conceiving God to be the Fountain of Wisdom, I
thought it right and necessary to solicit his Assistance for
obtaining it; to this End I form'd the following little Prayer,
which was prefix'd to my Table of Examination; viz.

> *O Powerful Goodness! bountiful Father! merciful
> Guide! Increase in me that Wisdom which discovers my
> truest Interests; Strengthen my Resolutions to perform
> what that Wisdom dictates. Accept my kind Offices to
> thy other Children, as the only Return in my Power for
> thy continual Favours to me.*

I us'd also sometimes a little Prayer which I took from
Thomson's Poems, viz.

> *Father of Light and Life, thou Good Supreme,*
> O teach me what is good, teach me thy self!
> Save me from Folly, Vanity and Vice
> From every low Pursuit, and fill my Soul
> *With Knowledge, conscious Peace, & Virtue pure,*
> Sacred, substantial, never fading Bliss!

The Precept of *Order* requiring that every Part of my
Business should have its allotted Time, one Page in my little
Book contain'd the following Scheme of Employment for
the Twenty-four Hours of a natural Day.

I enter'd upon this Plan for Self Examination, and
continu'd it *with occasional Intermissions* for some time. I

was surpriz'd to find myself so much fuller of Faults than I had *imagined, but I* had the Satisfaction of seeing them diminish. To avoid the Trouble of renewing now & then my little Book, which by scraping out the Marks of old Faults to make room for new Ones in a new Course, became full of Holes: I transferr'd my Tables to the old Ivory Leaves of a Memorandum Book, on which the Lines were drawn with red Ink that made a durable Stain, and I mark'd my Faults on those with a black Lead Pencil, which Marks I could easily wipe out with a wet Sponge. After a while I went thro' one Course only in a Year, and afterwards only one in several Years; till at length I omitted them entirely, but always carried my little Book with me. My Scheme of *Order*, gave me the most Trouble, and I found, that tho' it might be practicable where a Man's Business was such as to leave him Master of the Disposition of his Time, that of a Journeyman Printer for instance, it was not possible to be observ'd by a Master, who must mix with the World, and receive People of Business at their own Hours. *Order* too, with regard to Places for Things, Papers, &c. I found extreamly difficult to acquire. I had not been early accustomed to *Method*, & having an exceeding good Memory, I was not so sensible of the Inconvenience of Want of Method. This Article therefore cost me so much painful Attention & vex'd me so much, and I made so little Progress in Amendment, & had such frequent Relapses, that I was almost ready to give up the Attempt, and content my self with a faulty Character in that respect. Like the Man who in buying an Ax of a Smith my Neighbour, desired to have the broad whole of its Surface as bright as the Edge; the Smith consented to grind it bright for him if he would turn the Wheel. He turn'd while the Smith to fatigue him press'd the broad Face of the Ax hard & heavily on the Stone, which made the Turning very fatiguing. The Man came every now & then from the Wheel to see how the Work went on, and at length would take it as was without farther Grinding. No, says the Smith, Turn on, turn on; we shall have it bright by and by; as yet it's only speckled. *Yes,* says the Man' but—*I think I like a speckled Ax best.* And I believe this may have been the Case with many who have found the Difficulty of obtaining good, & breaking bad Habits *for want of some such Means as I employ'd* have given up the Struggle, & concluded that *a speckled Ax was best.* For something that pretended to be Reason was every now and then suggesting to me, that such extream Nicety as I exacted of my self might be a kind of Foppery in Morals, which if it were known would make me ridiculous; that a perfect Character might be envied and hated; and that a benevolent Man would for the sake of his Friends allow a few Faults in himself, to keep his Friends in Countenance. In Truth I found myself incorrigible with respect to *Order;* and now I am grown old and my Memory bad, I feel sensibly the want of it. But on the whole, tho' I never arrived at the Perfection I had been so ambitious of obtaining, yet I was made by the Endeavour a better Man than I otherwise should have been, if I had not attempted it; as those who aim at perfect Writing by imitating the engraved Copies, tho' they never reach the wish'd for Excellence of those Copies, their Hand is mended by the Endeavour, and is tolerable while it continues legible.[9]

It will be remark'd that, tho' my Scheme was not wholly without Religion there was in it none of the distinguishing Tenets of any particular Sect. I had purposely avoided them; for being fully persuaded of the Utility of and Excellency of my Method, and that it might be serviceable to People in all Religions, and intending some time or other to publish it, I would not have any thing in it that should prejudice any one of any Sect against it. I purposed writing a little Comment on each Virtue, in which I would have shown the Advantages of possessing it, the Mischief attending its opposite Vice; and I should have called my Book the *ART of Virtue*, because it would have shown the *Means* of obtaining Virtue; which would have distinguish'd it from mere Exhortation to be good, that does not instruct the Means; which is but like the Apostle's Man of verbal Charity, who only, without showing to the Naked & the Hungry *how* or where they might get Cloaths or Victuals, exhorted them to be fed & clothed. *James* II.15,16.

But it so happened that my Intention of writing & publishing this Comment was never fulfilled. I did indeed, from time to time, put down short Hints of the Sentiments, Reasonings, &c. to be made us of in it; some of which I have still by me: But private Business in the earlier part of my Life, and public Business have occasioned my postponing it. For it being connected in my Mind with a *great and extensive Project* that required the whole Man to execute, and which a Succession of Employs prevented my attending to, it has hitherto remain'd unfinish'd.

In this Piece it was my Design to enforce this Doctrine, that vicious Actions are not hurtful because they are forbidden, but forbidden because they are hurtful, the Nature of Man alone consider'd: That it was therefore every one's own Interest to be virtuous, who wish'd to be happy even in this World. And I should from this Circumstance, there being always in the World a great Number of Rich Merchants, Nobility, States and Princes, who have need of honest Instruments for the Management of their Affairs, and such being so rare have endeavoured to convince young Persons, no Qualities were so likely to make a poor Man's Fortune as those of Probity & Integrity.

My List of Virtues contain'd at first but twelve. But a Friend having inform'd me that I was generally thought proud; that my Pride show'd itself in Conversation; that I was not content with being in the right when discussing any Point, but was overbearing & rather insolent; of which he convinc'd me by mentioning several Instances; I determined endeavouring to cure myself of this Vice or Folly among the rest, and I added *Humilty* to my List. I cannot boast of much Success in acquiring the *Reality* of this Virtue; but I had a good deal with regard to the *Appearance* of it. I made it a rule to forbear all direct Contradiction of the Sentiments of others, and all positive Assertions of my own. I even forbid myself *agreable to the old Laws of our Junto*, the Use of every Word or Expression in the Language that imported a fix'd Opinion; such as *certainly, undoubtedly*, &c and I adopted instead of them, *I conceive, I apprehend,* or *I imagine* a thing to be so or so. When another asserted something, that I thought an Error, I deny'd my self the Pleasure of contradicting him abruptly, and of showing immediately some Absurdity in his Proposition; but I began by observing that in certain Cases or Circumstances his Opinion would be right, but that in the present case there *appear'd* or *seem'd* to me some Difference, &c. I soon found the Advantage of this Change in my Manners. The Conversations I engag'd in went on more pleasantly. The modest way in which I propos'd my Opinions, procur'd them an easier Reception and less Contradicition; *I had less Mortification when I was found to be in the wrong,* and I more easily prevail'd with others to give up their Mistakes & join with me when I happen'd to be in the right. And this Mode, which I at first put on, with some violence to natural Inclination, became at length so habitual to me, that perhaps for these Fifty Years past no one has ever heard a dogmatical Expression escape me. And to this Habit (*after my Character of Integrity*) I think it principally owing, that I had early so much Weight with my Fellow Citizens, when I proposed new Institutions, or Alterations in the old; and so much Influence in public Councils when I became a Member. For I was but a bad Speaker, never eloquent, *subject to much Hesitation in my choice of Words,* hardly correct in Language, and yet I generally carried my Points.

In reality there is perhaps no one of our natural Passions so hard to subdue as *Pride.* Disguise it, struggle with it, beat it down, stifle it, mortify it as much as you please, it is still alive, and will every now and then peep out and show itself. You will see it perhaps often in this History. For if I could conceive that I had compleatly overcome it, I should probably be proud of my Humility.[10]

13

PROMOTING VIRTUE & VIEWS

1731–1754

Increasing business success enabled Franklin to turn to broader fields for doing good. The new Library broadened his interest in practical means of promoting virtue while his almanac and newspaper offered the media for amusement and instruction as well as information. Adopting the comical style of Britain's favorite almanac, *Poor Robin*, Franklin created the famous Poor Richard figure who gained celebrity at home and abroad, as in France where he was called "Bonhomme Richard," and enduring fame for his role as straight man to Father Abraham in the all-time bestselling sketch, "The Way to Wealth," promoting thrift and industry as the way to the American dream. The *Pennsylvania Gazette*, while not so successful as the almanac, would nevertheless do well enough to enable Franklin to take early retirement at age forty-two.

Having mentioned a *great & extensive Project* which I had conceiv'd, it seems proper that some Account should be here given of that Project and its Object. Its first Rise in my Mind will appear in the following little Paper, accidentally preserv'd, viz.

Observations on my Reading History in Library, May 9, 1731
"That the great Affairs of the World, the Wars, Revolu-
tions, &c. are carried on and effected by Parties.
"That the View of these Parties is their present general
Interest, or what they take to be such, —
"That the different Views of these different Parties,
occasion all Confusion.
"That while a Party is carrying on a general Design,
each Man has his particular private Interest in
View.
"That as soon as a Party has gain'd its general Point,
each Member becomes Intent upon his particular
Interest, which thwarting others, breaks that Party
into Divisions, and occasions more Confusion.
"That few in Public Affairs act from a meer View of the
Good of their Country, whatever they may pretend; and tho' their Actings bring real Good to
their Country, yet Men primarily consider'd that
their own and their Country's Interest was united,
and did not act from a Principle of Benevolence.
"That fewer still in public Affairs act with a View to the
Good of Mankind.
"There seems to me at present to be great Occasion for
raising an united Party for Virtue, by forming the
Virtuous and good Men of all Nations into a
regular Body, to be govern'd by suitable good and
wise Rules, which good and wise Men may probably be more unanimous in their Obedience to,
than common People are to common Laws.
"I at present think, that whoever attempts this aright,
and is well qualified, cannot fail of pleasing God, &
of meeting with Success. —"
                                        B. F.

Revolving this Project in my Mind, as to be undertaken hereafter when my Circumstances should afford me the necessary Leisure, I put down from time to time on Pieces of Paper such Thoughts as occur'd to me respecting it. Most of these are lost; but I find one containing the Substance of an intended Creed, containing as I thought the Essentials of every known Religion, and free of every thing that might shock the Professors of any Religion. It is express'd in these Words: viz

"That there is one God who made all things.

"That he governs the World by his Providence.

"That he ought to be worshipped by Adoration, Prayer & Thanksgiving.

"But that the most acceptable Service to God is doing Good to Man.

"That the Soul is immortal.

"And that God will certainly reward Virtue and punish Vice either here or hereafter."

My Ideas at that time were that the Sect should be begun & spread at first among young and single Men only; that each Person to be initiated should not only declare his Assent to such Creed, but should have exercis'd himself with the Thirteen Weeks Examination and Practice of the Virtues as in the before-mention'd Model; that the Existence of such a Society should be kept a Secret till it was become considerable, to prevent Solicitations for the Admission of improper Persons; but that the Members should each of them search among his Acquaintance for ingenuous well-disposed Youths, to whom with prudent Caution the Scheme should be gradually communicated. That the Members should engage to afford their Advice Assistance and Support to each other in promoting one another's Interest Business and Advancement in Life. That for Distinction's

Sake we should be call'd the Society of the *Free and Easy:*
Free, as being by the general Practice and Habits of the Virtues, free from the Dominion of Vice, and particularly by
the Practice of Industry & Frugality, free from Debt, which
exposes a Man to Confinement and a Species of Slavery to
his Creditors. This is as much as I can now recollect of the
Project, except that I communicated it in part to two young
Men, who adopted it with Enthusiasm. But my then narrow Circumstances, and the Necessity I was under of sticking close to my Business, occasion'd my Postponing the
farther Prosecution of it at that time, and my multifarious
Occupations public & private oblig'd me to continue postponing, so that it has been omitted till I have no longer
Strength or Activity left sufficient for such an Enterprize.
Tho' I am still of Opinion that it was a practicable Scheme;
and might have been very useful, by forming a great Number of good Citizens. And I was not discourag'd by the seeming Magnitude of the Undertaking, as I have always thought
that one Man of tolerable Abilities may work great Changes,
& accomplish great Affairs among Mankind, if he first forms
a good Plan, and, cutting off all Amusements or other
Employments that would divert his Attention, makes the
Execution of that same Plan his sole Study and Business.

In 1732 I first printed my Almanack, under the Name
of *Richard Saunders;* it was continu'd by me about 25 Years,
and commonly call'd *Poor Richard's* Almanack. I endeavour'd to make it both entertaining and useful, and it accordingly came to be in such Demand that I reap'd
considerable Profit from it, vending annually near ten
Thousand. And observing that it was generally read, scarce
any Neighbourhood in the Province being without it, I
consider'd it as a proper Vehicle for conveying Instruction
to the common People, who bought scarce any other Books.

I therefore filled all the little Spaces that occurr'd between the Remarkable Days in the Calendar, with Proverbial Sentences, chiefly such as inculcated Industry and Frugality, as the Means of procuring Wealth and securing Virtue, it being more difficult for a Man in Want to act always honestly, as (to use here one of those Proverbs) *it is hard for an empty Sack to stand upright.* These Proverbs, which contained the Wisdom of many Ages and Nations, I assembled and form'd into a connected Discourse prefix'd to the Almanack of 1757, as the Harangue of a wise old Man to the People attending an Auction. The bringing all these scatter'd Counsels thus into a Focus, enabled them to make greater Impression. The Piece *being universally approved* was copied in all the Newspapers of the Continent, reprinted in Britain on a Broadside to be stuck up in Houses, two Translations were made of it in French, and great Numbers bought by the Clergy & Gentry to distribute gratis among their poor Parishioners and Servants. In Pennsylvania, as it discouraged useless Expence in foreign Superfluities, some thought it had its Share of Influence in producing that growing Plenty of Money which was observable for several Years after its Publication .

I consider'd my Newspaper also as another Means of spreading useful Knowledge and communicating Instruction, & in that View frequently reprinted in it Extracts from the Spectator and other moral Writers, and sometimes publish'd little Pieces of my own which had been first compos'd for Reading in our Junto. Of these are a Socratic Discourse tending to prove, that, whatever might be his Parts and Abilities, a vicious Man could not properly be called a Man of Sense. And a Discourse on Self denial, showing that Virtue was not Secure, till its Practice became a Habitude, free from the Opposition of contrary Inclinations. These may be found in the Papers about the beginning of 1735.[1]

"Self-Denial Not the Essence of Virtue" appeared 18 February and "A Man of Sense" 11 February.[2]

In the Hurry of other Business an Advertisement was brought to me to be printed; it signified that such a Ship lying at such a Wharff, would sail for Barbadoes *in such a Time, and that Freighters and Passengers might agree with the Captain at such a Place; so far is what's common: But at the Bottom of this odd Thing was added: "N. B. No Sea Hens nor Black Gowns will be admitted on any Terms." I printed it and receiv'd my Money; and the Advertisement was stuck up around Town as usual. I had not so much Curiosity at that time to enquire the Meaning of it, nor did I in the least imagine it would give so much Offence. Several good Men [were] very angry with me on this Occasion; they [were] pleas'd to say I have too much Sense to do such things ignorantly; that if they were Printers they would not have done such a thing on any Consideration; that it could proceed from nothing but my abundant Malice against Religion and the Clergy: They therefore declare'[d] they will not take any more of my Papers, nor have any farther Dealing with me; but will hinder me of all the Custom they can. All this is very hard![3]*

I believe it had been better if I had refused to print the said Advertisement.[4] . . . I never saw the Word "Sea-Hens" before in my Life; nor have I yet ask'd the Meaning of it and tho' I had certainly known that "Black Gowns" in that Place signified the Clergy of the Church of England, yet I have that confidence in the generous good Temper of such of them as I know, as to be well satisfied such a trifling mention of their Habit give them no Disturbance.[5]

In the slang of the time, "Sea Hens" referred to seagoing prostitutes.

Notwithstanding the Rashness and Inexperience of Youth which is most likely to be prevail'd to do things that ought not to be done; yet I have avoided printing such Things as usually give Offence either to Church or State, more than any Printer that has followed the Business in this Province before.

I take leave to conclude with an old Fable, which some of my Readers have heard before, and some have not. A certain well-meaning Man and his Son, were travelling towards a Market Town, with an Ass which they had to sell. The Road was bad; and the old Man therefore rid, but the Son went a-foot. The first Passenger they met, asked the Father if he was not ashamed to ride by himself, and suffer the poor Lad to wade along thro' the Mire; this induced him to take up his Son behind him: He had not travelled far, when he met others, who said, they were two unmerciful Lubbers to get both on the Back of that poor Ass, in such a deep Road. Upon this the old Man gets off, and let his Son ride alone. The next [passenger] they met called the Lad a graceless, rascally young Jackanapes, to ride in that Manner thro' the Dirt, while his aged Father trudged along on Foot; and they said the old Man was a Fool, for suffering it. He then bid his Son come down, and walk with him, and they travelled on leading the Ass by the Halter; 'til they met with another Company, who called them a Couple of senseless Blockheads, for going both on Foot in such a dirty Way, when they had an empty Ass with them, which they might ride upon. The old Man could bear no longer; "My son," said he, "it grieves me much that we cannot please all these People: Let us throw the Ass over the next Bridge, and be no farther troubled with him."

Had the old man been seen acting this last Resolution, he would probably have been call'd a Fool for troubling himself about the different Opinions of all that were pleas'd to find Fault with him: Therefore, tho' I have a Temper almost as complying as his, I intend not to imitate him in this last Particular. I consider the variety of Humours among Men, and despair of pleasing every Body; yet I shall not therefore leave off Printing. I shall continue my Business. I shall not bury my Press and melt my Letters.[6]

In the Conduct of my Newspaper I carefully excluded all Libelling and Personal Abuse, which is of late Years become so disgraceful to our Country. Whenever I was solicited to insert any thing of that kind and the Writers pleaded the Liberty of the Press, and that a Newspaper was like a Stage Coach in which any who would pay had a Right to a Place, my Answer was, that I would print the Piece separately if desired, and the Author might have as many Copies as he pleased to distribute himself, *but that I would not take upon me to spread his Detraction, and* that having contracted with my Subscribers to furnish them with what might be either useful or entertaining, I could not fill their Papers with private Altercation in which they had no Concern without doing them manifest Injustice. Now many of our Printers make no Scruple of gratifying the Malice of Individuals by false Accusations of the fairest Characters among ourselves, augmenting Animosity even to the producing of Duels, and are moreover so indiscreet as to print scurrilous Reflections on the Government of neighbouring States, and even on the Conduct of our best National Allies, which may be attended with the most pernicious Consequences. These Things I mention as a Caution to young Printers, & that they may be encouraged not to pollute their Presses and disgrace their Profession by such infamous Practices, but refuse steadily; as they may see by my Example, that such a Course of Conduct will not on the whole be injurious to their Interests.

In 1733, I sent one of my Journeymen to Charleston, South Carolina where a Printer was wanting. I furnish'd him with a Press and Letters, on an Agreement of Partnership, by which I was to receive One Third of the clear Profits, & pay One Third of the Expence. He was a Man of Learning and an honest, but ignorant in Matters of Account; and tho' he sometimes made me Remittances, I could get no Account from him, nor any satisfactory State of our Partnership while he lived. On his Decease, the Business was continued by his Widow, who being born & bred in Holland, where the Knowledge of Accompts makes a Part of Female Education, she not only sent me as clear an Account as she could find of the Transactions past, but continu'd to account with the greatest Regularity & Exactitude every Quarter afterwards; and manag'd the Business with such Success that she not only brought up reputably a Family of Children, but at the Expiration of the Term was able to purchase of me the Printing-House and establish her Son in it. I mention this Affair chiefly for the Sake of recommending that Branch of Education for our young Females, as likely to be of more Use to them & their Children in Case of Widowhood than either Music or Dancing, by preserving them from Losses by Imposition of crafty Men, and enabling them to continue perhaps a profitable mercantile House till a Son is grown up fit to undertake and go on with it, to the lasting Advantage and enriching of the Family.[8]

After ten Years Absence from Boston, I made a Journey thither to visit my Relations, which I could not sooner well afford. In returning I call'd at Newport, to see my Brother then settled there with his Printing-House. Our former Differences were forgotten, and our Meeting was very cordial and affectionate. He was fast declining in his Health, and requested of me that in case of his Death which he apprehended not far distant, I would take home his Son, then but 10 Years of Age, and bring him up to the Business.

This I accordingly perform'd, sending him a few Years to the Grammar School before I took him into the Office.

Jemmy Franklin, when with me, was always dissatisfied and grumbling. When I was last in Boston, his aunt bid him go to a shop and please himself, which the gentleman did, and bought a suit of clothes on my account dearer by one half, than any I ever afforded myself, one suit excepted; which I don't mention by way of complaint, for he and I are good friend, but only to show you the nature of boys.[9] His Mother carry'd on the Business till he was grown up, when I assisted him with an Assortment of new Types, those of his Father being in a Manner worn out. Thus it was that I made my Brother ample Amends for the Service I had depriv'd him of by leaving him so early.[10]

14

TAKING CARE OF BUSINESS

1736–1739

The printing business absorbed most of his time, yet
Franklin learned to translate from French to German,
faithfully attended the Junto, Masons, and Library Company, and wrote regularly for the *Pennsylvania Gazette* and
Poor Richard's Almanac, while beginning a distinguished
career in public service as postmaster and politician.
Siding with the legislature against the proprietary government, he engaged in political controvery while at the same
time he promoted civic improvements in public safety.

I had begun in 1733 to study Languages. I soon made
myself so much a Master of the French as to be able to read
the Books with Ease. I then undertook the Italian. An Acquaintance who was learning it also us'd often to tempt me
to play Chess with him. Finding this took up too much of
the Time I had to spare for Study, I at length refus'd to play
any more, unless on this Condition, that the Victor in every Game, should have a Right to impose a Task, either in
Parts of the Grammar to be got by heart, or in Translation,
which Tasks the Vanquish'd was to perform upon Honour
before our next Meeting. As we play'd pretty equally we
thus beat one another into that Language. I afterwards with

a little Pains-taking acquir'd as much of the Spanish as to read their Books also. I have already mention'd that I had only one Years Instruction in a Latin School, which was when very young, after which I neglected that Language entirely. But when I had attained an Acquaintance with the French, Italian and Spanish, I was surpriz'd to find, on looking over a Latin Testament, that I understood so much more of that Language than I had imagined; which encouraged me to apply my self to the Study of it, with more Success, as those preceding Languages greatly smooth'd my Way. From these Circumstances I have thought that there is some Inconsistency in our common Mode of Teaching Languages. We are told that it is proper to begin first with the Latin, and having acquired that it will be more easy to acquire those modern Languages which are deriv'd from it; and yet we do not begin with the Greek in order more easily to acquire Latin. It is true, that if you can clamber to the Top of a Stair Case without using the Steps, you will more easily gain them in descending: but if you begin with the lowest you will with more Ease ascend to the Top. And I would therefore offer it to the Consideration of those who superintend the Education of our Youth, whether, since many of those who begin with the Latin, quit the same after some Years Study, without having made any great Proficiency, so that their time has been lost, it would not have been better to have begun them with the French, proceeding to the Italian &c. for tho' after spending the same time they should quit the Study of Languages, & never arrive at the Latin, they would have acquir'd another Tongue or two that might be useful to them in common Life.[1]

Our Club, the Junto, was found so useful, & afforded such Satisfaction to the Members, that several were desirous of introducing their Friends, which could not well be done without going beyond what we had settled as a convenient Number, viz. Ten. We had from the Beginning made it a Rule to keep our Institution a Secret, which was pretty well observ'd. The intention was to avoid Applications of improper Persons for Admittance, some of whom perhaps we might find it difficult to refuse. I was one of those who were against any Additions to our Number, but instead of it made in Writing a Proposal, that every Member separately should endeavour to form a subordinate Club, with the same Rules respecting Queries, &c. and without acquainting them of the Connection with the Junto. The Advantages propos'd were the Improvement of so many young Citizens by the Use of our Institutions; our better Acquaintance with the general Sentiments of the Inhabitants on any Occasion, as the Junto-Member might propose what Queries we should desire, and was to report to Junto what pass'd in his separate Club; the Promotion of our particular Interests in Business by more extensive Recommendations, and the Increase of our Influence in public Affairs by spreading thro' the several Clubs the Sentiments of the Junto.

The Project was approv'd, and every Member undertook to form his Club; but they did not all succeed. Five or six only were compleated, which were call'd by different Names, as the Vine, the Union, the Band, &c. They were useful to themselves, & afforded us a good deal of Amusement, Information & Instruction, besides answering in some considerable degree our Views of influencing the public Opinion on particular Occasions, of which I shall give some Instances hereafter in course of time as they happened.

My first Promotion was being chosen in 1736 Clerk of the General Assembly. The Choice was made that Year without Opposition; but the Year following when I was again propos'd (the Choice, like that of the Members annual) a new Member made a Speech against me, in order to favour some other Candidate. I was however chosen; which was the more agreable to me, as besides the Pay for immediate Service as Clerk, the Place gave me a better Opportunity of keeping up and securing an Interest among the Members, which secur'd to me the Business of Printing the Votes, Laws, Paper Money and other occasional Jobbs for the Public, which on the whole was very profitable. I therefore did not like the Opposition of this new Member, who was a Gentleman of Fortune, Education & Talents that were likely to give him in time great Influence with the House, which indeed afterwards happened. I did not however aim at gaining his Favour by any servile Respect to him, but took another Method. Having heard that he had in his Library a certain very curious Book, I wrote a Note to him expressing my Desire of perusing it and requesting he would do me the Favour of lending it to me for a few Days. He sent it immediately; and I returne'd it in about a Week, with another Note expressing strongly my Sense of the Favour. When we next met in the House he spoke to me with great Civility (which he had never done before). And he ever afterwards manifested a Readiness to serve me on all Occasions, so that we became great Friends, & our Friendship continu'd to his Death. This is another Instance of the Truth of the old Maxim which says, "He that has once done you a Kindness will be more ready to do you another, than he whom you yourself have obliged." And it shows how much better it is prudently to remove, than to resent, return & continue inimical Proceedings.[2]

In 1736 I lost one of my Sons, a fine Boy of 4 Years old, by the Small Pox taken in the common way. I long regretted that I had not given it to him by Inoculation, which I mention for the Sake of Parents, who omit that Operation on the Supposition that they should never forgive themselves if a Child died under it; my Example showing that the Regret may be the same either way, and that therefore the safer should be chosen.[3]

In 1737, Col. Spotswood, late Governor of Virginia, & then Postmaster, General, being dissatisfied with the Conduct of his Deputy at Philadelphia, respecting Negligence in rendering, & Inexactitude of the Accounts, took from him the Commission & offered it to me. I accepted it readily, and found it of great Advantage; for tho' the Salary was small, it facilitated the Correspondence that improv'd my Newspaper, encreas'd the Number demanded, as well as the Advertisements inserted, so that it came to afford me a very considerable Income. My old Competitor's Newspaper declin'd proportionably, and I was satisfy'd without retaliating his Refusal, while Postmaster, to suffer my Papers being carried by the Riders. He suffer'd greatly from his Neglect in due Accounting; and I mention it as a Lesson to those who may manage Affairs for others which should always be done and Remittances made with great Clearness and Punctuality. Such a Conduct is the most powerful Recommendation to new Employments & Increase of Business.[4]

Early in 1738, after Franklin became involved in a scandal over the death of a young man during a Masonic mock initiation, news reached his parents in Boston who expressed concern about his religious views.

I imagine a Man must have a good deal of Vanity who believes, and a good deal of Boldness who affirms, that all the Doctrines he holds, are true; and all he rejects, are false. And perhaps the same may be justly said of every Sect, Church

and Society of Men when they assume to themselves that In-
fallibility which they deny to the Popes and Councils. I think
Opinions should be judg'd of by their Influences and Effects;
and if a Man holds none that tend to make him less Virtuous
or more vicious, it may be concluded he holds none that are
dangerous; which I hope is the Case with me.[5] *. . . What an*
Arminian or an Arian is, I cannot say that I very well know;
the Truth is, I make such Distinctions very little my Study; I
think vital Religion has always suffer'd, when Orthodoxy is
more regarded than Virtue. And the Scripture assures me,
that at the last Day, we shall not be examin'd what we thought,
but what we did; and our Recommendation will not be that
we said, "Lord, Lord," but that we did GOOD to our Fellow
Creatures. See Matthew 26.[6]

I began now to turn my Thoughts a little to public Affairs, beginning however with small Matters. The City
Watch was one of the first Things that I conceiv'd to want
Regulation. It was managed by the Constables of the respective Wards in Turn. The Constable warn'd a Number
of Housekeepers to attend him for the Night. Those who
chose never to attend paid him Six Shillings a Year to be
excus'd, which was suppos'd to be for hiring Substitutes:
but was in Reality much more than was necessary for that
purpose, and made the Constableship a Place of Profit. And
the Constable for a little Drink often got such Ragamuffins
about him as a Watch, that reputable Housekeepers did not
chuse to mix with. Walking the Rounds too was often neglected, and most of the Night spent in Tippling. I thereupon wrote a Paper to be read in Junto, representing these
Irregularities, but insisting more particularly on the Inequality of this Six Shilling Tax of the Constables, respecting the Circumstances of those who paid it, since a poor
Widow Housekeeper, all whose Property to be guarded by

the Watch did not perhaps exceed the Value of Fifty Pounds, paid as much as the wealthiest Merchant who had Thousands of Pounds-worth of Goods in his Stores. On the whole I proposed as a more effectual Watch, the hiring of proper Men to serve constantly in that Business; and as a more equitable way of supporting the Charge, the levying a Tax that should be proportion'd to Property. This Plan being approv'd by the Junto, was communicated to the other Clubs, but as arising in each of them. And tho' the Plan was not immediately carried into execution, yet by preparing the Minds of People for the Change, it paved the Way for the Law pass'd a few years after, when the Members of our Clubs were grown into more Influence.[7] ...

After some time I drew a Bill for Paving the City, and brought it into the House. It was just before I went to England in 1757 and did not pass till I was gone, and then with an Alteration in the Mode of Assessment, which I thought not for the better, but with an additional Provision for lighting as well as Paving the Streets, which was a great Improvement. It was by a private Person giving a Sample of the Utility of Lamps by placing one at his Door, that People were first impress'd with the Idea of enlightening all the City. The Honour of this Improvement has also been ascrib'd to me, but it belongs truly to that Gentleman [John Clifton].[8] ...

In the early 1750s, the House passed Junto-supported bills for regulating the watch, paving, and lighting. At that time Philadelphia had an estimated population of fifteen thousand with two or three thousand houses.[9] After describing in detail a plan he had submitted for Dr. John Fothergill ("one of the best Men I have known") on cleaning London's streets, Franklin concluded with a hint of daylight savings time.

Requiring the Dust swept up before the Shops are open is very practicable in the Summer, when the Days are long. For in walking thro' the Strand and Fleet street one Morning at 7 aClock I observ'd there was not one shop open tho' it had been Day-light near four Hours. The Inhabitants of London chusing voluntarily to live much by Candle Light, and sleep by Sunshine; and yet complain of the Duty on Candles and the high Price of Tallow.

Some may think these trifling Matters not worth Attention: But when they consider, that tho' Dust blown into the Eyes of a single Person or a single Shop on a windy Day, is but of small Importance, yet the Number of Instances in a populous City give it a Weight & Consequence; perhaps they will not censure very severely those who bestow some of Attention to Affairs of this seemingly low Nature. The Happiness of Man consists not so much in great Pieces of good Fortune that seldom occur, but in little Advantages that occur every Day. Thus if you teach a poor young Man to shave himself and keep his Rasor in order, you may contribute more to the Happiness of his life than if you gave him 1000 Guineas. The Money may be soon spent, and the Regret only remaining of having foolishly spent it. But *in the other Case* he escapes the frequent Vexation of waiting for a Barber, & their sometimes, dirty Fingers, offensive Breaths and dull Razors. He shaves when most convenient to him, and has the daily Pleasure of its being done with a good Instrument. With these Sentiments I have written the preceding Pages, hoping they may afford some Hints which some time or other may be found useful to a City I love, having lived many Years in it very happily; and perhaps to some of our Towns in America.[10]

15

PROMOTING THE
GREAT AWAKENING

1739–1740

Franklin's growing success in business coincided with the
intercolonial phase of the Great Awakening, the religious
revival energized by Methodist Rev. George Whitefield.
During his second visit in 1739–40, Whitefield enjoyed a
symbiotic relationship with Franklin, who promoted his
tours, sermons, and pamphlets while profiting from their
publication distributed through a network of partners
along the seaboard. William Parks, who published the
Virginia Gazette, could boast of communication links
from Boston to Charleston (22 June 1739), for the colonies
now had at least sixteen print shops. Whitefield exploited
the new American newspaper-reading public. He used
plain, scriptural language along with illustrations from
everyday life rather than erudite classics, and he kept his
publications brief. During Spring 1740 news and reprints
from Whitefield's sermons dominated Franklin's newspaper along with advertisements for those published by
Franklin the printer. His narrative below echoes the
promotional pieces in his *Pennsylvania Gazette* of that
spring.[1]

———

In 1739 arriv'd among us from England the Rev. Mr Whitefield, who had made himself remarkable there by speaking as an itinerant Preacher. He was at first permitted to preach in some of our Churches; but the Clergy taking some Dislike to him, soon refus'd him their Pulpits and he was oblig'd to preach in the Fields. The Multitudes of all Sects and Denominations that attended his Sermons were enormous, and the Effect on his Hearers extraordinary, notwithstanding his Abuse of them, by assuring them they were naturally "half Beasts and half Devils." It was wonderful to see the

> Whitefield had used this phrase in commenting on the Pharisee and the Publican (Luke 18: 9–14)."Would [the publican] be angry if any one had told him, that, by nature, he was half a devil and half a beast."[2]

Change soon made in the Manners of our Inhabitants; from being thoughtless or indifferent about religion, it seem'd as if all the World were growing Religious; so that one could not walk thro' the Town in an Evening without Hearing Psalms sung in different Families of every Street. And it being found inconvenient to assemble in the open Air, subject to its Inclemencies, the Building of a House to meet in was no sooner propos'd and Persons appointed to receive Contributions, but sufficient Sums were soon receiv'd to purchase the Ground and erect the Building which was 100 feet long & 70 broad, about the Size of Westminster-hall; and the Work was carried with such Spirit as to be finished in a much shorter time than could have been expected. Both House and Ground were vested in Trustees, for the Use of any Preacher of any religious Persuasion who might desire to say something to the People of Philadelphia, so that even if the Mufti of Constantinople were to send a Missionary to preach Mahometanism to us, he would find a Pulpit at his Service. The Contributions being made by People of different Sects promiscuously, Care was taken in the Nomination of Trustees to avoid giving a Predominancy to any one Sect, so that one of each was appointed, viz. one Church of England-man, one Presbyterian, one Baptist, one Moravian, &c.

Mr Whitfield, in leaving us, went preaching all the Way thro' the Colonies to Georgia. The Settlement of that Province had lately been begun; but instead of being made with hardy Husbandmen accustomed to Labour, it was with Families of broken Shopkeepers and other insolvent Debtors, taken out of the Goals, who being set down in the Woods, unqualified for clearing Land, & unable to endure the Hardships of a new Settlement, perish in Numbers, leaving many helpless Children unprovided for. The Sight of their miserable Situation inspir'd the benevolent Heart of Mr Whitfield with the Idea of building an Orphan House in which they might be supported and educated. In returning northward he preach'd up this Charity & made large Collections for he had a wonderful Power over the Hearts & Purses of his Hearers, of which I myself was an Instance. I did not disapprove of the Design, but as Georgia was then destitute of Materials & Workmen, and it was propos'd to send them from Philadelphia at a great Expence, I thought it would have been better to have built the House here & brought the Children to it. This I advis'd, but he was resolute in his first Project, and I thereupon resolv'd to contribute nothing. Happening however to attend one of his Sermons, in the course of which I perceived he intended to finish with a Collection, I silently resolving he should get nothing from me, I had in my Pocket a Handful of Copper, Money, three or four Dollars, and five Pistoles in Gold. As he proceeded I began to soften, and concluded to give the

Coppers. Another Strike of his Oratory made me asham'd of that, and determin'd me to give the Silver; & he finish'd so admirably, that I empty'd my Pocket wholly into the Collector's Dish, Gold and all.

At this Sermon there was one of our Club, who being of my Sentiments respecting the Building in Georgia, and suspecting a Collection had in Precaution emptied his Pockets before he came from home; towards the Conclusion of the Discourse however, he felt a strong Desire to give, and apply'd to a Neighbour who stood near him to borrow some Money for the Purpose. The Application was unfortunately to the only Man in the Company who had the firmness not to be affected by the Preacher. His Answer was, "At any other time, Friend H[opkinso]n, I would lend to thee freely; but not now; for thee seems to be out of thy Senses."

Some of Mr Whitfield's Enemies affected to suppose that he would apply these Collections to his own private Emolument; but I, who was intimately acquainted with him (being employ'd in printing his Sermons & Journals, &c.) never had the least Suspicion of his Integrity but am to this day decidedly of Opinion that he was in all his Conduct, a perfectly *honest Man*. And methinks my Testimony

> In contrast to his energetic defense of Hemphill, Franklin kept quiet about the decades of public controversy over Whitefield's financing, perhaps because it focused on the kind of sloppy accounting that Franklin abhorred.

ought to have the more Weight, as I had no religious Connection. He us'd indeed sometimes to pray for my Conversion, but never had the Satisfactionn of believing that his Prayers were heard. Ours was a mere civil Friendship, sincere on both Sides, and lasted to his Death.

Upon one of his Arrivals from England at Boston, he wrote to me that he should come soon to Philadelphia, but knew not where he should lodge when once there, as he understood his old kind Host Mr Benezet was remov'd to Germantown. My Answer was, "You know my House; if you can make shift with its scanty accommodations you will be most heartily welcome." He reply'd, that if I made that kind Offer for Christ's Sake, I should not miss of a Reward. And I return'd, "Don't let me be mistaken; it was not for Christ's Sake, but for your Sake." One of our common Acquaintance jocosely remark'd, that knowing it to be the Custom of the Saints, when they receiv'd any favour, to suppose it coming from Heaven to shift the Burthen of the Obligation from off their own Shoulders, and place it elsewhere, but I was determin'd to fix it on Earth.

The last time I saw him was in London, when he consulted me about his Orphan House Concern, and his Purpose of appropriating it to the Establishment of a College.

He had a loud and clear Voice, and articulated his Words & Sentences so perfectly that he might be heard and understood at a great Distance, especially as his Auditories, however numerous, observ'd the most exact Silence. He preach'd one Evening from the Top of the Court House Steps, which are in the Middle of Market Street, and on the West Side of Second Street which crosses it at right angles. Both Streets were fill'd with his Hearers at a considerable Distance. Being among the hindmost in Market Street, I had the Curiosity to learn how far he could be heard, by retiring down the Street towards the River, and I found his Voice distinct till I came near Front-Street, when some Noise in that Street obscur'd it. Imagining then a Semi-Circle, of which my Distance should be the Radius, and that it was fill'd with Auditors, to each of whom I allow'd two square feet, I computed that he might well be heard by more than Thirty-Thousand. This reconcil'd me to the

Accounts of his having preach'd sometime to 25000 People in the Fields, and to the antient Histories of Generals haranguing whole Armies, of which I had sometimes doubted.

> According to the *Pennsylvania Gazette* for 15 November 1739, Whitefield preached four nights from the Courthouse porch to "near 6000 People" in the street "who stood in an awful Silence to hear him."

By hearing him often I came to distinguish easily between Sermons newly compos'd, & those which he had often preach'd in the Course of his Travels. His Delivery of the latter was so improv'd by frequent Repetitions, that every Accent, every Modulation of Voice, was so perfectly well tun'd and well plac'd, that without being interested in the Subject, one could not help being pleas'd with the Discourse, a Pleasure of the same kind with that receiv'd from an excellent Piece of Musick. This is an Advantage itinerant Preachers have over those who are stationary: as the latter cannot improve their Delivery of a Sermon by so many rehearsals.

His Writing and Printing from time to time gave great Advantage to his Enemies. Unguarded Expressions *and even erroneous Opinions* delivered in Preaching might have been afterwards explain'd, or qualify'd by others that might have accompany'd them; or they might have been deny'd; But *Litera scripta manet.* His Critics attack'd him violently, and with so much Appearance of Reason as to diminish the Number of his Votaries, and prevent their Encrease: So that I am of Opinion, if he had never written any thing he would have left behind a much more numerous Sect. And his Reputation might have been still growing, even after his Death; as there being nothing of his Writing to be found on which to found a Censure; and give him a lower Character, his Proselites would be less at Liberty to feign for him as great a Variety of Excellencies, as their enthusiastic Admiration of him might wish him to have possessed.

My Business was now continually augmenting, and my Circumstances growing daily easier, my Newspaper having become very profitable, as being for a time almost the only one taken in this and the neighbouring Provinces. I experienc'd too the Truth of the Observation, that "after getting the first hundred Pound, it is more easy to get the second": Money itself being of a prolific Nature.

The Partnership at Carolina having succeeded, I was encourag'd to engage in others, and to promote several of my Workmen who had behaved well, by establishing them with Printing-Houses in different Places, on the same Terms with that in Carolina. Most of them did well, being enabled at the End of our Term, Six Years, to purchase the Types of me; and go on for themselves, by which means several Families were raised.

Partnerships often finish in Quarrels, but I was happy in this, that mine were carry'd on and ended amicably; owing I think a good deal to the Precaution of having explicitly settled in our Articles every thing to be done by or expected from each Partner, so that there was nothing to dispute, which Precaution I would therefore recommend to all who enter into Partnerships, for whatever Esteem Partners may have for each other at the time of the Contract, little Jealousies and Disgusts may arise, with Ideas of Inequality in the Care & Burthen of the Business, &c. which are attended often with Breach of Friendship & of the Connection, Lawsuits and other disagreable Consequences.[3]

Having in 1742 invented an open Stove, for the better warming of Rooms and at the same time saving Fuel, as the fresh Air admitted was warmed in Entring, I made a Present of the Model to Mr Robert Grace, one of my early

Friends, who having an Iron Furnace, found the casting of the Plates for the Stove a profitable Thing, as they were growing in Demand. Gov. Thomas had been so please'd with the Construction of this Stove, that he offer'd to give me a Patent for the sole Vending of them for a Term of Years; but I declin'd it from a Principle that has ever weigh'd with me on such Occasions, viz. *That as we who now live enjoy great Advantages from the Inventions of others, we should be glad of an Opportunity to serve others by any inventions of ours, and this we should do freely and generously.* An Ironmonger in London, however, after making a small Change in the Machine, which rather hurt its Operation, got a Patent for it there, and made a little Fortune by it. And this is not the only Instance of Patents taken out for my Inventions by others, tho' not always with the same Success. And I never contested them, as having no Desire of profiting by Patents my self, and hating Disputes.

His inventions, besides the stove, that received patents for others included a carriage wheel and a copperplate engraving process for ceramics.[4] Those that escaped such piracy included his armonica, convertible chair, three-wicked lamp, laundry mangle, u-shaped anchor, and improved bifocals.

16

PROMOTING PROVINCIAL DEFENSE

1740s

Thus far in Franklin's time, the warfare among Britain, France, and Spain had been limited in North America. Guerilla fighting on the western frontier hardly affected Philadelphians. When in 1747, appearance of a Spanish fleet on the Delaware frightened them, Quakers' pacifism would not allow funds for defense, so Franklin appealed to the community. This activity risked his political future and government business.

I had on the whole abundant Reason to be satisfied with my being established in Pennsylvania. There were however two things that I regretted: There being no Provision for defence, nor for a compleat Education of Youth. No Militia nor any College. I therefore in 1743 drew up a Proposal for establishing an Academy; & at that time thinking the Rev. Mr [Richard] Peters, who was then out of Employ, a fit Person to superintend such an Institution, I communicated the Project to him. But he having more profitable Views, which succeeded, declin'd the Undertaking. And not knowing another at that time suitable for such a Trust, I let the

Scheme lie for some Years dormant. I succeeded better the next Year, 1744, in proposing and establishing a Philosophical Society.[1]

> The projected society, planned with Philadelphian John Bartram and New Yorker Cadwallader Colden, came to nothing. Apparently potential colleagues preferred clubs, chess, or coffee houses to "the Curious amusements of natural observations."[2]

With respect to Defence, Spain having been several Years at War against Britain, and being at length join'd by France, and the laboured Endeavours of Governor [George] Thomas with our Quaker Assembly to pass a Militia Law, & make other Provisions for Security of the Province having prov'd abortive, I determined to try what might be done by a voluntary Association of the People. To promote this I first wrote & published a Pamphlet, intitled *Plain Truth*, in which I stated our Danger in strong Lights, with the Necessity of Union & Discipline for our Defence, and promis'd to propose in a few Days an Association to be signed for that purpose. The Pamphlet had a surprizing Effect. I was call'd upon for the Instrument of Association: And having settled the Draft of it with a few friends, I appointed a Meeting of the Citizens in the large Building before mentioned; It was full.

I had prepared a Number of printed Copies, and provided Pens and Ink dispers'd all over the Room. I harangu'd them a little on the Subject, and then distributed the Papers which were eagerly signed, not the least Objection being made. When the Company separated, & the Papers were collected we found some Thousand of Hands; and other Copies being dispers'd in the Country the Subscribers amounted at length to upwards of Ten Thousand. These all furnish'd themselves with Arms; form'd themselves into

Companies, and Regiments, chose their own Officers, & met every Week to be instructed in the manual Exercise, and other Parts of military Discipline. The Women, by a Subscription among themselves, provided Silk Colours, which they presented to the Companies, painted with different Devices and Motto's which I furnish'd.[3]

The *Pennsylvania Gazette* (12 January, 26 April 1748) described the flags with such images as Liberty holding a spear topped by a liberty cap. Most of the mottoes were in Latin but an exception was Number IX: "In God We Trust."[4]

The Officers of the 12 Companies composing the Philadelphia regiment, being met, chose me for their Colonel; but conceiving myself unfit, I declin'd & recommended Mr [Thomas] Lawrence, a fine Person and Man of Influence, who was accordingly appointed. I then propos'd a Lottery to defray the Expence of Building a Battery below the Town and furnishing it with Cannon. It filled expeditiously and the Battery was soon erected, the Merlons being of Logs & fill'd with Earth. We bought some old Cannon from Boston, but these not being sufficient, we wrote to England for more, soliciting at the same Time our Proprietaries for some Assistance, tho' without much Expectation of obtaining it.

Mean while Colonel Lawrence, Mr William Allen, Abraham Taylor, Esquire, and myself were sent to New York by the Associators, commission'd to borrow some Cannon of Governor [George] Clinton. He at first refus'd us, but at Dinner with his Council where there was great Drinking of Madeira Wine, as the Custom at that Place then was, he soften'd by degrees, and said he would lend us Six. After a few more Bumpers he advanc'd to Ten. And at length he very good-naturedly conceded Eighteen. They were fine Cannon, 18 pounders, with their Carriages, which we soon transported and mounted on our Battery, where the Associators kept nightly Guard while the War lasted. And among the rest I regularly took my Turn of Duty there as a common Soldier.

My Activity in these Operations was agreable to the Governor and Council; they took me into Confidence, & I was consulted in every Measure wherein their Concurrence was thought useful to the Association. Calling in the Aid of Religion, I propos'd to them the Proclaiming a Fast to implore the Blessing on our Undertaking. They embrac'd the Motion, but as it was the first Fast ever thought of in the Province, the Secretary had no Precedent from which to draw the Proclamation. My Education in New England, where a Fast is proclaim'd every Year, was here of Advantage. I drew it in the accustomed Stile, it was translated into German, printed in both Languages and divulg'd thro' the Province. This gave the Clergy of the different Sects (except Quakers) an Opportunity of Influencing their Congregations to join in the Association; and it would probably have been general among them if the Peace had not soon interven'd.

> Franklin generally sided with the Quaker-dominated Assembly but came under their fire for supporting efforts to raise funds for defense. He goes on to tell how the Assembly finally in July 1745 voted four thousand Pounds for gunpowder by semantic subterfuge.

It was thought by some of my Friends that by my Activity in these Affairs, I should offend the Quakers, and thereby lose my Interest in the Assembly where they were a great Majority. A young Gentleman who had likewise some Friends in the House, and wished to succeed me as their Clerk, acquainted me that it was decided to displace me at the next Election, and he therefore in good Will advis'd me to resign, as more consistent with my Honour than being turn'd out. My Answer to him was, that I had read or heard of some Public Man, who made it a Rule never to ask for an Office, and never to refuse one when offer'd to him. I approve, says I, of his Rule, and will practise it with a small Addition; I shall never *ask*, never *refuse*, nor ever *resign* an Office. If they will have my Office of Clerk to dispose of to another, they shall take it from me. I will not by giving it up, lose my Right of some time or other making Reprisals on my Adversaries. I heard however no more of this. I was chosen again unanimously as usual, at the next Election. Possibly they might have been pleas'd if I would voluntarily have left them; but they did not care to displace me on Account merely of my Zeal for the Association; and they could not well give another Reason.

Indeed I had some Cause to believe, that the Defence of the Country was not disagreeable to them, provided they were not requir'd to assist in it. And I found that a much greater Number of them than I could have imagined, tho' against offensive War, were clearly for the defensive. Many Pamphlets pro & con were publish'd on the Subject, and some by good Quakers in favour of Defence, which I believe convinc'd most of the younger People.

A Transaction in our Fire Company gave me some Insight into the prevailing Sentiments. It had been propos'd that we should encourage the Scheme for building a Battery by laying out the present Stock, then about Sixty Pounds, in Tickets of the Lottery. By our Rules no Money could be dispos'd of but by the next Meeting after the Proposal. The Company consisted of Thirty Members, of which Twenty-two were Quakers, & Eight only of other Persuasions. We eight punctually attended the Meeting; but tho' we knew that some of the Quakers would join us, we were by no means sure of a Majority. Only one Quaker, Mr James Morris, appear'd to oppose the Measure. He express'd Sorrow that it had ever been propos'd, as he said *Friends* were all against it, and it would create such Discord as might break up the Company. We told him, that we saw no Reason for that; we were the Minority, and if *Friends* were against the Measure and outvoted us, we must and should, agreable to the Usage of all Societies, submit. When the Hour for Business arriv'd, it was mov'd to put the Vote. He allow'd we might do it by the Rules, but as he could assure us that a Number of Members intended to be present for the purpose of opposing it, it would be but candid to allow a little time for their appearing. While we were disputing this, a Waiter came into the Room to tell me two Gentlemen below desir'd to speak with me. I went down to them and found they were two of our Quaker members. They told me there were eight of them assembled at a Tavern just by; that they were determin'd to come and vote with us if there should be occasion, which they hop'd would not be the Case; but desir'd we would not call for their Assistance if we could do without it, as their Voting for such a Measure might embroil them with their Elders & Friends.[5]

Franklin's anecdote reflects the trend among second-generation Quakers to curb their dogma. Immigration had been cutting into their majority, but they still retained power. In the elections of 1740–45, they raised representation in the Assembly from 46 to 83 per cent.[6]

Being thus secure of a Majority, I went up, and after a little seeming Hesitation, agreed to allow another Hour. This Mr Morris allow'd to be extreamly fair. Not one of his opposing Friends appear'd, at which he express'd great Surprize; and at the Expiration of the Hour, we carry'd the Resolution Eight to one. And as of the 22 Quakers, eight were ready to vote with us and Thirteen by their Absence could not oppose the Measure, I afterwards estimated the Proportion of Quakers sincerely against Defence as one to twenty one only. For these were all regular Members of the Society, and in good Reputation among them.

The Honourable James Logan, who had always been of that Sect, was one who wrote an Address to them, declaring his Approbation of defensive War, and supporting his Opinion by many strong Arguments: He put into my Hands Sixty Pounds to be laid out in Lottery Tickets for the Battery, with Directions to apply what Prizes might be drawn wholly to that Service. He told me an Anecdote of Wm Penn respecting Defence. He came over from England with that Proprietary as his Secretary. It was War Time, and their Ship was chas'd by an armed Vessel. Their Captain prepar'd for Defence, but told Wm Penn and his Company that he did not expect their Assistance, and they might retire into the Cabin; which they did, except James Logan, who chose to stay upon Deck, and was quarter'd to a Gun. The suppos'd Enemy prov'd a Friend; so there was no Fighting. But when the Secretary went down to communicate the Intelligence, Wm Penn rebuk'd him severely for staying upon Deck and undertaking to assist in defending the Vessel, contrary to the Principles of *Friends*, especially as it had not been required by the Captain. This Reproof being before all the Company, piqu'd the Secretary, who answer'd, "I being thy Servant, why did thee not order me to come down: but thee was willing enough that I should stay and help to fight the Ship when thee thought there was Danger."

My being many Years in the Assembly, the Majority of which were constantly Quakers, gave me frequent Opportunities of seeing the Embarrasment given them by their

Principles against War, when Application was made to them by Order of the Crown to grant Aids for military Purposes. They were unwilling to offend Government by a direct Refusal on the one hand, and their Friends the Body of Quakers on the other, by a Compliance contrary to the Principles. Hence a Variety of Evasions to avoid complying, and Modes of disguising the Compliance when it became unavoidable. The common Mode at last was to grant Money "for the King's Use," and never to enquire how it was applied. But when the Application was not directly from the Crown, that Phrase was found not so proper, and some other was to be invented. As when Powder was wanting (I think it was for the Garrison at Louisburg), and the Government of New England solicited a Grant of some from Pennsilvania, which was much urg'd on the House by Governor Thomas, they could not grant Money to buy Powder, because that was an Ingredient of War, but they voted Three Thousand Pounds, to be put into the Hands of the Governor, for the Purchasing of Bread, Flour, Wheat, "or other Grain." Some of the Council advis'd the Governor not to accept Provisions, as not being the Thing he had demanded. But he reply'd, "I shall accept it, for I understand very well their Meaning: 'Other Grain is Gunpowder;'" which he accordingly bought; and they never objected to it.

It was in Allusion to this Fact, that when we feared the Success of our Proposal in favour of the Lottery, I said to my friend [Philip] Syng, one of our members, "If we fail, let us move the Purchase of a Fire Engine with the Money; the Quakers can have no Objection to that: and then if you nominate me, and I you, as a Committee for that purpose, we will buy a great Gun, which is certainly a 'Fire Engine.'" "I see," says he, "you have improv'd by being so long in the

Assembly; your Project would be a Match for their Wheat 'or *other Grain.*'"

These Embarassments that the Quakers suffer'd from having establish'd it as a Principle, that no kind of War was lawful, *and which once being published they could not after-wards, however they might change their minds, easily get clear of,* reminds me of what I think a more prudent Conduct in another Sect among us; that of the Dunkers. I was acquainted with one of its Founders, Michael Welfare, soon after it appear'd. He complain'd to me that they were grievously abus'd by the Zealots of other Persuasions, and charg'd with Principles and Practices to which they were utter Strangers. I told him this had always been the case with new Sects; and that to put a Stop to such Abuse, I imagin'd it might be well to publish the Articles of their Belief and the Rules of their Discipline. He said that it had been propos'd but not agreed to, for this Reason: "When we were first drawn together as a Society, it had pleased God to inlighten our Minds so far, as to see that many Doctrines which we once esteemed Truths were Errors, & that others which we had esteemed Errors were real Truths. From time to time he has been pleased to afford us further Light, and our Principles have been improving, & our Errors diminishing. Now we are not sure that we are arriv'd at the Perfection of Spiritual Knowledge; and we fear that if we should once print our Confession of Faith, we should feel ourselves bound & confin'd by it, and unwilling to receive farther Improvement; and our Successors still more so, as conceiving what we had done to be something sacred, never to be departed from." This Modesty in a Sect is perhaps a singular Instance in the History of Mankind, every other Sect supposing itself in Possession of all Truth, and that those who differ are so far in the Wrong: Each like a Man travelling in a foggy Weather: Those before him on the Road he sees wrapt up in the Fog, as well as those behind him, and the People in the Fields on each side; but near him all is clear. Tho' in truth he is as much in the Fog as any of them.[8]

17

ESTABLISHING AN ACADEMY

1749

Franklin's narrative lumps his carefully crafted plan for the Philadelphia Academy in with other, many less important, public services, perhaps because it had been an exercise in futility. His idea of pairing English and classical curricula had been subverted by trustees. In the last summer of his life, he blamed himself for not having opposed them "with sufficient Zeal and Earnestness" while recognizing that other duties had "tended much to weaken" his influence.[1]

Peace being concluded, and the Association Business therefore at an End, I turn'd my Thoughts again to the Affair of establishing an Academy. . . . *As in the Scheme of the Library I had provided only for English Books, so in this new Scheme my Ideas went no farther than to procure the Means of a good English Education.*

Peace being concluded, and the Association Business therefore at an End, I turn'd my Thoughts again to the Affair of establishing an Academy. The first Step I took was to write and publish a Pamphlet intitled, *Proposals relating to the Education of Youth in Pennsylvania.* This I distributed among the principal Inhabitants gratis; and as soon as I could suppose their Minds a little prepared by the Perusal of it, I set on foot a Subscription for Opening and Supporting an Academy; it was to be paid in Quotas yearly for Five Years; by so dividing it I judg'd the Subscription might be larger, and I believe it was so, amounting to no less than Five thousand Pounds.

In the Introduction to these Proposals, I stated their Publication not as an Act of mine, but of some *publick-spirited Gentlemen*; avoiding as much as I could, according to my usual Rule, the presenting my self to the Publick as the Author of any Project for their Benefit.

The Subscribers, to carry the Project into immediate Execution chose out of their Number Twenty-four Trustees, and appointed Mr [Tench] Francis, then Attorney General, and my self, to draw up Constitutions for the Government of the Academy, which being done and signed, a House was hired, Masters engag'd and the Schools opened, I think in the same Year 1749. But the Scholars encreasing fast, the House was soon found too small, and we were looking out for a Piece of Ground properly situated, with Intention to build, when Fortune threw into our way a House ready built, which with a few Alterations might well serve our purpose; this was the Building before mentioned erected by the Hearers of Mr Whitefield, and was obtain'd for us in the following Manner:

It is to be noted, that the Contributions to this Building being made by the People of different Sects, Care was taken in the Nomination of Trustees, in whom the Building & Ground was to be vested, that a Predominancy should not be given to any Sect, lest in time it might be a means of appropriating the whole to the Use of such Sect, contrary to the original Intention; it was therefore that one of each Sect was appointed, viz. one Church-of-England-man, one Presbyterian, One Baptist, one Moravian, &c. These in case of Vacancy by Death were to fill it by Election from among the Contributors. The Moravian happen'd not to please his Colleagues, and on his Death, they resolved to have no other of that Sect. The Difficulty then was, how to avoid having two of some other Sect, by means of the new Choice. Several Persons were named and for that Reason not agreed to. At length one of them mention'd me with the Observation that I was of no Sect, which prevail'd with them to chuse me.

The Enthusiasm which existed when the House was built, had long since abated, and the Trustees had not been able to pay the Ground Rent, nor discharge some other Debts the Building had occasion'd, which embarrass'd them greatly. Being now a Member of both Sets of Trustees, those for the Building & those for the Academy, I had an Opportunity of negociating with both, & brought them finally to an Agreement, by which the Trustees for the Building were to cede it to those of the Academy, the latter undertaking to discharge the Debt, and to keep open in the Building a large Hall for occasional Preachers according to the original Intention, and maintain a School for the Instruction of poor Children. Writings were accordingly drawn, and on paying the Debts the Trustees of the Academy were put in Possession of the Premises, and purchasing some additional Ground, the whole was made fit for our purpose, and the Scholars remov'd into the Building.

The whole Care and Trouble of agreeing with the Workmen, purchasing Materials, and superintending the Work fell upon me, and I went thro' it chearfully, as it did not then interfere with my private Business, having the Year before taken a very able, industrious & honest Partner, Mr David Hall, with whose Character I was well acquainted, as he had work'd for me four Years. He took off my Hands all

Care of the Printing-Office, paying me punctually my Share of the Profits. The Partnership continued Eighteen Years, successfully for us both.[2]

> Hall, Franklin's partner from 1748 to 1766, was originally intended as a partner in the Caribbean, but he married a relative of Deborah Franklin and remained in Philadelphia at a salary reported at one thousand pounds a year.[3]

The Trustees of the Academy after a while were incorporated by a Charter from the Governor; their Funds were increas'd by Contributions in Britain, and Grants of Land from the Proprietaries, to which the Assembly has since made considerable Addition, and thus was establish'd the present University of Philadelphia.

> Chartered in 1743, the academy became a college in 1755. Franklin was replaced as head of the Trustees nine years before the college became the University of Pennsylvania in 1756.

I have been continued one of its Trustees from the Beginning, now near forty Years, and have had the very great Pleasure of seeing a Number of the Youth who have receiv'd their Education in it, distinguish'd by their Abilities, serviceable in public Stations, and Ornaments to their Country.[4]

18

Retiring to Public Service

1748–1753

Retiring at forty-two left Franklin another forty-two years to engage in local, state, national, and world affairs successively. When he was chosen alderman in 1751, his mother said: "I am glad to hear that you are so respected in your toun for them to chuse you alderman alltho I dont know what it means nor what better you will be of it beside the honer of it."[11] Successful campaigning for the Library Company, the Association, a fire company, and the academy earned him fame as fund-raiser for other projects while consulting for the Governor and Council and serving on the Assembly sparked the career in politics, public policy, and diplomacy that would consume much of his omnicompetent career.

When I disengag'd my self as above mentioned from private Business, I flatter'd myself that I had secur'd leisure during the rest of my Life, for Philosophical Studies and Amusements; and I proceeded in my Electrical Experiments with great Alacrity; but the Publick now considering me as a Man of Leisure, laid hold of me for their Purposes; every part of our Civil Government, and almost at the same time, imposing some Duty upon me. The Governor put me into the Commission of the Peace; the Corporation of the City chose me of the Common Council, and soon after an Alderman; and the Citizens at large chose me a Burgess to represent them in the Assembly. The latter Station was the more agreable to me, as I was at length tired with sitting there to hear Debates in which as Clerk I could take no part, and which were often so unentertaining, that I amus'd my self with making magic Squares, or Circles, or any thing to avoid Weariness. And I conceiv'd my becoming a Member would enlarge my Power of doing Good. I would not however insinuate that my Ambition was not flatter'd by all these Promotions. It certainly was. *For considering my low Beginning they were great Things to me.* And they were still more pleasing, as being so many Testimonies of the public good Opinion, and by me entirely unsolicited.

The Office of Justice of the Peace I try'd a little, by attending a few Courts, and sitting on the Bench to hear Causes.

> In June 1749 when Franklin sat on the Court of Common Pleas with three other judges, none of them had had legal training either.[3]

But finding that more Knowledge of the Law than I possess'd, was necessary to act in that Station with Credit, I gradually withdrew from it, excusing myself by my being oblig'd to attend the higher Dutys of a Representative. My Election to this Trust was repeated every Year for Ten Years, without my ever asking any Elector for his Vote, or signifying directly or indirectly any Desire of being chosen. On taking my Seat in the House, my Son was appointed Clerk.[4]

> In April 1750 Franklin kept his mother informed of his little family and a month later wrote a will providing for

them, as though realizing the risks in playing with electricity which, indeed, six months after that almost killed him.[5]

Will is now 19 Years of Age, a tall proper Youth, and much of a Beau. He acquir'd a Habit of Idleness . . . but begins of late to apply himself to Business, and I hope will become an industrious Man. He imagin'd his Father had got enough for him; But I have assur'd him that I intend to spend what little I have, my self; if it please God that I live long enough. . . . [Seven-year-old] Sally grows a fine Girl, and is extreamly industrious with her Needle, and delights in her Book, and perfectly Dutiful and obliging, to her Parents and to all. . . . For my own Part, at present I pass my time agreably enough. I enjoy (thro' Mercy) a tolerable Share of Health; I read a great deal, ride a little, do a little Business for my self, more for others; retire when I can, and go Company when I please; so the Years roll round, and the last will come; when I would rather have it said, "He lived usefully," than "He died rich."[6]

> In June 1750 his will distributed his estate, naming Deborah and William executors, then concluded with a passage retained in an otherwise substantially revised will seven years later before he departed for England.

And now humbly returning sincere Thanks to God for producing me into Being, and conducting me hitherto thro' Life so happily, so free from Sickness, Pain and Trouble, and with such a Competency of this World's Goods as might make a reasonable Mind easy: That he was pleased to give me such a Mind, with moderate Passions, or so much of his gracious Assistance in governing them; and to free it early of Ambition, Avarice and Superstition, common Causes of much Uneasiness to Men. That he gave me to live so long in a Land of Liberty, with a People that I love, and rais'd me, tho' a Stranger, so many Friends among them; bestowing on me moreover a loving and prudent Wife, and dutiful Children. For these and all his other innumerable Mercies and Favours, I bless that Being of Beings who does not disdain to care for the meanest of his Creatures. And I reflect on those Benefits received with greater Satisfaction, as they give me such a Confidence in his Goodness, as will, I hope, enable me always in all things to submit freely to his Will, and to resign my Spirit chearfully into his Hands whenever he shall please to call for it; reposing myself securely in the Lap of God and Nature as a Child in the Arms of an affectionate Parent.[7]

The year ... [1753] a Treaty being to be held with the Indians at Carlisle, the Governor sent a Message to the House, proposing that they should nominate some of their Members to be join'd with some Members of Council as Commissioners for that purpose.[8]

> The four-day conference was convened by Indians from Virginia and Pennsylvania frontiers after the French threatened them. They asked the British for arms, protection for their fur trade, and restrictions on selling rum to their peoples. "The Rum ruins us."[9] Satisfying pacifist Quakers by calling the arms, "Presents" (customary gifts), Pennsylvania was finally able to send a wagonload of weapons only to have it arrive too late to be of any use. Franklin published a complete report of the proceedings.

The House nam'd the Speaker (Mr [Isaac] Norris) and my self; and being commission'd we went to Carlisle, and met the Indians accordingly. As these People are extreamly apt to get drunk, and when so are very quarrelsome & disorderly, we strictly forbad all the Tavern Keepers the selling any Liquor to them; and when they complain'd of this Restriction, we promis'd that if they would continue sober during the Treaty, we would give them Plenty of Rum when Business was over. They promis'd this; and they kept their Promise—because they could get no Liquor—and the Treaty was conducted very orderly, and concluded to mutual Satisfaction.[10]

> The "satisfaction," however, was all on the part of the Pennsylvanians. Since the arms did not arrive in time, the Indians lost faith and turned instead to the Virginians for protection.[11]

They then claim'd and receiv'd the Rum. This was in the Afternoon. They were near 100 Men, Women & Children, and were lodg'd in temporary Cabins built in the Form of a Square just without the Town. In the Evening, hearing a great Noise among them, the Commissioners walk'd out to see what was the Matter. We found they had made a great Bonfire in the Middle of the Square. They were all drunk Men and Women, quarreling and fighting. Their dark-colour'd Bodies, half naked, running after and beating one another with Firebrands, accompanied by their horrid Yellings, form'd a Scene the most resembling our Ideas of Hell that could well be imagin'd. There was no appeasing the Tumult, and we retir'd to our Lodging. At Midnight a Number of them came thundering at our Door, demanding more Rum; of which we took no Notice. The next Day, sensible they had misbehav'd in giving us that Disturbance, they sent three of their old Counsellors to make their Apology. The Orator acknowledg'd the Fault, but laid it upon the Rum; and then endeavour'd to excuse the Rum, by saying, "The great Spirit who made all things made every thing for some Use, and whatever Use he design'd them for, that Use they should always be put to; Now, when he made Rum, he said, '*Let this be for Indians to get drunk with.'* And so it must be so."—And indeed if it be the Design of Providence to extirpate these Savages in order to make room for Cultivators of the Earth, it seems not impossible that Rum may be the appointed Means. It has already annihilated all the Tribes who formerly inhabited the Seacoast.[12]

> Franklin is alluding to the theory that civilization passes through stages from "savages" or hunters, through shepherds, farmers, and fabricators.[13] Contemporary with his comment on liquor, Jefferson's *Notes on Virginia* estimated that about one third of Virginia's Indians had been wiped out by "liquors, the small-pox, war, and an abridgement of territory.[14]

In 1751, Dr Thomas Bond, a particular Friend of mine, conceiv'd the Idea of establishing a Hospital in Philadelphia, for the Reception and Cure of sick persons, whether Inhabitants of the Province or Strangers. A truly beneficent Design, which has been ascribed to me, but was really his. He was zealous & active in endeavouring to procure Subscriptions towards it; but the Proposal being a Novelty in America, and at first not well understood, he met with small Success. At length he came to me, with the Compliment that he found there was no such thing as carrying a public Spirited Project through, without my being concern'd in it; "for," says he, "I am often ask'd by those to whom I propose Subscribing, 'Have you consulted Franklin upon this Business?' and 'What does he think of it?'—And when I tell them that I have not (supposing it rather out of your Line), they do not subscribe, but say they will consider of it."

I enquired into the Nature, & probable Utility of his Scheme, and receiving from him a very satisfactory Explanation, I not only subscrib'd to it myself, but engag'd heartily into endeavouring to procure Subscriptions from others. But previously to the Solicitation, I endeavoured to prepare the Minds of the People by writing on the Subject in the Newspapers, which was my usual Custom in such Cases, but which he had omitted. The Subscriptions afterwards were more free and generous, but beginning to flag, I saw they would be insufficient without some Assistance from the Assembly, and therefore propos'd to petition for it, which was done. The Country Men did not at first relish the Project. They objected that it could only be serviceable to the City, and therefore the Citizens should alone be at the Expence of it; and they doubted whether the Citizens themselves generally approv'd of it: My Alleging on the contrary, that it met with such Approbation as to leave no doubt of our being able to raise 2000 Pounds by voluntary Donations, they considered as a most extravagant Supposition, and utterly impossible.

On this I form'd my Plan; and having obtain'd Leave to bring in a Bill, the which was obtain'd chiefly on the Consideration that they could throw it out if they did not like it, I drew it so as to make the important Clause a conditional One, viz. "That when the said Contributors shall have met and chosen their Managers and Treasurer, *and shall have raised, by their Contributions a Capital Stock of 2000 Pounds Value* (the Yearly Interest of which is to be applied to the Accommodating of the Sick Poor in the said Hospital, free of Charge for the Diet, Attendance, Advice and Medicines) and *shall make the same appear to the Satisfaction of the Speaker of the Assembly* for the time being; that *then* it shall and may be lawful for the said Speaker, and he is hereby required to sign an Order on the Provincial Treasurer for the Payment of Two Thousand Pounds in two yearly Payments, to the Treasurer of the said Hospital, to be applied to the Founding, Building and Finishing of the Same." This Condition carried the Bill through; for the Members who had oppos'd the Grant, and now conceiv'd they might have the Credit of being charitable without the Expence, agreed to its Passage; And then in soliciting Subscriptions, we urg'd the conditional Promise of the Law as an additional Motive to give, since every Man's Donation would be doubled. *Thus the Clause work'd both ways.* The Subscriptions accordingly soon exceeded the requisite Sum, and we claim'd and receiv'd the Public Gift, which enabled us to carry the Design into Execution. A convenient and handsome Building was soon erected, the Institution has by Experience been found useful, and flourishes to this Day. And I do not remember any of my political maneuvres, the Success of which gave me at the time more Pleasure. *Or that in after-thinking of it, I more easily excus'd my self for having made some Use of Cunning.*[15]

It was about this time that another Projector, the Rev. Gilbert Tennent, came to me, with a Request that I would assist him in procuring a Subscription for erecting a new Meeting-house. It was to be for the Use of a Congregation he had gathered among the Presbyterians who had been followers of Mr Whitefield. Unwilling to make myself disagreable to my fellow Citizens, by too frequently soliciting their Contributions, I absolutely refus'd to be concern'd. He then desir'd I would furnish him with a List of the Names of Persons I knew by Experience to be generous and public-Spirited. I thought it would be unbecoming in me, after their kind Compliance with my Solicitations, to mark them out to be worried by other Beggars, and therefore refus'd to give such a List. He then desir'd I would at least give him my Advice. That I will do, says I; and, in the first Place, I advise you to apply to all those whom you know will give something; next to those whom you are uncertain whether they will give or not; and show them the List of those who have given: and lastly, do not neglect those who you are sure will not give, for in some of them you may be mistaken. He laugh'd, and thank'd me, and said he would take my Advice. He did so, for he ask'd of *every body*; and obtain'd a much larger Sum than he expected, with which he erected the large and very elegant Meeting-house that stands in Arch Street.[16]

Having been for some time employed by the Postmaster General of America, as his Comptroller, in regulating the Offices, and bringing the Officers to account, I was upon his Death in 1753 appointed, jointly with Mr William Hunter, to succeed him.

> While auditing American post offices, Franklin formed a network of intercolonial friendships, including William Hunter, publisher of the *Williamsburg Gazette*, who linked him to such Virginians as Washington and Jefferson.

The American Office had never hitherto paid any thing to that of Britain. We were to have 600 Pounds a Year if we could make it out of the Office. To do this, a Variety of Improvements were necessary; some of these were inevitably at first expensive; so that in the first four Years the Office became above 900 Pounds in debt to us. But it soon after began to repay us, and before I was displac'd, by a Freak of the Ministers, of which I shall speak hereafter, we had brought it to yield *three times* as much Revenue to the Crown as the Post-Office of Ireland. Since that imprudent Transaction, it has receiv'd—Not one Farthing.

The Business of the Post-Office occasion'd my taking a Journey this Year to Boston, where the College of Cambridge of their own Motion, presented me with the Degree of Master of Arts. Yale College in Connecticut, had before given me a similar Compliment. Thus without studying in any College I came to partake of their Honours. They were confer'd in Consideration of my Improvements in the electrical Branch of Natural Philosophy.[17]

19

EXPERIMENTING WITH ELECTRICITY

1743–1753

Entertained by Dr. Archibald Spencer's tricks with glass rods, Franklin did not try experimenting with them until Peter Collinson, the Library's agent in London, sent equipment along with an article from *Gentleman's Magazine* for April 1745 reporting on exciting experiments in Germany.[1] In the next decade Franklin would report discovering that electricity consisted of positive and negative charges; lightning was electricity; and sharp-tipped rods could arrest lightning. He would thereby achieve international fame invaluable for future diplomacy.

In 1746 [1743] being at Boston, I met there with a Dr Spence, who was lately arrived from Scotland, and show'd me some electric Experiments. They were very imperfectly perform'd, as he was not very expert; but being on a Subject quite new to me, they equally surpriz'd and pleas'd me. Soon after my Return to Philadelphia, our Library Company receiv'd from Mr Peter Collinson, F.R.S. of London, a Glass Tube, with some Account of the Use of it in making such Experiments.² *In 1745, he sent over an Account of the new German Experiments in Electricity. This was the first Notice I had of this curious Subject, which I afterwards prosecuted with some Diligence, being encouraged by the friendly Reception he gave to the Letters I wrote to him upon it.*³

I eagerly seiz'd the Opportunity of repeating what I had seen at Boston, and by much Practice acquir'd great Readiness in performing those also which we had an Account of from England, adding a Number of new Ones. I say much Practice, for my House was continually full for some time, with People who came to see these new Wonders. To divide a little this Incumbrance among my Friends, I caused a Number of similar Tubes to be blown at our Glass-House, so they furnish'd themselves, so that we had several Performers. Among these the principal was Mr [Ebenezer] Kinnersley, an ingenious Neighbour, who being out of Business, I encouraged to undertake showing the Experiments for Money, and drew up for him two Lectures, in which the Experiments were rang'd in such Order and accompanied with such Explanations, in such Method, as that the foregoing should assist in Comprehending the following.

> Kinnersley's lectures began in May 1747. He gave the first public lectures on Franklin's theory of the sameness of lightning and electricity two years later. Franklin's enemies subsequently accused him of plagiarising from these lectures.⁴

He procur'd an elegant Apparatus for the purpose, in which all the little Machines that I had roughly made for myself were nicely form'd by Instrument-makers. His Lectures were well attended and gave great Satisfaction; and after some time he went thro' the Colonies exhibiting them in every capital Town, and pick'd up some Money. In the

West India Islands indeed it was with Difficulty the Experiments could be made, from the general Moisture of the Air.[5]

His learned friend James Logan encouraged Franklin to send regular reports to Collinson beginning in March 1747. Collinson would read them to the Royal Society in London, and Franklin would send copies to friends in America, including Cadwallader Colden of New York and James Bowdoin of Massachusetts, so that they soon formed an informal intercolonial scientific society of their own.[6] To his brother, however, he reported how, in trying to electrocute a turkey in winter 1750, he nearly electrocuted himself by grasping a metal conductor—and laughed about it:

I am ashamed to have been guilty of so notorious a Blunder; a Match for that of the Irishman, Sister told me of, who to divert his Wife pour'd the Bottle of Gun Powder on the live Coal; or of that Other, about to steal Powder, made a Hole in the Cask with a Hott Iron.[7]

Oblig'd as we were to Mr Colinson for his present of the Tube, &c. I thought it right he should be inform'd of our Success in using it, and wrote him several Letters containing Accounts of our Experiments. He got them read in the Royal Society, where they were not thought worth so much Notice as to be printed in their Transactions. One Paper which I wrote for Mr Kinnersley, on the Sameness of Lightning with Electricity, I sent to Dr [John] Mitchel, one of the Members too of that Society; who wrote me word that it had been read but was laught at by the Connoisseurs.

Many members were virtuosi, or merely curious science buffs rather than scientists. The *Gentleman's Magazine* reported that they "ridiculed" the theory.[8]

The Papers however being shown to Dr [John] Fothergill, he thought them of too much value to be stifled, and advis'd the Printing of them. Mr Collinson then gave them to [Edward] Cave for publication

> Fothergill, leader of British Quakers, kept in close touch with transatlantic affairs and would later be Franklin's physician while in London. Collinson, as a Quaker, would turn to him for advice.

in his *Gentleman's Magazine;* but he chose to print them separately in a Pamphlet, and Dr Fothergill wrote the Preface. Cave it seems judg'd rightly for his Profit; for by the Additions that arriv'd afterwards they swell'd to a Quarto Volume, which has had five Editions, and cost him nothing for Copy-money.[9]

> *Experiments & Observations on Electricity* appeared in April 1751. The Royal Society's Transactions reviewed it favorably for "great variety of curious and well-adapted experiments."[10] The Count de Buffon had it translated to irritate antagonists Jean Antoine Nollet and René Réaumur.[11]

It was however some time before these Papers were much taken Notice of in England. A Copy happening to fall into the Hands of the Count de Buffon, a Philosopher of great Reputation in France, he prevail'd with M. [T.F.] Dalibard to translate them into French, and they were printed at Paris. The Publication offended the Abbe Nollet, who had form'd a Theory of Electricity, which then had the Vogue throughout Europe. He could not at first believe that such a Work came from America, & said it must have been fabricated by his Enemies at Paris, to oppose his System. Afterwards having been assur'd that there really existed such a Person as Franklin of Philadelphia, which he had doubted, he wrote and published a Volume of Letters, chiefly address'd to me, defending his Theory, & denying the Verity of my Experiments and of the Positions deduc'd from them. I once purpos'd answering the Abbe, and actually began the Answer. But on Consideration that my Writings contain'd only a Description of Experiments, which any one might repeat & verify, or of Observations offer'd as Conjectures, & not delivered dogmatically, therefore not laying me under any Obligation to defend them; and reflecting that a Dispute between two Persons writing in different Languages might be lengthened much by mistranslations, and thence misconceptions of one anothers Meaning, much of one of the Abbe's Letters being founded on an Error in the Translation; I concluded to let my Papers shift for themselves;[12]

> Fothergill's preface had said that Franklin "exhibits" existence of electrical charges, but Dalibard translated it as "discovered."[13]

believing it was better to spend what time I could spare from public Business in making new Experiments than in Disputing about those already made. I therefore never answer'd M. Nollet and the Event gave me no Cause to repent my Silence; for my Book was translated from the French into the Italian, German and Latin Languages, and the Doctrine it contain'd was by Degrees universally adopted by the Philosophers of Europe in preference to that of the Abbe, so that he lived to see himself the last of his Sect; except Mr [M-J Brisson] his Eleve & immediate Disciple.

What gave my Book the more sudden and general Celebrity, was the Success of one of its propos'd Experiments, made by Messrs Dalibart & Delor, at Marly la Ville for drawing Lightning from the Clouds. This engag'd the public

Attention every where. M. Delor, who had an Apparatus for experimental Philosophy, and lectur'd in that Branch of Science, undertook to repeat what he call'd "the Philadelphia Experiments," and after they were perform'd before the King & Court, all the Curious of Paris flock'd to see them. I will not swell this Narrative with an Account of that capital Experiment, nor of the infinite Pleasure I receiv'd in the Success of a similar one I made soon after with a Kite at Philadelphia; as both are to be found in all the Histories of Electricity.[14]

> Dalibard & Delor used a pointed rod to attract lightning and ground it harmlessly (May 1752). Franklin described the celebrated kite-and-key experiment in the *Pennsylvania Gazette* (19 October 1752) as demonstrating "the Sameness of the Electrical Matter with that of Lightning." His friend Joseph Priestley's *History & Present State of Electricity* described it in 1767 (pp. 179–81).[15]

Dr. [Edward] Wright, an English Physician then at Paris, wrote to a Friend who was of the Royal Society an Account of the high Esteem my Experiments were in among the Learned abroad, and of their Wonder that my Writings had been so little noticed in England. The Society on this resum'd the Consideration of the Letters that had been read to them, and Dr. Watson drew up a summary Account of all I had afterwards sent to England on the Subject, which he accompanied with an Eulogium on the Writer.[16]

> Hardly "an Eulogium," William Watson's summary only compared his own work to Franklin's, egregiously overlooking the lightning rod.[17]

This Summary was then printed in their Transactions: And some Members of the Society in London, particularly Mr [John] Canton, having verified the Experiment of pocuring

Lightning from the Clouds by a Pointed Rod, and acquainting them with the Success, they soon made me more than Amends for the Slight with which they had before treated me: Without my having made any Application for that Honour, they chose me a Member, and voted that I should be excus'd the customary Payments, which would have amounted to twenty-five Guineas, so that ever since I have receiv'd their Transactions gratis. They also presented me with the Gold Medal of Sir Godfrey Copley for the year 1753, which was delivered accompanied by a very handsome Speech of the President Lord Macclesfield, in which I was highly honoured.[18]

> Franklin was the first to win the coveted Copley Medal under a new system stressing "improving natural knowledge." In 1756 he was also honored with life membership in the new Royal Society of Arts for advancing technology (which still calls its American Fellows, "Franklin Fellows"). Being honored by both societies recognized his combining Newtonian theoretical science and Baconian applied science.[19]

The Tatler [no. 151] tells us of a Girl who was observ'd to grow suddenly proud, and none could guess the Reason, till it came to be known that she had got on a pair of new Silk Garters. . . . I think I will not hide my new Garters under my Petticoats, but take the Freedom to show them: a Letter in the politest Terms to the Royal Society, to return the [French] Kings Thanks and Compliments in an express Manner to Mr. Franklin of Pennsilvania, for the Useful Discoveries in Electricity, and Application of the pointed Rods to prevent the terrible Effects of Thunderstorms. On reconsidering this Paragraph, I fear I have not so much Reason to be proud as the Girl had; for a Feather in the Cap is not so useful a Thing, or so serviceable to the Wearer, as a Pair of good Silk Garters.[20]

Collinson notified Franklin of his medal in early 1753, sent the medal in early 1754, but the membership in the Royal Society was not until mid-1756, by which time Franklin's attention had shifted to a hunt for the Northwest Passage and then to meteorology until being totally distracted by the impending war with France on Pennsylvania's frontier.

20

PROMOTING A UNITED FRONT

1754

With the outbreak of fighting on the frontier, Franklin's intercolonial network broadened. In late May 1754, twenty-two-year-old George Washington of the Virginia militia in the Ohio Valley attacked a small party of French, killing ten, among whom was one claimed by the French to be an unarmed diplomat. Capturing Washington, they had him sign a confession (which he could not read since it was in French) that he had "assassinated" the diplomat, a document the French circulated in Europe as proof of British aggression in starting the French-Indian War (1754–63). As Deputy Postmaster-General, Franklin was caught up in the action and as a commissioner attended intercolonial strategy conferences. Commanding Pennsylvania troops engaged in building forts, he took part in the same activity that had led Washington into the Ohio Valley but without international infamy.

In 1754, War with France being again apprehended, a Congress of Commissioners from the different Colonies was by an Order receiv'd from England to be assembled at Albany, there to confer with the Chiefs of the Six Nations, concerning the Means of defending both their Country and that of the Colonies. Our Governor, Mr Hamilton, having receiv'd this Order, acquainted the House with it, requesting they would furnish proper Presents for the Indians to be given on this Occasion; and nam'd the Speaker (Mr [Isaac] Norris) and my self, to be join'd by [John] Penn & Mr Secretary [Rev. Richard] Peters, as Commissioners to attend for Pennsylvania. The House approv'd the Nomination, and provided the Goods for the Present, and the Commissioners set out for the Congress, met those from New Hampshire, Massachusetts, Rhode-island, Connecticut, New York at Albany about the Middle of June.

> When New York Governor George Clinton heard rumors that Mohawks had joined the French, he called the conference to persuade the Six Nations to unite with the British colonies for mutual defense. New Yorkers and New Englanders wished the Iroquois to fight with them; the Pennsylvanians wished them to remain neutral. Franklin urged that an intercolonial union would be the best defense.

In our Way thither, I projected and drew up a Plan for the Union of all the Colonies in one Form under one Government so far as was necessary for Defence, and other important general Purposes. As we pass'd thro' New York, I show'd my Project to Mr James Alexander & Mr [Archibald] Kennedy, two Gentlemen of great Knowledge in public Affairs, and being fortified by their Approbation I ventur'd to lay it before the Congress. I found that several others of the Commissioners had plans of the same kind. A previous Question was first taken whether a Union should be established, which passed in the Affirmative. A Committee was then appointed to consider the Plans and report. Mine happen'd to be prefer'd, and with a few Amendments was accordingly reported.[1]

On Reflection it now [1789] seems probable, that if the foregoing Plan or something like it, had been adopted and carried into Execution, the subsequent Separation of the Colonies from the Mother Country might not so soon have happened, nor the Mischiefs suffered on both sides have occurred, perhaps during another Century. For the Colonies, if so united, would have really been, as they then thought themselves, sufficient to their own Defence, and being trusted with it, as by the Plan, an Army from Britain, for that purpose would have been unnecessary: The Pretences for framing the Stamp-Act would then not have existed, nor the other Projects for drawing a Revenue from America to Britain by Acts of Parliament, which were the Cause of the Breach, and attended with such terrible Expence of Blood and Treasure: so that the different Parts of the Empire might still have remained in Peace and Union. But the Fate of this Plan was singular. For tho' after many Days through Discussion of all its Parts in Congress it was unanimously agreed to, and Copies ordered to be sent to the Assembly of each Province for Concurrence, and one to the Ministry in England for the Approbation of the Crown. The Crown disapprov'd of it, as having plac'd too much Weight in the democratic Part of the Constitution; and every Assembly as having allow'd too much to Prerogative. So it was totally rejected.[2]

But such Mistakes are not new. History is full of the Errors of States & Princes. The best public Measures are seldom *adopted from previous Wisdom, but forc'd by the Occasion.*[3]

Our Governor of Pennsylvania in sending it down to the House, express'd his Approbation of the Plan "as appearing to him to be drawn up with good Clearness & Strength of Judgment, and therefore recommended it as well worthy their closest & most serious Attention."[4] The

House however, by the Management of a certain Member, took it up when I happen'd to be absent, which I thought not very fair, and reprobated it without paying any Attention to it at all, to my no small Mortification. Governor [Thomas] Hutchinson, too, who was one of the Congress, lik'd it so well.[5]

> The "unknown Member," most likely Isaac Norris, objected to the plan as weakening the Assembly's control of appropriations.[6]

In my Journey to Boston this Year, I met at New York with our new Governor, Mr [Robert Hunter] Morris, just arriv'd there fom England, with whom I had been before acquainted. He brought a Commission to supercede Mr Hamilton, who, tir'd with the Disputes his Proprietary Instructions had subjected him to, had resigned. Mr Morris ask'd me, if I thought he might expect as uncomfortable an Administration. I said, No; you may on the contrary have a very comfortable one, if you only take care not to enter into any Dispute with the Assembly.

"My dear Friend," says he,"how can you advise my avoiding Disputes. You know I love Disputing; it is one of my greatest Pleasures: However, to show the Regard I have for your Counsel, I promise you I will if possible avoid them."

He had some Reason for loving to dispute, being eloquent, an acute Sophister, and therefore generally successful in argumentative Conversation. He had been indeed brought up to it from a Boy, his Father (as I have heard) accustoming his Children to dispute with one another before him while sitting at Table after Dinner. In the Course of my Observation, these disputing, contradicting & confuting People are generally unfortunate in their Affairs. They get Victory sometimes, but they never get Good Will, which

would be of more use to them. We parted, he going to Philadelphia, and I to Boston. In returning, I met at New York
with the Votes of the Assembly, by which it appear'd that
notwithstanding his Promise to me, he and the House were
already in high Contention, and it was a continual Battle
between them, as long as he remain'd in the Province,
retain'd the Government. I had my Share of it; for as I got
back to my Seat in the Assembly, I was put on every Committee for answering his Speeches and Messages, and by
the Committee always directed to make the Drafts.[7]

> Morris had arrived in October 1754 while Franklin was at
> Boston and thus missed two months of the legislative
> battle. Typical of his counterpunching on his return he
> said of Morris, "If, after the Experience we have had of our
> Governor, we could be astonished at any Thing that comes
> from him, we should be so at his Message of the 22d
> instant."[8]

Our Answers as well as his Messages were often tart, and
sometimes indecently abusive. And as he knew I wrote for
the Assembly, one might have imagined that when we met
we could hardly avoid cutting Throats. But he was such a
good-natur'd a Man, that no personal Difference between
him and me was occasion'd by it, and we often supp'd together.

One Afternoon we met in the Street. "Franklin," says
he, "you must go home with me and spend the Evening. I
am to have some Company that you will like;" and taking
me by the Arm he led me to his House. He had before told
me Jokingly that he much admir'd the Idea of Sancho Panza
when it was propos'd to give him a Government, requested
it might be a Government of *Blacks*, as then, if he could
not agree with his People he might sell them. One of his
Friends who sat next me, says, "Franklin, why do you con-

tinue to side with these damn'd Quakers? Had not you better sell them? the Proprietor would give you a good Price."

"The Governor," says I, "has not yet *black'd* them enough." He had indeed labour'd hard to blacken them in all his Messages, but they wip'd off his Colouring as fast as he laid it on, and laid it in return thick upon his own Face; so that finding he was likely to be negrify'd himself, he too grew tir'd of the Contest, and quitted the Government.

These public Quarrels were all at bottom owing to the Proprietaries, who when any Expence was to be incurr'd for the Defence of their Province, with incredible Meanness instructed their Governors to pass no Act for laying the necessary Taxes, unless their Estates were in the same Act expressly excused; and had even taken Bonds of these Governors to comply with such Instructions. The Assemblies for three Years held out against this Injustice. At length Capt. [William] Denny, who was Governor Morris's Successor, ventur'd to disobey those Instructions; how that was brought about I shall show hereafter.

But I am got forward too fast with my Story; there are still some Transactions to be mentioned that happened during the Administration of Governor Morris.[9] ...

The order of events during 1755: conferring with General Braddock, April; teaming with Quakers against taxes, October; and building forts, December. Omitted here is an episode of April in which Franklin assists Josiah Quincy in obtaining a loan from the Assembly to assist defense of Massachusetts.

The British Government not chusing to permit the Union of the Colonies, as propos'd at Albany, and to trust that Union with their Defence, lest they should thereby grow too military, and feel their own Strength, Suspicions & Jealousies at this time being entertain'd of them; sent over General Braddock with two Regiments of Regular English troops for that purpose. He landed at Alexandria in Virginia, and thence march'd to Frederic Town in Maryland, where he halted for Carriages.[10]

> When Governor Morris warned Braddock that the Assembly would prove recalcitrant, the general warned them he would use "unpleasant methods" to secure cooperation, including decent postal service.[11]

Our Assembly, apprehending from some Information, that he had conceived violent Prejudices against us, sent me to wait upon him, not as from them, but as Postmaster General, under the guise of proposing to settle with him the Mode of conducting with most Celerity and Certainty the Dispatches between him and the Governors of the several Provinces, with whom he must necessarily have continual Correspondence. My Son accompanied me on this Journey. We found the general at Frederic Town, waiting impatiently for the Return of those he had sent thro' the back Parts of Maryland & Virginia to collect Waggons. I staid with him several Days, and had full Opportunity of removing all his Prejudices, by the Information of what the Assembly had done to assist him and facilitate his Operations.[12]

> The Assembly had appropriated one thousand pounds,[13] which Morris vetoed, telling Braddock that Quakers had obstructed the aid. Franklin's mission was thus to placate Braddock, including supplying horses and wagons borrowed on his own security. Braddock's defeat in July would leave Franklin facing financial ruin.

When I was about to depart, The Returns of Waggons were brought in, by which it appear'd that they amounted only to twenty-five, and not all of those were in serviceable

Condition. The General and all the Officers were surpriz'd, declar'd the Expedition was then impossible, and exclaim'd against the Ministers for landing them in a Country destitute of the Means of conveying their Stores, Baggage, &c not less than 150 Waggons being necessary. I happen'd to say, I thought it was pity they had not been landed rather in Pennsylvania, as in that Country every Farmer had his Waggon. The General eagerly laid hold of my Words, and said, "Then you, Sir, who are a Man of Interest there, can probably procure them for us; and I beg you will undertake it."

I ask'd what Terms were to be offer'd the People to induce Owners of the Waggons; and I was desir'd to put on Paper the Terms that appear'd to me necessary. This I did, and they were immediately agreed to, and a Commission and Instructions accordingly prepar'd immediately. What these Terms were will appear in the Advertisement I publish'd which from the great and sudden Effect it produc'd, being a Piece of some Curiosity.

> Published as a broadside, the "curiosity" was a subtly veiled threat to the farmers of (mostly) German origin that if they did not cooperate, Braddock would unleash Sir John St. Clair the Hussar, who would treat them as harshly as they had been used to in the old country.

I receiv'd of the General about 800 Pounds Sterling to be disburs'd in Advance-money to the Waggon-owners &c. but that being insufficient, I advanc'd upwards of 200 more, and in two Weeks, the 150 Waggons with 259 carrying Horses were on their March for the Camp. The Advertisement promised Payment according to the Valuation, in case any Waggon or Horse should be lost. The Owners however, alledging they did not know General Braddock, or what Dependance might be had on his Promise, insisted on my Bond for the Performance, which I accordingly gave them.

While I was at the Camp, supping with the Officers of Col. [Thomas] Dunbar's Regiment, he represented to me his Concern for the Subalterns, who he said were generally not in Affluence, and could ill afford to lay in the Stores that might be necessary in so long a March thro' a Country where nothing was to be purchas'd. I said nothing to him of my Intention, but wrote the next Morning to the Committee of Assembly, who had the Disposition of some public Money, recommending the Case of these Officers to their Consideration, and proposing that a Present should be sent them of Necessaries & Refreshments. My Son, who had had some Experience of a Camp Life, drew up a List for me, which I inclos'd in my Letter. The Committee approv'd, and used such Diligence, that conducted by my Son, the Stores arrived at the Camp as soon as the Waggons. They consisted of 20 Parcels, each containing

6 lb Loaf Sugar
6 lb good Muscovado Ditto
1 lb good Green Tea
l lb good Bohea Ditto
6 lb good ground Coffee
6 lb Chocolate
1/2 hundredweight best white Biscuit
1/2 lb Pepper
1 Quart best white Wine Vinegar
1 Gloucester Cheese
1 Kegg containing 20 lb good Butter
2 Doz. old Madeira Wine
2 Gallons Jamaica Spirits
1 Bottle Flour of Mustard
2 well-cur'd Hams
1/2 Doz dry'd Tongues

6 lb Rice
6 lb Raisins.[14]

Pacifists in the Assembly were quite willing to support the military with food and drink to counter the Governor's charge that they were subverting provincial defense.[15]

These 20 Parcels well pack'd were plac'd on as many Horses, each Parcel with the Horse, being intended as a Present for one Officer. They were very thankfully receiv'd, and the Kindness acknowledg'd by Letters to me from the Colonels of both Regiments in the most grateful Terms. The General too was highly satisfied with my Conduct in procuring him the Waggons, &c. thanking me repeatedly and requesting my farther Assistance in sending Provisions after him. I undertook this also, and was busily employ'd in it till we heard of his Defeat, advancing, for the Service, of my own Money, upwards of 1000 Pounds Sterling, of which I sent him an Account. It came to his Hands luckily for me a few Days before the Battle, and he return'd me immediately an Order on the Paymaster for the round Sum of 1000 Pounds Sterling leaving the Remainder to the next Account. I consider this Payment as good Luck; having never been able to obtain the Remainder; of which more hereafter.

This General was I think a brave Man, and might probably have made a Figure as a good Officer in some European War. But he had too much self-confidence, too high an Opinion of the Validity of Regular Troops, and too mean a One of both the Americans and Indians. George Croghan, our Indian Interpreter, join'd him on his March with 100 of those People, who might have been of great Use to his Army as Guides, Scouts, &c. if he had treated them kindly; but he slighted & neglected them, and they gradually left him.[16]

Croghan's official report said he brought only fifty Indians, who insisted on setting up their own bivouac; all but eight disappeared when Braddock insisted squaws could not come along after they fraternized with his troops.[17]

In Conversation with him one day, he was giving me some Account of his intended Progress. "After taking Fort Du Quesne," says he, "I am to proceed to Niagara; and having taken that, to Frontenac, if the Season will allow time; and I suppose it will; for Duquesne can hardly detain me above three or four Days; and I see nothing that can obstruct my March to Niagara."

Having revolv'd in my Mind the long Line his Army must make in their March, by a very narrow Road to be cut thro' the Woods & Bushes; & what I had read of a former Defeat of 1500 French who invaded the Iroquois Country, I had conceiv'd some Doubts, & some Fears for the Event: But I ventur'd only to say, "To be sure, if you arrive well before the Place, with these fine Troops so well provided with Artillery, that Place, as yet not compleatly fortified, and as we hear with no very strong garrison, can probably make but a short resistance. The only Danger I apprehend of Obstruction to your March, is from Ambuscades of Indians, who by constant Practice are dextrous in laying & executing them. And the long and slender Line your Army must make, may expose it to be attack'd by Surprize in its Flanks, and to be cut like a Thread into several Pieces, which from their Distance cannot come up in time to support each other."

He smil'd at my Ignorance, & reply'd, "These Savages may indeed be formidable to your raw American Militia; but, Sir, upon the King's regular & disciplin'd troops, it is impossible they should make any Impression." I was conscious of an Impropriety in my Disputing with a military Man in Matters of his Profession, and said no more.

The Enemy however did not take Advantage of his Army which I apprehended its long Line of March expos'd it to, but let it advance without Interruption till within 9 Miles of the Place; and then in a more open Part of the Woods than any they had pass'd, attack'd its advanc'd Guard, by a heavy Fire from behind Trees & Bushes; which was the first Intelligence the General had of an Enemy's being near him. This Guard being disorder'd, the General called the Troops up to their Assistance, which was done in great Confusion thro' Waggons, Baggage and Cattle; and presently the Fire came upon their Flank; the Officers being on Horseback were more easily distinguish'd, and pick'd out as Marks, and fell very fast; and the Soldiers were crowded together in a Huddle, having or hearing no Orders, and standing to be shot at till two thirds of them were killed, and then seiz'd with a Pannick the whole fled with Precipitation.

The Waggoners took each a Horse out of his Team, and scamper'd; their Example was immediately follow'd by others, so that all the Waggons, provisions, Artillery and Stores were left to the Enemy. The General being wounded was brought off with Difficulty, his Secretary Mr [William, Jr.] Shirley was killed, and out of 86 Officers 63 were killed or wounded, and 714 Men killed out of 1100. These 1100 had been picked Men out of the whole Army,[18] the

> Franklin, unsure of these figures, made a note in the column of the manuscript to check them. The English reported 62 officers killed or wounded out of 96; 914 men out of 1373. The French listed 23 dead and 16 wounded out of a force totaling 250 French and 650 "Sauvages."

Rest had been left with Col. [Thomas Dunbar] and the heavier Part of the Stores, Provisions and Baggage. The Flyers, without being pursu'd, arriv'd at Dunbar's Camp, and the Pannick they brought with them instantly seiz'd him and all his People. And tho' he had now above 1000 Men, and the Enemy who had beaten Braddock did not exceed 400, Indians and French together; instead of Proceeding and endeavouring to recover some of the lost Honour, or posting his Troops so as to guard in some Degree the Frontier, he order'd all the Stores to be destroy'd, that he might have more Horses to assist his Flight towards the Settlements. He was there met with Requests from the Governors of Virginia & Maryland that he would post his Troops on the Frontiers so as to afford some Protection to the Inhabitants; but he continu'd his March thro' all the Country, not thinking himself safe till he arriv'd at Philadelphia, where the Inhabitants could protect him. This whole Transaction gave us Americans the first Suspicion that our exalted Ideas of the Prowess of British Regulars had not been well founded.

In their first March too, from their Landing till they got beyond the Settlements, they had plundered and stript the Inhabitants, totally ruining some poor Families, by disabling them to planting their Corn or do anything, besides insulting, abusing & confining the People if they remonstrated. This was enough to put us out of Conceit of such Defenders if we had really wanted any. How different was the Conduct of our French Friends in 1781, who during a March thro' the most inhabited Part of our Country, from Rhodeisland to Virginia, near 700 Miles, occasion'd not the smallest Complaint, for the Loss of a Pig, a Chicken, or even an Apple!

Capt. [Robert] Orme, who was one of the General's Aid de Camps, and being grievously wounded was brought off with him, and continu'd with him to his Death, which happen'd in a few Days, told me, that he was totally silent, all the first Day, and at Night only said, "Who'd have thought it?" that he was silent again the following Days, only saying

at last, "We shall know how to deal with them better another time;" and dy'd a few Minutes after.

The Secretary's Papers with all the General's Orders,
Instructions and Correspondence falling into the Enemy's
Hands, they selected and translated a Number of Articles,
which they printed to prove the hostile Intentions of the
British Court before the Declaration of War. Among these
were some Letters of the General to the Ministry speaking
highly of the great Service I had rendered the Army, & recommending me to their Notice.[19]

> Franklin's files had a commendation from Braddock by 12
> June 1755.[20] As reprinted by the French among the general's
> captured papers, it is dated 5 June and praises Franklin's
> service as "almost the first Instance of Integrity, Address
> and Ability that I have seen in all these Provinces."[21]

David Hume too, who was some Years after secretary to
Lord Harcourt when Minister in France, and afterwards to
Gen. Conway when Secretary of State, told me he had seen
among the Papers in that Office Letters from Braddock
highly commending me. But the Expedition having been
unfortunate, my Service it seems was not thought of much
Value, for those Recommendations were never of any Use
to me.

As soon as the Loss of the Waggons was generally known,
all the Owners came upon me for the Valuation which I
had given Bond to pay. Their Demands gave me a great
deal of Trouble, my assuring them that I had apply'd to
General Shirley by Letter, but he being gone to Oswego, a
very remote Place, an Answer could not soon be receiv'd,
and they must have Patience; all this was not sufficient to
satisfy, and some began to sue me. General Shirley at length
reliev'd me from this terrible Situation, by appointing Commissioners to examine the Claims and ordering Payment.

They amounted to near twenty Thousand Pound, which would have ruined me.

Before we had the News of this Defeat, the two Doctors Bond came to me with a Subscription Paper, for raising Money to defray the Expence of a grand Fire Work, which it was intended to exhibit at a Rejoicing on receipt of the News of our Taking Fort Duquesne. I looked grave and said, "It would, I thought, be time enough to prepare for the Rejoicing when we knew we should have occasion to rejoice."

They seem'd surpriz'd that I did not immediately comply with their Proposal. "Why the D——l," says one of them, "you surely don't suppose that the Fort will not be taken?"

"I don't know that it will not be taken; but I know that the Events of War are subject to great Uncertainty." The Subscription was dropt, and the Projectors thereby miss'd the Mortification they would have undergone if the Firework had been prepared. Dr. Bond on some other Occasions afterwards said, that he did not like my forebodings.

Governor Morris who had continually harass'd the Assembly with Message after Message before the Defeat of Braddock, to beat them into the making of Acts to raise Money for the Defence of the Province without Taxing among others the Proprietary Estates, and had rejected all their Bills for not having an exempting Clause, now redoubled his Attacks, the Danger & Necessity being greater. The Assembly however continu'd firm, believing they had Justice on their side, and that it would be giving up an essential Right, if they suffered the Governor to amend their Money-Bills. In one of the last, indeed, his last Amendment was only of a single Word; the Bill express'd that all Estates real and personal were to be taxed, those of the Proprietaries *not* excepted. His Amendment was: for *not* read *only.* A small but very important Alteration! However, when the News of this Disaster reach'd England, our Friends there whom I had taken care to furnish all the Assembly's Answers to the Governor's Messages, rais'd some Clamour against the Proprietaries for their Meanness & Injustice in giving their Governors such Instructions, some going so far as to say that as they obstruct'd the Defence of their Province, they forfeited their Right to it. They were intimidated by this, and sent immediate Orders to their Receiver General to pay 5000 Pounds of their Money to whatever the Sum that might be given to the Assembly, for such Purpose. This being notified to the House, was accepted in Lieu of their Share of a general Tax, and the Bill pass'd with an exempting Clause accordingly. By this Act I was appointed one of the Commissioners for disposing of the Money, 60,000 Pounds. I had been active in modelling it, and procuring its Passage; and had at the same time drawn a Bill for establishing and disciplining a voluntary Militia, which I carried thro' the House without much Difficulty, as Care was taken in it to leave the Quakers at their Liberty.[22]

> The Assembly's success turned hollow when the Proprietors paid their share with a portfolio of bad debts and Franklin's militia bill was vetoed in London.[23]

21

Soldiering on the Frontier

1756

In a shrewd move for public support, Governor Morris put Franklin in charge of civil and military commands along the northern frontier. On Franklin's return, the new militia named him colonel and treated him with triumphal honors, further aggravating the Proprietors towards him. At least he outlasted Governor Morris.

To promote the Association necessary to form the Militia, I wrote a Dialogue, stating and answering all Objections I could think of to such a Militia, which was printed & had a good Effect. While the several Companies in the City & Country were forming and learning their Exercise, the Governor prevail'd with me to take Charge of our Northwestern Frontier, which was infested by the Enemy, and provide for the Defence of the Inhabitants by building a Line of Forts. I undertook this Business, tho' I did not conceive my self well-qualified for it. He gave me full Powers and a Parcel of blank Commissions to be given to whom I thought fit. I had little Difficulty in raising Men, having soon 560 under my Command. My Son who had in the preceding War been an Officer in the Army rais'd against Canada, was my Aid de Camp, and of great Use to me.[1]

At sixteen, William Franklin had been an ensign during much of 1747, stationed at Albany for an expedition against Canada that never came off.

The Indians had burnt Gnadenhut, a Village settled by the Moravians, and massacred the Inhabitants, but the Place was nevertheless thought a good Situation for one of the Forts. In order to march thither, I assembled the Companies at Bethlehem, the chief Establishment of those People.[2]

As to our Lodging ['twas] on real feather Beds, in warm Blankets, and much more comfortable than when we lodg'd at our Inn, the first Night after we left Home, for the Woman being about to put very damp Sheets on the Bed we desired her to air them first; half an hour afterwards, she told us the Bed was ready, and the Sheets well aired. I got into Bed, but jumped out immediately, finding them as cold as Death, and partly frozen. She had aired them indeed, but it was out upon the hedge.[3]

As we drew near [Bethlehem], we met a Number of Waggons, and many People moving off with their Effects and Families being terrified by the Defeat [at Gnadenhut], and the Burnings and Murders committed in the Township on New Year's Day. We found this Place fill'd with Refugees, the Workmen's Shops, and even the Cellars being crouded with Women and Children; and we learnt that Lehi Township is almost entirely abandoned by the Inhabitants.[4]

I was surprized to find [Bethlehem] in so good a Posture of Defence. The Destruction of Gnadenhut had made them apprehend Danger. The principal Buildings were defended by a Stockade. They had purchased a Quantity of Arms & Ammunition from New York, and had even plac'd Quantities of small paving Stones between the Windows of their high Stone Houses, for their Women to throw down upon the Heads of any Indians that should attempt to force into them. In Conversation with Bishop [Augustus] Spanenberg, I mention'd my Surprize; as knowing they had obtain'd an Act of Parliament exempting them from military Service Duties, as conscientiously scrupulous of bearing Arms. He answer'd me, "That it was not one of their establish'd Principles; but that at the time of their obtaining that Act, it was thought to be a Principle with many of their People. On this Occasion, however, they found it adopted by but a few." It seems they were either deceiv'd in themselves, or deceiv'd the Parliament, but Common Sense aided by present Danger, will sometimes be too strong for whimsicall Opinions.

It was in the Beginning of January when we set out upon this Business of Building Forts. The Moravians procur'd us five Waggons for our Tools, Stores, Baggage, &c. Just before I left Bethlehem, Eleven Farmers who had been driven from their Plantations by the Indians came to me, requesting they might be supply'd with Fire Arms, to go back and fetch off their Cattle. I gave them each a Gun with suitable Ammunition. We had not march'd many Miles before it began to rain, and it continu'd raining all Day. There were no Habitations on the Road to shelter us, till we arriv'd near Night at the House of a German, and in his Barn we were all huddled together as wet as Water could make us. It was well we were not attack'd in our March, for our Men could not keep their Gunlocks dry. The Indians are dextrous in Contrivances for that purpose, which we had not. They met that Day the poor Farmers above-mentioned & kill'd ten of them. He that escap'd inform'd that their Guns would not go off, the Priming being wet with the Rain. The next Day being fair, we continu'd our March and arriv'd at

Gnadenhut. There was a Saw Mill near, round which were left several Piles of Boards, with which we soon hutted ourselves; an Operation the more necessary at that inclement Season, as we had no Tents. *Our first Work was to bury more effectually the Dead we found there, half interr'd by the Country People.*[5]

> Trooper Peter Williamson's *French & Indian Cruelty* (1758) described the scene: "To our great Consternation, we found little Occasion to bury our unhappy Comrades, the Swine (which in that Country are vastly numerous in the Woods) having devour'd their Bodies, and nothing but Bones strewed up and down were to be seen."[6]

The next Morning our Fort was plann'd and mark'd out, the Circumference measuring 455 feet, which would require as many Palisades to be made of Trees one with another of a Foot Diameter each. Our Axes, of which we had 70 were immediately set to work, to cut down Trees; and our Men being dextrous in the Use of them, great Dispatch was made. Seeing the Trees fall so fast, I had the Curiosity to look at my Watch when two Men began to cut at a Pine. In 6 Minutes they had it upon the Ground. Each Pine made three Palisades of 18 Feet long, pointed at one End. While these were preparing, our other Men, dug a Trench all round of three feet deep in which the Palisades were to be planted, and our Waggons, the Body being taken off, and the fore and hind Wheels separated by taking out the Pin which united the two Parts of the Perch, we had 14 Carriages to bring the Palisades fom the Woods to the Spot. When they were set up, our Carpenters built a Stage of Boards all round within, about 6 Feet high, for the Men to stand on and fire thro' the Loopholes. We had one swivel Gun which we mounted on one of the Angles; and thus our Fort (if such a magnificent Name may be given to so miserable a Stockade) was finished in a Week, tho' it rain'd so hard every other Day that the Men could not work.

This gave me occasion to observe, that when Men are employ'd they are best contented. For on the Days they work'd they were good-natur'd and chearful; and on idle Days they were mutinous and quarrelsome, finding fault with their Pork, the Bread, &c. and in continual ill-humour; which put me in mind of the Prudence of a Sea-Captain, who made it a Rule to keep his Men constantly at Work; and when his Mate once told him that they had done everything, and he could not find what farther to employ them about; "Then," says he, "make them scour the Anchor."

We had for our Chaplain a zealous Presbyterian Minister, Mr [Charles] Beatty, who complain'd to me that the Men did not generally attend his Prayers & Exhortations. When they enlisted, they were promis'd, besides Pay & Provisions, a Gill of Rum a Day, which was punctually serv'd out to them, and I observ'd they were as punctual in attending to receive it. Upon which I said to Mr Beatty, "It is perhaps below the Dignity of your Profession to act as Steward of the Rum. But if you were to deal it out, and only to those just after Prayers, you would have them all about you." He lik'd the Thought, and undertook the Office, and with the help of a few Hands to measure out the Liquor executed it to Satisfaction; and never were Prayers more generally & more punctually attended. So that I thought this Method perferable to the Punishments inflicted by some military Laws for Non-Attendance on Divine Service.[7]

This Fort, however contemptible, is a sufficient Defence against Indians who have no Cannon. Finding our selves now posted securely, and having a Place to retreat to on Occasion, we ventur'd out in Parties to scour the adjacent Country. We met with no Indians, but we found the Places on the neighbouring Hills where they had lain to watch our Proceedings. There was an Art in their Contrivance of these Places that seems worth mention. It being Winter, a Fire was necessary for them. But a common Fire on the Surface of the Ground would by its Light have discover'd their Position at a Distance. They had therefore dug Holes in the Ground about three feet Diameter, and some what deeper. We saw where they had with their Hatchets cut off the Charcoal from the Sides of burnt Logs lying in the Woods. With these Coals they had made Fires in the Bottom of the Holes, and we observ'd the Prints of their Bodies made by their laying all round with their Legs hanging down in the Holes to keep their Feet warm, which with them is an essential Point. This kind of Fire, so manag'd, could not discover them either by its Light, Flames, Sparks or even Smoke. It appear'd that their Number was not great, and it seems they saw we were too many to be attack'd by them with Prospect of Advantage.[8]

I had hardly finish'd this Business, and got my Fort well stor'd with provisions, when I receiv'd a Letter from the Governor, acquainting me that he had called the Assembly, and wish'd my Attendance there, if the Posture of Affairs on the Frontier was such that my remaining there was no longer necessary.[9]

Attacks on the frontier were bound to increase as new growth provided even more dense foliage for screens, but Morris's policy was to pit frontiersmen against urban Quakers and both against friendly tribes now thinking of allying themselves with the French.[10] He was replaced by William Denny, 20 August 1756. John Campbell, Fourth Earl Loudon, replaced General Shirley in July.

My three intended Forts being now compleated, and the Inhabitants contented to remain on their Farms under that Protection, I resolved to return. The more willingly as a New England Officer, experienc'd in Indian War, being on a Visit to our establishment, consented to accept the Command. I gave him a Commission, and parading the Garrison had it read before them, and introduc'd him to them as an Officer who from his Skill in Military Affairs, was much more fit to command them than myself; and giving them a little Exhortation took my Leave.

"Colonel" William Clapham had more skill as a con man than as anything else. He was unmasked soon after Franklin left.[11]

I was escorted as far as Bethlehem, where I rested a few Days, to recover from the Fatigue I had undergone.[12]

While at Bethlehem, I enquir'd a little into the Practices of the Moravians. Some of them accompanied me and all were very kind to me. I found they work'd for a common Stock, eat at common Tables, and slept in common Dormitorys, great Numbers together. In the Dormitories I observ'd Loopholes at certain Distances all along under the Ceiling, which I thought judiciously plac'd for Change of Air. I was at Church, where I was entertain'd with good Musick, the organ being accompanied with Violins, Hautboys, Flutes, Clarinets, &c. I understood that their Sermons were not usually preached to mix'd Congregations, of Men Women and Children, as is our common Practice; but that they assembled sometimes the married Men, at other times the Wives, then the young Men, the single Women, and the little Children, each Division by itself. The Sermon I heard was to the latter, who came in and plac'd themselves in Rows on Benches, the Boys under the Conduct of a young Man their Tutor, and the Girls conducted by a young Woman. The Discourse seem'd well adapted to their Capacities, and was delivered in a pleasing familiar Manner, coaxing them as it were to be good. They behav'd very orderly, but look'd pale and unhealthy, which made me suspect they were not allow'd sufficient Exercise.

I enquir'd concerning their Marriages, whether the Report was true that they were by Lot? I was told that Lots were us'd only in particular Cases. That generally when a young Man found himself dispos'd to marry, he inform'd the Elders of it, who consulted the Elders that govern'd the young Women. As these Elders of the different Sexes were well acquainted with Tempers & Dispositions of their respective Pupils, they could best judge what Matches were suitable, and their Judgments were generally acquiesc'd in. But if for example it should happen that two or three young Women were found to be so *equally* proper for the young Man, the Lot was then recurr'd to. I objected, "If the Matches are not made by mutual Choice of the Parties, some of them may chance to be very unhappy." "And so they may," answer'd my Informer, "if you let them chuse for themselves."—Which I could not deny.[13]

The first Night being in a good Bed, I could hardly sleep, it was so different from my hard Lodging on the Floor of the Hut at Gnaden, wrapt only in a Blanket or two.[14]

Being return'd to Philadelphia, I found the Association went on swimmingly, the Inhabitants that were not Quakers having pretty generally come into it, form'd themselves into Companies, and chosen their Captains, Lieutenants and Ensigns according to the new Law. Dr B. visited me, and gave me an Account of the Pains he had taken to spread a general good Liking to the Law, and ascrib'd much to those Endeavours. I had had the Vanity to ascribe all to my Dialogue; However, not knowing but that he might be in the Right, I let him enjoy his Opinion.

The Officers meeting chose me Colonel of the Regiment. We paraded about 1200 Men, with a Company of Artillery who had been furnish'd with 6 brass Field Pieces, which they had made themselves so expert in the Use of as to fire twelve times in a Minute. The first Time I review'd my Regiment, they accompanied me to my House, and would salute me with some Rounds fired before my Door, which shook down and broke several Glasses of my Electrical Apparatus. And my new Honour prov'd not much less Brittle; for all our Commissions were soon after broke by a Repeal of the Law in England.

> The repeal came in October 1756. Dates of the other events: elected colonel, 28 February; parade, 18 March; escorted to lower ferry, 19 March (but Franklin insisted the troops carried drawn swords for only about 200 yards).[15]

During the short time of my Colonelship, being about to set out on a Journey to Virginia, the Officers of my Regiment hearing of it, took it into their heads that it would be proper for them to escort me out of town as far as the Lower Ferry. Just as I was getting on Horseback, they came to my door, between 30 & 40, mounted, and all in their Uniforms. I had not been acquainted with the Project, or I should have prevented it, being naturally averse to the assuming of State on any Occasion, & I was a good deal chagrin'd at their Appearance. I could not avoid their accompanying me. What made it worse, was, that as soon as we began to move, they drew their Swords, and rode with them naked all the way. Somebody wrote an Account of this to the Proprietor.[16]

I wonder who could think it worth their While to send such trifling News to England, or how it has been represented so as to give Offence. This was the only Instance of the kind: For tho' a greater Number met me at my Return, they did not ride with drawn Swords, having been told that Ceremony was improper, unless to compliment some Person of great Distinction. I, who am totally ignorant of military Ceremonies, and above all things averse to making Show and Parade, or doing any useless Thing that can serve only to excite Envy or provoke Malice, suffer'd at the Time much more Pain than I enjoy'd Pleasure, and have never since given the Opportunity for anything of the Sort.[17]

It gave [Thomas Penn] great Offence. No such Honours had been paid him when in the Province; and he said it was only proper to Princes of the Blood Royal; which may be true for aught I know, who was, and still am, ignorant of the Etiquette in such Cases. This silly Affair however greatly increas'd his Rancour against me, which was before considerable, on account of the Part I had in the Dispute between him & the Assembly, respecting the Exemption of his Estate from Taxation, which I had always oppos'd very warmly, & not without severe Reflections on his Meanness & Injustice in contending for it. He accus'd me to the Ministry as being the great Obstacle to the King's Service, & by my Influence in the House the proper Forming of the Bills for raising Money; and he instanc'd this Parade with my Officers as a Proof of my having an Intention to take the Government of the Province out of his Hands by Force. He also apply'd to Sir Everard Fauckener, then Post Master General, to deprive me of my Office. But this had no other Effect, than to procure from Sir Everard a gentle Admonition.[18]

It had been Thomas Penn who had recommended Franklin to Sir Everard just the year before, but paranoid reports from Rev. Richard Peters (as the one about the naked swords) strained the relationship.[19]

Notwithstanding the continual Wrangle between the Governor and the Assembly, in which I as a Member had so large a Share, there still subsisted a civil Intercourse between that Gentleman & myself, and we never had any personal Difference. I have sometimes since thought his little or no Resentment against me for the Answers it was known I drew up to his Messages, might be the Effect of Habit, being bred a Lawyer, he might consider us both as merely Advocates for contending Clients in a Suit, he for the Proprietaries & I for the Assembly. He would therefore sometimes call in a friendly way to advise with me on difficult Points, and sometimes, tho' not often, take my Advice. When the News arriv'd of Braddock's Defeat, the Governor sent in haste for me, to consult on Measures for preventing the Desertion of the back Counties. I forget now the Advice I gave, but I think it was, that Dunbar should be written to and prevail'd with if possible to post his Troops on the Frontier for their Protection, till by Reinforcements from the Colonies he might be able to proceed on the Expedition. And after my Return from the Frontier, he would have had me undertake the Conduct of such an Expedition with Provincial Troops, for the Reduction of Fort Duquesne, Dunbar & his Men being otherwise employ'd; and he propos'd to commission me as General. I had not so good an Opinion of my military Abilities as he profess'd to have; and I believe his Professions exceeded his real Sentiments: but probably he might think that my Popularity would facilitate the Raising of the Men, and my Influence in Assembly the Grant of Money to pay them: and that perhaps without taxing the Proprietary Estate. Finding me not so forward to engage in the Business as he expected, the Project was dropt: and he soon after left the Government, being superseded by Capt. Denny.[20]

22

MAKING A MISSION
TO LONDON

1756–1757

With his new-found fame for science, the Assembly sent Franklin to petition to control its own appropriations. His departure, however, was delayed by negotiations demanded by Lord Loudon, by almost three weeks waiting for Loudon's permission to sail. In the mean time, Franklin's enemies warned associates in London he was a mischief-make motivated solely by self-interest.[1] Proprietor Thomas Penn, however, feared neither his infamy nor fame. He was confident that those who would decide the issue cared little about his reputation as a scientist or a subversive.

Our new Governor, Capt. [William] Denny, brought over for me the Medal of the Royal Society, which he presented to me at an Entertainment given him by the City. He accompanied it with very polite Expressions of his Esteem for me, having long been acquainted with my Character. After Dinner, when the Company as was customary at that time, were engag'd in Drinking, he took me aside into another Room, and acquainted me that he had been

advis'd by his Friends in England to cultivate a Friendship
with me, as one who was capable of giving him the best
Advice, & of contributing most effectually to the making
his Administration easy. That he therefore desired of all
things to have a good Understanding with me; and he begg'd
me to be assur'd of his Readiness on all Occasions to render me every Service in his Power. He said much to me also
of the Proprietor's good Dispositions towards the Province, and of the Advantage it might be to us all, and to me
in particular, if the Opposition that had been so long
continu'd to his Measures, were dropt, and Harmony
restor'd between him and the People, in which it was
thought no one could be more serviceable than my self,
and I might depend on more than adequate Acknowledge-
ments & Recompences, &c. &c. &c. The Drinkers finding
we did not return immediately to the Table, sent us a De-
canter of Madeira, which the Governor made liberal Use
of, and in proportion became more profuse of his Solicitations and Promises. My Answers were to this purpose, that
my Circumstances, Thanks to God, were such as to make
Proprietary Favours unnecessary to me; and that being a
Member of the Assembly I could not possibly accept of any;
that however I had no personal Enmity to the Proprietary,
and that whenever the Measures he propos'd should appear to be for the Good of the People, no one should es-
pouse and forward them more zealously than myself, my
past Opposition having been founded on the evident Intention of the Measures propos'd to serve the Proprietary
Interest with general Prejudice to that of the People. That I
was obliged to him (the Governor) for his Professions of
Regard to me, and that he might rely on every thing in my
Power to make his Administration as easy to him as possible, hoping at the same time that he had not brought with

him the same unfortunate Instructions his Predecessor had
been hamper'd with. On this he did not then explain himself. But when he afterwards came to do Business with the
Assembly it appear'd again, & the Disputes were renewed,
but between us personally no Enmity arose; we were often
together, he was a Man of Letters, had seen much of the
World and was very entertaining & pleasing in Conversation. He gave me the first Information that my old Friend
Ralph was still alive, that he was esteem'd one of the best
political Writers in England, had been employ'd in the Dispute between Prince Frederic and the King, and had
obtain'd a Pension of Three Hundred a Year; that his Reputation was indeed small as a Poet, Pope having damn'd it in
his Dunciad, but his Prose was thought as good as any
Man's.

The Assembly finally, finding the Proprietary obsti-
nately persisted in manacling their Deputies with Instructions inconsistent not only with the Privileges of the People,
but with the Service of the Crown, resolv'd to petition the
King against them, and appointed me their Agent to go
over to England to present & support the Petition. The
Assembly had sent up a Bill to the Governor granting a
Sum of Sixty Thousand Pounds for the King's Use, which
the Governor refus'd in Compliance with his Instructions.
I had agreed with Captain [William] Morris of the Packet
at New York for my Passage, and my Stores were put on
board, when Lord Loudon arriv'd at Philadelphia, expresly,
as he told me to endeavour an Accomodation between the
Governor and Assembly, that his Majesty's Service might
not be obstructed by their Dissensions: Accordingly he
desir'd the Governor & myself to meet him, that he might
hear what was said on both sides. We met and discuss'd the
Business. In behalf of the Assembly I urg'd all the Argu-

ments that may be found in the publick Papers of that Time, & the Governor pleaded his Instructions, the Bond he had given to observe them, and his Ruin if he disobey'd; Yet seem'd not unwilling to hazard himself if Lord Loudon would advise it. This his Lordship did not chuse to do, but rather urg'd the Compliance of the Assembly, and intreated me to use my Endeavours with them for that purpose; declaring he could spare none of the King's Troops for the Defence of our Frontiers, and that if we did not continue to provide for that Defence they must remain expos'd to the Enemy.

Seeing it unavoidable, I acquainted the House with what had pass'd in this and having presented them with a Set of Resolutions I had drawn up, declaring their Rights, & that they did not relinquish their Claim to these but only suspended their Exercise thro' Force, against which they protested, they finally at length agreed to drop that Bill and frame another agreable to the Proprietary Instructions. This of course pass'd, and I was then at Liberty to proceed on my Voyage: but in the meantime the Pacquet had sail'd in which had been my Sea-Stores, which was some Loss to me, and my only Recompence was his Lordship's Thanks for my Service, the Credit of obtaining the Accommodation falling to his Share.[2]

> Thomas Penn credited Loudon with the accommodation and blamed Franklin for trying to obstruct this and other measures. "All these republican schemes are chiefly insisted on by Mr. Franklin, who is coming to England for redress of their Grievances."[3]

He set out for New York before me, and as the Time for dispatching the Pacquet Boats, and there were two then remaining there, one of which he said was to sail very soon, I requested to know the time, that I might not miss her by any Delay of mine. His Answer was, "I have given out that she is to sail on Saturday next, but I may let you know *entre nous,* that if you are there by Monday morning you will be in time, but do not delay longer." By some Accidental Hindrance at a Ferry, it was Monday Noon before I arrived, and I was much afraid she might have sailed as the Wind was fair, but I was soon made easy by the Information that she was still in the Harbour, and would not till the next Day.[4]

> Cause of the delay was Loudon's insistence on awaiting reinforcements from England for an attack on Quebec. Records show that Franklin left Philadelphia on 4 April, arrived in New York four days later, boarded ship a month later, anchored off Sandy Hook on 20 June and finally sailed 23 June.[6]

One would imagine that I was now on the very point of Departing for Europe. I thought so; but I was not then so well acquainted with his Lordship's Character, of which *Indecision* was one of the Strongest Features. It was about the Beginning of April that I came to New York, and I think it was near the end of June before we sail'd. There were then two of the Pacquet Boats which had been long in Port, but were detain'd for the General's Letters, which were always to be ready to-morrow. Another Pacquet arriv'd, and she too was detain'd. We were the first to be dispatch'd, as having been there longest. Passengers were engag'd in all, & extreamly impatient to be gone, and the Merchants uneasy about their Letters, the Orders they had given for Insurance (it being War-time). But their Anxiety avail'd nothing; his Lordships Letters were not ready. And yet whoever waited on him found him always at his Desk, his Pen in hand, and concluded he must needs write abundantly.

Going my self one Morning to pay my Respects, I found

in his Antechamber one Innis, a Messenger of Philadelphia, who had come from thence express, with a Pacquet from Governor Denny for the General. He deliver'd to me some Letters from my Friends there, which occasion'd my enquiring when he was to return & where he lodg'd, that I might send some Letters by him. He told me he was to call to-morrow at nine for the Generals' Answer to the Governor, and should set off immediately. I put my Letters into his Hands the same Day. A Fortnight after I met him again in the same Place. "So you are soon return'd, Innis!"

"*Returned;* No, I am not *gone* yet. I have call'd here by Order every Morning for these two Weeks past for his Lordship's Letter, and it is not yet ready."

"Is it possible, when he is so constantly so great a Writer, for I see him often at his Scritore."

"Yes," says Innis, "but he is like St. George on the Signs, *always on horseback, and never rides on.*" This Observation of the Messenger was it seems well found; for when in England, I understood that Mr Pitt gave it as one Reason for Removing this General, and sending Amherst & Wolf, to replace him *that the Ministers never heard from him, and could not tell what he was doing.*

> Loudon was indeed replaced for not corresponding. Another complaint was that his correspondence with Franklin slighted Governor Denny.[5]

This daily Expectation of Sailing, and the Ship being down to Sandy hook, the Passengers thought it best to be on board, lest by a sudden Order the Ships should sail, and they be left behind. There if I remember right we were about Six Weeks, consuming our Sea Stores, and oblig'd to procure more. At length the Fleet sail'd, the General and all his Army on board, bound to Lewisburg with Intent to besiege and take that Fortress; all the three Packet-Boats in

Company. Ours was ordered to attend the General's Ship, ready to receive his Dispatches when they should be ready. We were out 5 Days before we got them, and then our Ship quitted the Fleet and steered for England. The other two Packets he still detain'd, carrying them with him to Halifax, where he staid some time to exercise the Men in sham Attacks upon sham Forts, then alter'd his Mind as to besieging Louisburg, and return'd to New York with all his Troops. During his Absence the French and Savages had taken Fort George on the Frontier of that Province, and massacred many of the Garrison after Capitulation.

I saw afterwards in London, Capt. [John] Bonnell, who commanded one of those Packets. He told me, that when he had been detain'd a Month, he acquainted his Lordship that his Ship was grown foul, and to a degree that must necessarily hinder her fast Sailing, a Point of consequence for a Packet Boat, and requested an Allowance of Time to heave her down and clean her Bottom. He was ask'd how long time that would require. The Captain answer'd, "Three Days." The General reply'd, "If you can do it in one Day, I give leave; otherwise not; for you must certainly sail the Day after to-morrow." So he never obtain'd leave tho' detained afterwards from day to day during full three Months. I saw also in London a Major, one of Bonnell's Passengers, who was so enrag'd against his Lordship for so deceiving and detaining him so long at New-York, and then carrying him to Halifax, and back again, that he swore he would sue him for Damages, and if he could not recover them, he would cut his Th[roat]. Whether he did nor not I never heard; but as he represented the Injury to his Affairs it was very considerable.

On the whole I wonder'd much, how such a Man came to be entrusted with so important a Business as the Conduct of a great Army: but having since seen more of the great World, and the means of obtaining & Motives for giving Places, my Wonder diminishes. General [William] Shirley, on whom the Command of the Army devolved upon the Death of Braddock, tho' not bred a Soldier, would in my Opinion have made a much better Campaign than that of 1757, which was frivolous, expensive and disgraceful to the Nation beyond Conception: For tho' Shirley was not a bred Soldier, he was sensible and sagacious in himself, and attentive to good Advice from others, capable of forming judicious Plans, quick and active in carrying them into Execution. Loudon, instead of defending the Colonies with his great Army, left them totally expos'd while he paraded it idly at Halifax, by which means Fort George was lost; and he derang'd all our mercantile Operations, & distress'd our Trade by a long Embargo on the Exportation of Provisions, on pretence of keeping Supplies from being obtain'd by the Enemy, but in reality for beating down their Price in Favour of the Contractors, in whose Profits some said, perhaps from Suspicion only, he had a Share. And when at last the Embargo was taken off, by neglecting to send Notice of it to Charlestown, the Carolina Fleet was detain'd near three Months longer, whereby their Bottoms were so much damag'd by the Worm, that a great Part of them founder'd in the Passage home.

Shirley was I believe sincerely glad of being reliev'd from so burthensom a Charge. I was at the Entertainment given by the City of New York, to Lord Loudon on his taking upon him the Command. Shirley tho' superseded, was present also. There was a great Company of Officers, Citizens and Strangers, and some Chairs having been borrowed in the Neighbourhood, there was one among them very low which fell to the Lot of Mr. Shirley. Perceiving it as I sat by him, I said, "They have given you, Sir, too low a Seat." "No matter," says he; "for I find *a low Seat* the easiest!"

While I was, as aforemention'd, detain'd at New York, I receiv'd all the Accounts of the Provisions, &c. that I had furnish'd to Braddock, some of which could not sooner be obtain'd from the different Persons I had employ'd to assist in the Business. I presented them to Lord Loudon, desiring to be paid the Ballance. He caus'd them to be regularly examin'd by the proper Officer, who, after comparing every Article with its Voucher, certified them to be right, and the Ballance due, for which his Lordship promis'd to give me an Order on the Paymaster. This, however, was put off from time to time; and tho' I called often for it by Appointment, I did not get it.[6]

> Loudon's diaries record Franklin visiting nine times during March and April, and that he thought Franklin's charges too high. Franklin, however, reported this reply: "The Country gave near as much more to persuade the People to serve Braddock."[7]

At length, just before my Departure, he told me he had on better Consideration concluded not to mix his Accounts with those of his Predecessors. "And you," says he, "when in England, have only to exhibit your Accounts to the Treasury, and you will be paid immediately." On my observing that it was hard I should be put to any Trouble to obtain the Money I had advanc'd, as I charg'd no Commissions for my Service, "O, Sir," says he, "you must not think of persuading me that you are no Gainer. We understand better these Affairs, and know that every one concern'd in supplying the Army finds means in the doing it to fill his own Pockets." I assur'd him that was not my Case, and that I had not profited a Farthing; but he appear'd clearly not to believe me; and indeed I have since learnt that immense

Fortunes are often made in such Employments. As to my Ballance, I am not paid it to this Day, of which more hereafter.[8]

Our Captain of the Pacquet had boasted much before we sail'd, of the Swiftness of his Ship. Unfortunately when we came to Sea, she proved the dullest of 96 Sail, to his no small Mortification. After many Conjectures respecting the Cause, when we were near another Ship almost as dull as ours, which however gain'd upon us, the Captain order'd all hands to come aft and stand as near the Ensign Staff as possible. We were, Passengers included, about forty Persons. While we stood there the Ship mended her Pace, and soon left our Neighbour far behind, which prov'd clearly what he suspected, that she was loaded too much by the Head. The Casks of Water it seems had been all plac'd forward. These he therefore order'd to be remov'd farther aft; on which the Ship recover'd her Character, and prov'd the best Sailer in the Fleet. The Captain said she had once gone at the Rate of 13 Knots, which is 13 Miles per hour. We had on board as a Passenger Captain [Archibald, Jr.] Kennedy of the Navy, who contended that it was impossible, and that no Ship ever sailed so fast, and that there must have been some Error in the Division of the Log-Line, or some Mistake in heaving the Log. A Wager ensu'd between the two Captains, to be decided when there should be sufficient Wind. Kennedy thereupon examin'd rigorously the Log-line, and being satisfy'd with that, he determin'd to throw the Log himself. Accordingly some Days after when the Wind blew very fair & fresh, and the Captain of the Packet ([Walter] Lutwidge) said he believ'd She then went at the Rate of 13 Knots, Kennedy made the Experiment, and own'd his Wager lost. The above Fact I give for the sake of the following Observation.

It has been remark'd as an Imperfection in the Art of Ship-building, that it can never be known till she is try'd, whether a new Ship will or will not be a good Sailer; for that the Model of a good sailing Ship has been exactly follow'd in a new One, which has been prov'd on the contrary remarkably dull. I apprehend this may be partly occasion'd by the different Opinions of Seamen respecting the Modes of lading, rigging & sailing of a Ship. Each has his System. And the same Vessel laden by the Judgment & Orders of one Captain shall sail better or worse than when by the Orders of another. Besides, it scarce ever happens that a Ship is form'd, fitted for the Sea, & sail'd by the same Person. One Man builds the Hull, another riggs her, a third lades and sails her. No one of these has the Advantage of knowing all the Ideas & Experiences of the others, & therefore cannot draw just Conclusions from the whole. Even in the simple Operation of Sailing when at Sea, I have often observ'd different Judgments in the Officers who commanded the successive Watches, the Wind being the same. One would have the Sails trimm'd sharper or flatter than another, so that they seem'd to have no certain Rule to govern by. Yet I think a Set of Experiments might be instituted, first to determine the most proper Form of the Hull; next the Dimensions and properest Place for the Masts; then the Form & Quantity of Sails, and the Position as the Wind may be; and lastly the Disposition of her Lading. This is the Age of Experiments; and such a Set accurately made & combin'd would be of great Use. I am therefore persuaded that ere long some ingenious Philosopher will undertake it; to whom I wish Success.

We were several times chas'd on our Passage, but outsail'd every thing, and in thirty Days had Soundings. We had a good Observation, and the Captain judg'd himself so near our Port (Falmouth) that if we made a good Run in the Night we might be off that Harbour in the Morning, and by running in the Night might escape the Notice of the Enemy's Privateers, who often cruis'd near the Entrance of the Channel. Accordingly all the Sail was set that we could possibly make, and the Wind being very fresh & fair, we went right before it, & made great Way. The Captain after his Observation, shap'd his Course as he thought so as to pass wide of the Scilly Isles: but it seems there is sometimes a strong Indraft setting up St. George's Channel which deceives Seamen, and caus'd the Loss of Sir Cloudsley Shovel's Squadron. This was probably the Cause of what happen'd to us. We had a Watchman plac'd in the Bow to whom they often call'd, "Look well out before there;" and he as often answer'd, "Aye, Aye!" But perhaps had his Eyes shut, and was half asleep at the time: they sometimes answering as mechanically: For he did not see a Light just before us, which had been hid by the Studding Sails from the Man at the Helm & the rest of the Watch; but by an accidental Yaw of the Ship was discover'd, & occasion'd a great Alarm, we being very near it, *the Light appearing to me as big as a Cart Wheel. It was Midnight, &* Our Captain was fast asleep. But Capt. Kennedy jumping upon Deck, & seeing the Danger, order'd the Ship to wear round, all Sails standing. An Operation dangerous to the Masts, but it carried us clear, and we escap'd Shipwreck, for we were running right upon the Rocks on which the Lighthouse was erected. This Accident & Deliverance impress'd me with the Utility of Lighthouses, and made me resolve to encourage the building more of them in America, if I should live to return there.

In the Morning it was found by the Soundings, &c. that we were near our Port, but a thick Fog hid the Land from our Sight. About 9 aClock the Fog began to rise, and seem'd to be lifted up from the Water like the Curtain at a Playhouse, discovering underneath the Town of Falmouth, the Vessels in its Harbour, & the Fields that surrounded it. A most pleasing Spectacle to those who had been so long without any other Prospects, than the uniform View of a vacant Ocean! And it gave us the more Pleasure, as we were now freed from the Anxieties which the State of War occasion'd.[9]

The bell ringing for church, we went thither immediately, and with hearts full of gratitude, return'd thanks to God for the mercies we had receiv'd: were I a Roman Catholic, perhaps I should on this occasion vow to build a chapel to some saint; but as I am not, if I were to vow at all, it should be to build a lighthouse.[10]

I set out immediately with my Son for London, and we only stopt a little by the Way to view Stonehenge on Salisbury Plain, and Lord Pembroke's House and Gardens, with his very curious Antiquities at Wilton. We arriv'd in London on the 27th of July 1757.[11]

By November 1789 Franklin had completed the drafts of his memoir that he had been composing since Summer 1771. Gravely ill, medicated with opiates, and unsure of how to go on with it, he had copies made for French and English friends. Subsequently, he felt well enough to add seven pages, recording the end of his conflict with Thomas Penn, a segment that must have been composed on his deathbed. He died 17 April 1790.

23

LOBBYING IN LONDON

1757–1762

Along with his son William and their two servants, Franklin stayed with Peter Collinson at the Bear Inn for a few days before settling in as lodger with Margaret Stevenson on Craven Street, his address in London thereafter. His mission, to force Thomas Penn's respect for the Assembly's control over its own appropriations, must have seemed impossible, since the wife of the Privy Council president was Penn's sister-in-law. Further adding to Franklin's burden, his principal antagonist before the Court was Penn's adviser, a recognized authority on colonial law, Fernando John Paris. But Franklin outlived him. Paris died a few months after the hearing recorded in the concluding pages of Franklin's autobiographical manuscript as represented in the first twenty-three chapters of this book.

I went first to visit Dr Fothergill, to whom I was strongly recommended, and whose Counsel respecting my proceedings I was advis'd to obtain. He was against an immediate Application to the Government, and thought the Proprietaries should first be personally apply'd to, who might possibly be induc'd by the Interposition & Persuasion of some private Friends to accommodate Matters amicably.

Dr. John Fothergill, leader of British Quakers, served as Franklin's London physician.

I then called on my old Friend and Correspondent Mr Peter Collinson, who told me that John Hanbury, the great Virginia Merchant, had desired to be informed as soon as I should arrive, that he might carry me to Lord Granville's, who wish'd to see me as soon as possible. I agreed to go with him the next Morning. Accordingly Mr Hanbury call'd for me and took me in his Carriage to that Nobleman's, who receiv'd me with great Civility; and after some Questions respecting the present State of Affairs in America, & Discourse thereupon, he said to me, "You Americans have wrong Ideas of the Nature of your Constitution; you contend that the King's Instructions to his Governors are not Laws, and think yourselves at Liberty to regard or disregard them at your own Discretion. But those Instructions are not like the Pocket Instructions given to a Minister going abroad, for regulating his Conduct in some trifling Point of Ceremony. They are first drawn up by Judges learned in the Laws; they are then considered, debated & perhaps amended in Council, after which they are signed by the King. They are then, so far as relates to you, *the Law of the Land*; for THE KING IS THE LEGISLATOR OF THE COLONIES."

I told his Lordship this was new Doctrine to me. I had always understood from our Charters, that our Laws were to be made by our Assemblies, and presented to the King for his Royal Assent, but that being once given the King could not repeal or alter them. And as the Assemblies could not make permanent Laws without his Assent, so neither could he make a Law for them without theirs. He assur'd me I was totally mistaken in the Matter. I did not think so however. And his Lordship's Conversation having a little alarm'd me as to what might be the Sentiments of the Court concerning us, I wrote it down as soon as I return'd to my Lodgings. I recollected that about 20 Years before, a Clause in a Bill brought into Parliament by the Ministry, propos'd to make the King's Instructions Laws in the Colonies, which Clause was thrown out by the Commons, for which we ador'd them as our Friends & Friends of Liberty, till by their Conduct towards us in 1765, it seem'd that they had refus'd that Point of Sovereignty to the King, only that they might reserve it for themselves.[1]

I had had a violent cold and something of a fever, but it was almost gone. However, it was not long before I had another severe cold, which continued longer than the first, attended by a great pain in my head, the top of which was very hot, and when the pain went off, very sore and tender. These fits of pain continued sometimes longer than at others; seldom less than 12 hours, and once 36 hours. I was now and then a little delirious: they cupped me on the back of the head which seemed to ease me for the present; I took a great deal of bark, both in substance and infusion, and too soon thinking myself well, I ventured out twice, to do a little business and forward the service I am engaged in, and both times got fresh cold and fell down again.[2]

> Given his physical condition, Franklin must have shown little patience during his meeting with Thomas Penn, who insisted that the Assembly had no rights or privileges other than those granted by William Penn's charter. Franklin held firm.

After some Days, Dr Fothergill having spoken to the Proprietaries, they agreed to a Meeting with me at Mr J[ohn] Penn's House in Spring Garden. The Conversation at first consisted of mutual Declarations of Disposition to reasonable Accommodation; but I suppose each Party had its own Ideas of what should be meant by reasonable Accommodation. We then went into Consideration of our several Points of Complaint. The Proprietaries justify'd their Conduct as well as they could, and I the Assembly's. *"But,"* says I, *"Your Father's Charter expressly says that the Assembly of Pennsylvania shall have all the Power and Privileges of an Assembly according to the Rights of the Freeborn Subjects of England, and as is usual in any of the British Plantations in America."*

"Yes," says he, "but if my Father granted Privileges he was not by the Royal Charter impowered to grant, Nothing can be claim'd by such Grant. . . The Royal Charter was no Secret; they who came into the Province on my Father's Offer of Privileges, if they were deceiv'd, it was their own Fault;" and that he said with a Kind of triumphing laughing Insolence, such as a low Jockey might do when a Purchaser complained that He had cheated him in a Horse. I was astonished to see him thus meanly give up his Father's Character and conceived that Moment a more cordial and thorough Contempt for him than I ever before felt for any Man living . . . however, finding myself grow warm I made no other Answer to this than that the poor People were no Lawyers themselves and confiding in his Father did not think it necessary to consult any.[3]

In reporting this "low Jockey" observation to the Assembly in which Penn had many supporters, Franklin gave his antagonist excuse to reject him.

We now appeared very wide, and far enough from each other in our Opinions, to discourage all Hope of Agreement. However, it was concluded that I should give them the Heads of our Complaints in Writing, and they promis'd then to consider them.

I did so soon after; but they put the Paper into the Hands of their Solicitor Ferdinando John Paris, who manag'd for them all their Law Business in their great Suit with the neighbouring Proprietary of Maryland, Lord Baltimore, which had subsisted 70 Years, and wrote for them all their Papers & Messages in their Dispute with the Assembly. He was a proud angry Man; and as I had occasionally in the Assembly treated his Papers with some Severity, they being really weak in point of Argument, and haughty in Expression, he had conceiv'd a mortal Enmity to me, which discovering itself whenever we met, I declin'd the Proprietary's Proposal that he and I should discuss the Heads of Complaint between our two selves, and refus'd treating with any one but them. They then by his Advice put the Paper into the Hands of the Attorney and Solicitor General for their Opinion and Counsel upon it, where it lay unanswered a Year wanting eight Days, during which time I made frequent Demands of an Answer from the Proprietaries to no Effect. The Answer still was that they had not yet receiv'd the Opinion of the Attorney & Solicitor General:[4]

> Their opinions could only be against Franklin, since they were sent a document that distorted the "Heads" of his argument.[5]

What it was when they did receive it I never learnt, for they did not communicate it to me, but wrote a long Message to the Assembly *drawn & signed by Paris* reciting my Paper, complaining of its want of Formality as a Rudeness on my part, and offering a flimsy Justification of their Conduct, adding that they should be willing to accomodate Matters, if the Assembly would send over some *Person of Candour* to treat with them for that purpose, intimating thereby that I was not such.

The Want of Formality or Rudeness complain'd of was, probably my not having address'd the Paper to them with their assum'd Titles of true and absolute Proprietaries of the Province of Pensilvania, which I omitted as not thinking it necessary in a Paper the Intention of which was only to reduce to a Certainty by writing what in Conversation I had delivered *viva voce*. But during this

> But in 1759, Franklin had recognized the alleged "Rudeness" lay in his report to the Assembly in which he accused Thomas Penn of behavior becoming "a low Jockey." He confessed, "Indignation extorted it from me, and I cannot yet say that I much repent of it."[6]

Delay, the Assembly having prevail'd with Governor Denny to pass a Bill taxing the Proprietary Estate in common with the Estates of the People, which was the great Point in Dispute, they omitted answering the Message.

When this Act however came over, the Proprietaries counsell'd by Paris determin'd to oppose its receiving Royal Assent. Accordingly they petition'd the King in Council, and a Hearing was appointed, in which two Lawyers were employ'd by them against the Act, and two by me in Support of it. They alledg'd that the Act was intended to load the Proprietary Estate in order to spare those of the People, and that if it were suffer'd to continue in force, the Proprietaries would be ruined. We reply'd that the Act had no such Intention and would have no such Effect. That the Assessors were honest & discreet Men, under an Oath to assess fairly & equitably, & that any Advantage each of them might expect in lessening his own Tax by augmenting that of the Proprietaries was too trifling to induce them to perjure themselves. This is the purport of what I remember as urg'd by both Sides, except that we insisted strongly on the mischievous Consequences that must attend a Repeal; for that the Money, 100,000 pounds Sterling, being printed and given to the King's Use, & expended in his Service, & now in the Hands of the People, the Repeal would strike it dead in their Hands to the Ruin of many, & the total Discouragement of future Grants, and the Selfishness of the Proprietors in soliciting such a Catastrophe, merely from a groundless Fear of being taxed too highly, was insisted on in the strongest Terms.

On this Lord Mansfield, one of the Council, rose & beckoning to me, took me into the Clerk's Chamber, and ask'd me if I was really of Opinion that no Injury would be done the Proprietary estate in the Execution of the Act. I said, "Certainly." "Then," says he, "you can have little Objection to enter into an Engagement to assure that Point." I answer'd, "None, at all." He then call'd in Paris, and after some Discourse his Lordship's Proposition was accepted on both Sides; a Paper to the purpose was drawn up by the Clerk of the Council, which I sign'd with Mr [Robert] Charles, who was also an Agent of the Province for their common Affairs; when Lord Mansfield return'd to the Council Chambers where finally the Law was allowed to pass. Some Changes were however recommended to be made by a subsequent Law; which the Assembly did not think necessary. They look'd on my entering into the Engagement as an essential Service to the Province, since it secur'd the Credit of the Paper Money then spread over all the Country; and gave me their Thanks when I return'd.[7]

> When he returned November 1762 he had to wait until the following 16 March to be voted 2214 pounds Sterling for services since 1757 and then the end of March for the official vote of thanks.[8]

But the Proprietaries were enrag'd at Governor Denny for having pass'd the Act, & turn'd him out, with Threats of suing him for Breach of Instructions which he had given Bond to observe. He however having done it at the Instance of the General & for His Majesty's Service, and having some powerful Interest at Court, despised the Threats, and they were never put in Execution.

24

SKIRMISHING
WITH PARLIAMENT

1757–1765

In describing the fog over Falmouth as rising like a play-house curtain, Franklin used a fitting image for the opening of his dramatic career in diplomacy, the second act of which closes with the infamous scene of his being abused before the Privy Council in the aptly named "Cock Pit," public humiliation he would neither forgive nor forget. Meanwhile he found fame and friends, even on the sea. While sailing in a convoy he felt "like traveling in a moving Village, with all one's Neighbours about one," as he happily reported in June 1765 to his new Scots friend, Henry Home, Lord Kames.

You require my History from the time I set Sail for America. I left England about the End of August 1762, in Company with Ten Sail of Merchant Ships under Convoy of a Man of War. . . . On the first of November, I arriv'd safe and well at my own House, after an Absence of near Six Years, found my Wife and Daughter well, the latter grown quite a Woman, with many amiable Accomplishments acquir'd during my Absence, and my Friends as hearty and affectionate as ever, with whom my House was fill'd for many Days, to congratulate me on my Return. I had been chosen yearly during my Absence to represent the City of Philadelphia in our Provincial Assembly, and on my Appearance in the House they voted me 3000 pounds Sterling for my Services in England and their Thanks delivered by the Speaker. In February following, my Son arriv'd with my new Daughter, for, with my Consent and Approbation he married soon after I left England, a very agreable West India Lady.

> William Franklin had stayed behind to receive appointment as Royal Governor of New Jersey and to wed tawny Elizabeth Downes, 34, in a fashionable wedding, September 1762, fulfilling his father's ambition for a son to rise into the gentry.

I accompanied him into his Government, where he met with the kindest Reception from the People of all Ranks, and has lived with them ever since in the greatest Harmony. A River only parts that Province and ours, and his Residence is within 17 Miles of me, so that we frequently see each other. In the Spring of 1763 I set out on a Tour thro' all the Northern Colonies, to inspect and regulate the Post Offices in the several Provinces. In this Journey I spent the Summer, travelled about 1600 Miles, and did not get home 'till the Beginning of November. The Assembly sitting thro' the following Winter, and warm Disputes arising between them and the Governor I became wholly engag'd in Public Affairs: For besides my Duty as an Assemblyman, I had another Trust to execute, that of being one of the Commissioners appointed by Law to dispose of the publick Money appropriated to the Raising and Paying an Army to act against the Indians and defend the Frontiers. And then in December we had two Insurrections of the back Inhabitants of our Province, by whom 20 poor Indians were murdered that had from the first Settlement of the Province lived among us and under the Protection of our Government. This gave me a good deal of Employment, for as the Rioters threatned farther Mischief, and their Actions seem'd to be approv'd by an encreasing Party, I wrote a Pamphlet entitled a *Narrative* [of the Late Massacres] to strengthen the Hands of our weak Government, by rendring the Proceedings of the Rioters unpopular and odious. This had a good Effect; and afterwards when a great Body of them with Arms march'd towards the Capital in defiance of the Government, with an avowed Resolution to put to death 140 Indian Converts then under its Protection, I form'd an Association at the Governor's Request, for his and their Defence, we having no Militia. Near 1000 of the Citizens accordingly took Arms; Governor [John] Penn made my House for some time his Head Quarters, and did every thing by my Advice, so that for about 48 Hours I was a very great Man, as I had been once some Years before in a time of publick Danger; but the fighting Face we put on, and the Reasonings we us'd with the Insurgents (for I went at the Request of the Governor and Council with three others to meet and discourse them) having turn'd them back, and restor'd Quiet to the City, I became a less Man than ever: for I had by these Transactions made myself many Enemies among the Populace; and the Governor (with whose Family our publick Disputes had long plac'd me in an unfriendly Light, and the Services I had lately render'd him not being of the kind that make a Man acceptable) thinking it a favourable Opportunity, join'd the whole Weight of the Proprietary Interest to get me out of the Assembly, which was accordingly effected at the last Election [3 October 1764], by a Majority of about 25 in 4000 Voters. The House however, when they met in October, approv'd of Resolutions taken while I was Speaker, of petitioning the Crown for a Change of Government, and requested me to return to England to prosecute that Petition; which Service I accordingly undertook, and embark'd the Beginning of November last, being accompany'd to the Ship, 16 Miles, by a Cavalcade of three Hundred of my Friends, who fill'd our Sails with their good Wishes, and I arrived in 30 Days at London.[1]

> Embarking from Chester on the ship *King of Prussia*, on 7 November 1764, Franklin reached London the second week of December. By June 1766 he was being accused at home of working against repeal of the infamous Stamp Tax. Deborah Franklin, facing threats of an angry mob, told him, "I was very sure you had done nothing to hurt anybody [and] I had not given offense to any person at all . . . but if anyone came to disturb me, I would show a proper resentment" and "sent for a gun or two as we had none."[2] His testimony before Parliament, however, was instrumental in repealing the act. "I never in my Life," he said, "labour'd any Point more heartily than I did in obtaining the Repeal."[3] And he reported the repeal for the Philadelphia press with unguarded optimism.

The present Ministry, who have been true Friends to America in this Affair, purpose also to review the Acts of Trade, and give us every farther Relief that is reasonable. I hope therefore that Harmony between the two Countries will be restor'd, and all Mobs and Riots on our Side the Water totally cease. It will certainly become us on this Occasion to behave decently and respectfully with regard to the Government here, that we may not disgrace our Friends who have in a manner engag'd their Credit for us on that head. We now see that tho' the Parliament may sometimes possibly thro' Misinformation be mislead to do a wrong Thing towards America, yet as soon as they are rightly inform'd, they will immediately rectify it, which ought to confirm our Veneration for that most august Body, and Confidence in its Justice and Equity.[4]

> Although repealing the Stamp Act, Parliament asserted its supremacy by passing an act requiring quarters for troops sent to defend them. Franklin forecast the consequences, 25 February 1767.

An Act was pass'd to regulate the Quartering of Soldiers in America.... New York Assembly has refus'd to do it. And now all the Talk is to send a Force to compel them. ... Their Refusal is here called Rebellion, and Punishment is thought of. But sure I am, that, if Force is us'd, great Mischief will ensue, the Affections of the People of America to this Country will be alienated, your Commerce will be diminished, and a total Separation of Interests be the final Consequence.

Upon the whole, I have lived so great a Part of my Life in Britain [nine years], and have formed so many Friendships in it, that I love it and wish its Prosperity, and therefore wish to see that Union on which alone I think it can be secur'd and establish'd. As to America, the Advantages of such an Union to her are not so apparent. She may suffer at present under the arbitrary Power of this Country; she may suffer for a while in a Separation from it; but these are temporary Evils that she will outgrow. Scotland and Ireland are differently circumstanc'd. Confin'd by the Sea, they can scarcely increase in Numbers, Wealth and Strength so as to overbalance England. But America, an immense Territory, favour'd by Nature with all Advantages of Climate, Soil, great navigable Rivers and Lakes, &c. must become a great Country, populous and mighty; and will in a less time than is generally conceiv'd be able to shake off any Shackles that may be impos'd on her, and perhaps place them on the Imposers. In the mean time, every Act of Oppression will sour their Tempers, lessen greatly if not annihilate the Profits of your Commerce with them, and hasten their final Revolt: for the Seeds of Liberty are universally sown there, and nothing can eradicate them. And yet there remains among that People so much Respect, Veneration and Affection for Britain, that, if cultivated prudently, with kind Usage and Tenderness for their Privileges, they might be easily govern'd stiill for Ages, without Force or any considerable Expence. But I do not see here a sufficient Quantity of Wisdom that is necessary to produce such a Conduct, and I lament the Want of it.[5]

> The press on both sides of the Atlantic abused Franklin for his role in the Stamp Act controversy, but he assured his favorite sister Jane Mecom that he would rather be abused than ignored.

Such Enemies do a Man some good; while they think they are doing him harm, by fortifying the Character they would destroy; for when he sees how readily imaginary Faults and Crimes are laid to his Charge, he must be more apprehensive of the Danger of committing real Ones, as he can expect no Quarter, and therefore is more on his Guard to avoid or at least to conceal them.... Good Mr. Whitfield said to me once on such an Occasion: "I read the Libels writ against you," says he, "when I was in a remote Province, where I could not be inform'd of the Truth of the Facts; but they rather gave me this good Opinion of you *that you continued to be USEFUL to the Publick*: For when I am on the Road, and see Boys in a Field at a Distance, pelting a Tree, though I am too far off to know what Tree it is, I conclude it has FRUIT on it.[6]

25

COPING IN A CALM

1766–1770

In September 1766, Franklin could speak of "a dead Calm of Politicks."[1] In addition to Pennsylvania, he became agent for Georgia, New Jersey, and Massachusetts, increased duties which would keep him from home several more years, leaving family management to Deborah Franklin. She would not join him for fear of the long Atlantic crossing. The political calm allowed him to visit intellectual communities in Great Britain and Europe where he found tranquillity merely skin deep: "In America if one Mob rises and breaks a few Windows, or tars and feathers a single rascally Informer, it is called *Rebellion*: Troops and Fleets must be sent, and military Execution talk'd of as the decentist Thing in the World. Here indeed one would think Riots part of the Mode of Government."[2] At the same time, however, he had to ensure domestic tranquillity in Philadelphia, especially when daughter Sally insisted on marrying poor but honest Richard Bache. Mrs. Franklin sought his decision. She feared that denying the match would lead them to elope, and yet Bache had no prospects. From his safe distance (22 June 1767), Franklin offered only financial advice.

I must leave it to your Judgment to act in the Affair of your Daughter's Match as shall seem best. If you think it a suitable one, I suppose the sooner it is compleated, the better. In that case, I would only advise that you do not make an expensive feasting Wedding, but conduct every thing with Frugality and Economy, which our Circumstances really now require to be observed in all our Expences; For since my Partnership with Mr. Hall is expired [on 21 January 1766], a great source of our Income is cut off; and if I should lose the Post Office, which among the many Changes here is far from being unlikely, we should be reduc'd to our Rent and Interest of Money for a Subsistence, which will by no means afford the chargeable Housekeeping and Entertainments we have been used to; for my own Part I live here as frugally as possible not to be destitute of the Comforts of Life, making no Dinners for anybody, and contenting my self with a single Dish when I dine at home; and yet such is the Dearness of Living here in every Article, that my Expences amaze me. I see too by the Sums you have received in my Absence, that yours are very great, and I am very sensible that your Situation naturally brings you a great many Visitors which occasion an Expence not easily to be avoided, especially when one has been long in the Practice and Habit of it: But when People's Incomes are lessened, if they cannot proportionably lessen their Outgoings, they must come to Poverty. If we were young enough to begin Business again, it might be another Matter; but I doubt we are past it; and Business not well managed ruins one faster than no Business. In short, with Frugality and prudent Care we may subsist decently on what we have, and leave it entire to our Children; but without such Care, we shall not be able to keep it together; it will melt away like Butter in the Sunshine; and we may live long enough to feel the miserable Consequences of our Indiscretion.[3]

Sally did wed her young man, who, a few years later,
visited with her father in England. Franklin advised him to
go back to Philadelphia and open a shop where Sally could
assist him; as he wrote to her (29 January 1772).

In keeping a Store, if it be where you dwell, you can be
serviceable to him as your Mother was to me: For you are
not deficient in Capacity, and I hope are not too proud.
You might easily learn Accounts, and you can copy Letters
or write them very well upon Occasion. By Industry and
Frugality you may get forward in the World, being both of
you yet young. And then what we may leave you at our
Deaths may be a pretty Addition, tho' of itself far fom sufficient to maintain and bring up a Family. It is of the more
Importance for you to think seriously of this, as you may
have a Number of Children to educate.

She would have eight children before dying of cancer at
the age of sixty-five.

'Till my Return you need be at no Expence for Rent,
&c. as you are all welcome to continue with your Mother,
and indeed it seems to be your Duty to attend her as she
grows infirm, and takes much Delight in your Company
and the Child's. This Saving will be a Help in your Progress:
And for your Encouragement I can assure you that there is
scarce a Merchant of Opulence in your Town whom I do
not remember a young Beginner with as little to go on with,
and no better Prospects than Mr. Bache.[4]
I have staid too long in London this Summer, and now
sensibly feel the Want of my usual Journey to preserve my
Health. Therefore I this Morning [28 August 1767] am to
set for a Trip to Paris. Sir John Pringle, the Queen's Physician, goes with me. He has Leave for Six Weeks only, her
Majesty being again pregnant.[5]

All the way to Dover we were furnished with Post Chaises hung so as to lean forward, the Top coming down over one's Eyes, like a Hood, as if to prevent one's seeing the Country, which being one of my great Pleasures, I was engag'd in perpetual Disputes with the Innkeepers, Hostlers and Postillions about getting the Straps taken up a Hole or two before, and let down as much behind, they insisting that the Chaise leaning forward was an Ease to the Horses, and that the contrary would kill them. I suppose the Chaise leaning forward looks to them like a Willingness to go forward; and that its hanging back shows a Reluctance. They added other Reasons that were no Reasons at all, and made me, as upon a 100 other Occasions, almost wish that Mankind had never been endow'd with a reasoning Faculty, since they know so little how to make use of it, and so often mislead themselves by it; and that they had been furnish'd with a good sensible Instinct instead of it.[6]

I have been at Court. We went to Versailles and had the Honour of being presented to the King [Louis XV]; he spoke to both of us very graciously and chearfully, is a handsome Man, has a very lively Look, and appears younger than he is. . . . The King talk'd a good deal to Sir John, asking many Questions about our Royal Family; and did me too the Honour of taking some Notice of me.[7]

The Civilities we every where receive give us the strongest Impressions of the French Politeness. It seems to be a Point settled here universally that Strangers are to be treated with Respect, and one has just the same Deference shewn one here by being a Stranger as in England by being a Lady. The Custom House Officers at Port St. Denis, as we enter'd Paris, were about to seize 2 Dozen of excellent Bourdeaux Wine given us at Boulogne, and which we brought with us;

but as soon as they found we were Strangers, it was immediately remitted on that Account.

Travelling is one Way of lengthening Life, at least in
Appearance. It is but a Fortnight since we left London; but
the Variety of Scenes we have gone through makes it seem
equal to Six Months living in one Place. Perhaps I have suffered a greater Change too in my own Person than I could
have done in Six Years at home. I had not been here Six
Days before my Taylor and Peruquier had transform'd me
into a Frenchman. Only think what a Figure I make in a
little Bag Wig and naked Ears! They told me I was become
20 Years younger, and look'd very galante; so being in Paris
where the Mode is to be sacredly follow'd, I was once very
near making Love to my Friend's Wife.[8]

> In a remarkable meditation Franklin prefigures the theme
> of Abraham Lincoln's celebrated second inaugural address
> and the course of events to come while contemplating his
> awkward position in November 1768.

There is nothing I wish for more than to see [the dispute with Great Britain] amicably and equitably settled.
But Providence will bring about its own ends by its own
means; and if it intends the downfal of a nation, that nation will be so blinded by its pride and other passions as
not to see its danger, or how its fall may be prevented.

Being born and bred in one of the countries, and having lived long, and made many agreeable connections of
friendship in the other, I wish all prosperity to both; but I
have talked and written so much and so long on the subject, that my acquaintances are weary of hearing, and the
public of reading any more of it; which begins to make me
weary of talking and writing for them, especially as I do
not find that I have gained any point in either country, except that of rendering myself suspected by my impartial-

ity; in England of being too much an American, and in America of being too much an Englishman.[9]

> In mid-July 1770, Franklin worried that his activism
> would result in his losing his position at the Post Office,
> with its salary of three hundred pounds a year. He lived on
> that salary in London while sending home his agency
> salaries totaling some eleven hundred pounds a year.[10]

As to the Rumour . . . that I had been depriv'd of my Place in the Post Office on Account of a Letter I wrote to Philadelphia, it might have this Foundation, that some of the Ministry had been displeas'd at my Writing such Letters, and there were really some Thoughts among them of shewing that Displeasure in that manner. But I had some Friends too, who unrequested by me advis'd the contrary. And my Enemies were forc'd to content themselves with abusing me plentifully in the Newspapers, and endeavouring to provoke me to resign. In this they are not likely to succeed, I being deficient in that Christian Virtue of Resignation. If they would have my Office, they must take it—I have heard of some great Man, whose Rule it was with regard to Offices, "Never to ask for them," and "never to refuse them"; To which I have always added in my own Practice, "Never to resign them." As I told my Friends, I rose to that Office thro' a long Course of Service in the inferior Degrees of it: Before my time, thro' bad Management, it never produced the Salary annex'd to it; and when I receiv'd it, no Salary was to be allow'd if the office did not produce it. During the first four Years it was so far from defraying itself, that it became 950 pounds Sterling in debt to me and my Colleague. I had been chiefly instrumental in bringing it to its present flourishing State, and therefore thought I had some kind of Right to it. I had hitherto executed the

Duties of it faithfully, and to the perfect Satisfaction of my Superiors, which I thought was all that should be expected of me on that Account. As to the Letters complain'd of, it was true I did write them, and they were written in Compliance with another Duty, that to my Country. A Duty quite distinct from that of Postmaster. My Conduct in this respect was exactly similar with that I held on a similar Occasion but a few Years ago, when the then Ministry were ready to hug me for the Assistance I afforded them in repealing a former Revenue Act. My Sentiments were still the same, that no such Acts should be made here for America; or, if made should as soon as possible be repealed; and I thought it should not be expected of me, to change my Political Opinions every time his Majesty thought fit to change his Ministers. This was my Language on the Occasion; and I have lately heard, that tho I was thought much to blame, it being understood that every Man who holds an Office should act with the Ministry whether agreable or not to his own Judgment, yet in consideration of the goodness of my private Character (as they are pleas'd to compliment me) the office was not to be taken from me. Possibly they may still change their Minds, and remove me; but no Apprehension of that sort, will, I trust, make the least Alteration in my Political Conduct. My rule in which I have always found Satisfaction is, Never to turn aside in Publick Affairs thro' Views of private Interest; but to go strait forward in doing what appears to me right at the time, leaving the Consequences with Providence. What in my younger Days enabled me more easily to walk upright was, that I had a Trade; and that I could live upon a little; and thence (never having had views of making a Fortune) I was free from Avarice, and contented with the plentiful Supplies my Business afforded me. And now it is still more easy for me to preserve my Freedom and Integrity, when I consider, that I am almost at the End of my Journey, and therefore need less to complete the Expence of it; and that what I now possess thro' the Blessing of God may with tolerable Economy, be sufficient for me (great Misfortunes excepted) tho' I should add nothing more to it by any Office or Employment whatsoever.[11]

26

AGITATING FOR
ALL AMERICANS

1770–1774

Urging Americans to band together against British im-
ports and attacking official policy in countless London
newspaper articles earned Franklin a reputation as an
agent provocateur. He also confronted the Secretary of
State for America, Lord Hillsborough, in a skirmish
leading to a major political battle that both contestants
lost. He went to visit Hillsborough.

The Porter at first deny'd his Lordship, on which I left
my Name, and drove off. But before the Coach got out of
the Square, the Coachman heard a Call, turn'd, and went
back to the Door, when the Porter came and said, "His Lordship will see you, Sir." I was shown into the Levee Room,
where I found Governor (Francis) Barnard [ex-governor
of Massachusetts], who I understand attends there constantly. Several other Gentlemen were there attending, with
whom I sat down a few Minutes. When Secretary [John]
Pownall came out to us, and said his Lordship desired I
would come in.

I was pleas'd with this ready Admission, and Preference,

(having sometimes waited 3 or 4 Hours for my Turn) and being pleas'd, I could more easily put on the open chearful Countenance that Mr Strahan advis'd me to wear. His Lordship came towards me, and said, "I was dressing in order to go to Court, but hearing that you were at the Door, who are a Man of Business, I determin'd to see you immediately." I thank'd his Lordship and said that my Business at present was not much, it was only to pay my Respects to his Lordship and to acquaint him with my Appointment by the House of Representatives of Massachusetts Bay, to be their Agent here, in which Station if I could be of any Service—I was going to say, to the Publick—I should be very happy; but his Lordship whose Countenance chang'd at my naming that Province cut me short, by saying, with something between a Smile and a Sneer,

> L.H. I must set you right there, Mr. Franklin, you are not Agent.
>
> B.F. Why; my Lord?
>
> L.H. You are not appointed.
>
> B.F. I do not understand your Lordship. I have the Appointment in my Pocket.
>
> L.H. You are mistaken. I have later and better Advices. I have a Letter from Governor [Thomas] Hutchinson. He would not give his Assent to the Bill.
>
> B.F. There was no Bill, my Lord; it is a Vote of the House.
>
> L.H. There was a Bill presented to the Governor, for the Purpose of appointing you, and another, one Dr. [Arthur] Lee, I think he is call'd, to which the Governor refus'd his Assent.
>
> B.F. I cannot understand this, my Lord. I think There

must be some Mistake in it. Is your Lordship quite
sure that you have such a Letter?

L.H. I will convince you of it directly. *Rings the Bell.*
Mr. Pownall will come in and satisfy you.

B.F. It is not necessary that I should now detain your
Lordship from Dressing. You are going to Court. I
will wait on your Lordship another time.

L.H. No, stay. He will come in immediately. *To the
Servant.* Tell Mr. Pownall I want him. *Mr. Pownall
comes in.* Have not you at hand Governor
Hutchinson's Letter mentioning his Refusing his
Assent to the Bill for appointing Dr. Franklin
Agent?

Sec. P. My Lord?

L.H. Is there not such a Letter?

Sec. P. No, my Lord. There is a Letter relating to some
Bill for payment of Salary to Mr. [Dennis] DeBerdt
[previous Massachusetts agent] and I think to
some other Agent, to which the Governor had
refus'd his Assent.

L.H. And is there nothing in that Letter to the purpose
I mention?

Sec. P. No, my Lord.

B.F. I thought it could not well be, my Lord, as my
Letters are by the last Ships and mention no such
Thing. Here is an authentic Copy of the Vote of the
House appointing me, in which there is no
Mention of any Act intended. Will your Lordship
please to look at it? *(With some seeming
Unwillingness he takes it, but does not look into it).*

L.H. . . . . No such Paper shall be entere'd while I have
any thing to do with the Business. The House of
Representatives has no Right to appoint an Agent.

We shall take no Notice of any Agents but such as are appointed by Acts of Assembly to which the Governor gives his Assent. We have had Confusion enough already. Here is one Agent appointed by the Council, another by the House of Representatives; Which of these is Agent for the Province? Who are we to hear on Provincial Affairs? An Agent appointed by Act of Assembly we can understand. No other will be attended to for the future, I can assure you.

B.F. I cannot conceive, my Lord, why the Consent of the *Governor* should be thought necessary to the Appointment of an Agent for the People. It seems to me, that—

L.H. *(With a mix'd Look of Anger and Contempt)* I shall not enter into a Dispute with you, Sir, upon this Subject. . . . This Proceeding is directly contrary to express Instructions.

B.F. I did not know there had been such Instructions. I am not concern'd in any Offence against them, and—

L.H. Yes, your Offering such a Paper to be entred is an Offence against them *(Folding it up again, without having read a Word of it)*. No such Appointment shall be entred. When I came into the Administration of American Affairs, I found them in great Disorder; By my *Firmness* they are now something mended; and while I have the Honour to hold the Seals [of office] I shall continue the same Conduct, the same *Firmness.* I think My Duty to the Master I serve and to the Government of this Nation require it of me. If that Conduct is not approved, They may take my Office from me when they please. I

shall make 'em a Bow, and thank 'em. I shall resign
with Pleasure.[1] . . . But while I continue in it, I shall
resolutely persevere in the same FIRMNESS.
*(Spoken with great Warmth, and turning pale in his
Discourse, as if he was angry at something or somebody
besides the poor Agent; and of more Importance to
himself.)*

B.F. *(Reaching out his Hand for the Paper, which his
Lordship returned to him)* I beg your Lordship's
Pardon for taking up so much of your time. It is I
believe of no great Importance whether the
Appointment is acknowledged or not, for I have
not the least Conception that an Agent can *at
present* be of any Use, to any of the Colonies. I shall
therefore give your Lordship no farther Trouble.
(Withdrew.)[2]

About mid-August 1772, Franklin sought to have
Hillsborough impeached or censured for denying Americans their constitutional right of petition. Hillsborough
resigned after having failed to block a petition by the
Walpole Company in which Franklin, along with some
very important politicians, speculated in Ohio Valley land.
Franklin relished that resignation, hoping for better
treatment from Hillsborough's successor.[3]

As Lord Hillsborough in fact got nothing out of me, I
should rather suppose he threw me away as an orange that
would yield no juice, and therefore not worth more squeez-
ing. When I had been a little while returned to London I
waited on him to thank him for his civilities in Ireland,
and to discourse on a Georgia affair. The porter told me he
was not at home. I left my card, went another time, and
received the same answer, though I knew he was at home, a
friend of mine being with him. After intermissions of a week

each, I made two more visits, and received the same answer. The last time was on a levee day, when a number of carriages were at his door. My coachman driving up, alighted and was opening the coach door, when the porter, seeing me, came out, and surlily chid the coachman for opening the door before he had enquired whether my lord was home; and then turning to me, said, "My Lord is not home." I have never since been nigh him, and we have only abused one another at a distance. . . . I know him to be as double and deceitful as any man I ever met with. . . . I recollect that on my complaining of him to a friend at Court, . . . he told me, we Americans were represented by Hillsborough as an unquiet people not easily satisfied with any ministry, that however it was thought too much occasion had been given us to dislike the present and asked me, whether, if he should be removed, I could name another likely to be more acceptable to us, I said, "Yes, there is Lord Dartmouth: we liked him very well when he was at the head of the Board [of Trade] formerly, and probably should like him again." This I heard no more of, though I knew not that it had any effect.

As to my situation here nothing can be more agreeable, especially as I hope for less embarrassment from the new minister. A general respect paid me by the learned, a number of friends and acquaintance among them with whom I have a pleasing intercourse; a character of so much weight that it has protected me when some in power would have done me injury, and continued me in an office they would have deprived me of; my company so much desired that I seldom dine at home in winter, and could spend the whole summer in the country houses of inviting friends if I chose it. Learned and ingenious foreigners that come to England, almost all make a point of visiting me, for my reputation is still higher abroad than here; several of the foreign ambassadors have assiduously cultivated my acquaintance, treating me as one of their *corps*, partly I believe from the desire they have from time to time of hearing something of American affairs, an object become of importance in foreign courts, who begin to hope Britain's alarming power will be diminished by the defection of her Colonies; and partly that they may have an opportunity of introducing me to the gentlemen of their country who desire it. The K[ing] too has lately been heard to speak of me with great regard. These are flattering circumstances, but a violent longing for home sometimes seizes me, which I can no otherwise subdue but by promising myself a return next spring or next fall, and so forth. As to returning hither, if I once go back, I have no thoughts of it. I am too far advanced in life to propose three voyages more. I have some important affairs to settle at home, and considering my double expences here and there, I hardly think my salaries fully compensate the disadvantages. The late change however being thrown into the balance determines me to stay another winter.[4]

> On meeting Lord Dartmouth, the new Secretary of State for America, in November, Franklin put in a good word for his son William, governor of New Jersey.

I said I was happy to see his Lordship in his present Situation, in which for the good of both Countries I hoped he would long continue; and I begg'd Leave to recommend my Son to his Protection, "Who," says I, "Is one of your Governors in America." The Secretary [Pownal] then put in, "*And a very good Governor he is.*" "Yes," says my Lord, "He has been a good Governor, and has kept his Province in good Order, during Times of Difficulty.[5]

Franklin acknowledged political differences with his son, but hoped for the best.

You are a thorough government man, which I do not wonder at, nor do I aim at converting you. I only wish you to act uprightly and steadily, avoiding that duplicity, which in Hutchinson, adds contempt to indignation. If you can promote the prosperity of your people, and leave them happier than you found them, whatever your political principles are, your memory will be honored.[6]

Friends in high places gave Franklin access to politicians in high places. In their confrontations, he developed pride as an American and as Dr. Franklin that could risk a great fall.

I am not upon Terms with Lord North to ask any . . . Favour. Displeased with something he said relating to America, I have never been at his Levees, since the first. Perhaps he has taken that amiss. For [the last week we] met occasionally at Lord Le Despencer's, in our Return from [Oxford] . . . and he seem'd studiously [to avoid] speaking to me. I ought to be asham'd to say that on such [occasions] I feel myself to be as proud as any body. . . . We din'd, supped, and breakfasted together, without exchanging three Sentences.[7]

As agent for Massachusetts, Franklin relayed to Boston unauthorized copies of private letters between Governor Hutchinson and his lieutenant Andrew Oliver. The legislature petitioned for removal of Hutchinson, but he, in turn, sent Lord Dartmouth a copy of Franklin's "treasonable" letters to the legislature urging independence. When Franklin appeared before the Privy Council to argue that his agency was constitutional, his antagonists seized the occasion to indict him for theft of mail and for the alleged treason.

It is said here that the famous Boston letters were sent chiefly to . . . Mr. Wheatly. They fell into my hands, and I thought it my duty to give some principal people there a sight of them, very much with this view, that when they saw the measures they complained of, took their rise in a great degree from the representations and recommendations of their own countrymen, their resentment against Britain on account of those measures might abate, as mine had done, and a reconciliation be more easily obtained. In Boston, they concealed who sent them, the better to conceal who received and communicated them. And perhaps it is as well that it should continue to be a secret. Being of that country my self, I think those letters more heinous.[8]

> With respect to the letters said to be treasonable, Franklin insisted that he had merely urged the legislature to "avoid all tumults and violent measures" while continuing to argue their rights under the king and their own legislatures rather than the London Parliament, which he continued to attack in newspaper satires.

I have written two pieces here lately for the Public Advertiser, on American affairs, designed to expose the conduct of this country towards the colonies, in a short, comprehensive and striking view, and stated therefore in out-of-the-way forms, as most likely to take the general attention. The first was called, "Rules by which a great empire may be reduced to a small one;" the second, "An Edict of the King of Prussia." . . . In my own mind I preferred the first, as a composition for the quantity and variety of the matter contained, and a kind of spirited ending of each paragraph. But I find that others here generally prefer the second. I am not suspected as the author, except by one or two friends; and have heard the latter spoken of in the highest terms as the keenest and severest piece that has appeared here a long time. Lord Mansfield I hear said of it, that it "was very ABLE and very ARTFUL," indeed; and would do mischief by giving here a bad impression of the measures of government; and in the colonies, by encouraging them in their contumacy. It is reprinted in the Chronicle but stripped of all the capitalling and italicking, that intimate the allusions and mark the emphasis of written discourses, to bring them as near as possible to those spoken: printing such a piece all in one even small character, seems to me like repeating one of Whitfield's Sermons in the monotony of a school-boy. What made it the more noticed here was, that the people in reading it, were, as the phrase is, *taken in*, till they got half through it, and imagined it a real edict, to which mistake I suppose the king of Prussia's *character* must have contributed. I was down at Lord Le Despencer's when the post brought that day's papers. Mr. [Paul] Whitehead was there too . . . who runs early through all the papers, and tells the company what he finds remarkable. He had them in another room, and we were chatting in the breakfast parlour, when he came running in to us, out of breath, with the paper in his hand. "Here!" says he, "here's news for ye! *Here's the king of Prussia, claiming a right to this kingdom!*" All stared, and I as much as any body; and he went on to read it. When he had read two or three paragraphs, a gentleman present said, "Damn his impudence, I dare say, we shall hear by next post that he is upon his march with one hundred thousand men to back this." Whitehead, who is very shrewd, soon after began to smoke it, and looking in my face said, "I'll be hanged if this is not some of your American jokes upon us." The reading went on, and ended with abundance of laughing, and a general verdict that it was a fair hit: and the piece was cut out of the paper and preserved in my lord's collection.[9]

27

FAILING TO RECONCILE

1774–1775

The year 1774 opened and closed badly. In January, Franklin faced the Privy Council for publicizing private correspondence of Massachusetts officials. Solicitor-General Alexander Wedderburn publicly affronted him as a thief and a terrorist (news of the Boston Tea Party had arrived) who had assumed hubristic "self-created importance." Franklin maintained "a cool sullen Silence."[1] Subsequent loss of his post office was bad enough but much worse was news about Deborah Franklin. She had died in December even as he wrote complaining about not having heard from her. He sorely missed his "old and faithful Companion." "I every day become more sensible of the greatness of that Loss; which cannot now be repair'd."[2] Through playing chess he developed a direct line to the administration. William Pitt, Lord Chatham, reinflated Franklin's spirit by publicly visiting him, openly acknowledging his advice, and calling him, "An honour not to the English nation only, but to Human Nature."[1] Still, the Court of Chancery found him liable to arrest. When his final attempts at reconciliation failed, he sailed for home in March 1775, using the voyage to write in great

---

detail about what had happened since "the Affront" of January 1774.

About the Beginning of [November] being at the Royal Society, Mr. [Matthew] Raper one of our Members told me there was a certain Lady who had a Desire of Playing with me at Chess, fancying she could beat me, and had requested him to bring me to her; it was, he said, a Lady with whose Acquaintance he was sure I should be pleas'd, a Sister of Lord [Viscount Richard] Howe's, and he hop'd I would not refuse the Challenge. I said I had been long out of Practice, but would wait upon the Lady when he and she should think fit. He told me where her House was, and would have me call soon and without farther Introduction, which I undertook to do; but thinking it a little awkward, I postpon'd it; and on the 30th meeting him again, he put me in Mind of my Promise, and that I had not kept it, and would have me name a Day when he said he would call for me and conduct me. I nam'd the Friday following. He call'd accordingly. I went with him, play'd a few Games with the Lady [Caroline Howe], whom I found of very sensible Conversation and pleasing Behaviour, which induc'd me to agree most readily to an Appointment for another Meeting a few Days after, tho' I had not the least Apprehension that any political Business could have Connection with this new Acquaintance.[3]

A "second Chess Party" with Lady Caroline hinted at the secret negotiations that followed.

After Playing as long as we lik'd, we fell into a little Chat, partly on a Mathematical Problem, and partly about the new Parliament then just met, when she said, "And what is to be done with this Dispute between Britain and the Colonies? I hope we are not to have a Civil War."

"They should kiss and [be] Friends,"says I, "what can they do better? Quarrelling can be of Service to neither but is Ruin to both."

"I have often said," says she, "that I wish'd Government would employ you to settle the Dispute for 'em. I am sure no body could do it so well. Don't you think that the thing is practicable?" "Undoubtedly, Madam, if the Parties are dispos'd to Reconciliation; for the two Countries have really no clashing Interest to differ about. It is rather a Matter of Punctilio, which two or three reasonable People might settle in half an Hour. I thank you for the good Opinion you are pleas'd to express of me; But the Ministers will never think of employing me in that good Work, they chuse rather to abuse me."

"Ay," says She, "they have behav'd shamefully to you. And indeed some of them are now asham'd of it themselves."

I look'd upon this as accidental Conversation, thought no more of it.[4]

On Christmas Day, visiting Mrs. Howe, she told me as soon as I came in, that her Brother Lord Howe wish'd to be acquainted with me; that he was a very good Man, and she was sure we should like each other. I said I had always heard a good Character of Lord Howe, and should be proud of the Honour of being known to him. "He is just by," says she; "will you give me Leave to send for him?" "By all means, Madam, if you think proper." She rang for a Servant, wrote a Note, and Lord H. came in a few Minutes.

After some extreamly polite Compliments as to the general Motives for his desiring an Acquaintance with me, he said he had a particular one at this time, viz. the alarming Situation of our Affairs with America, which no one he was persuaded understood better than myself; . . . that he was unconnected with the Ministry except by some personal Friendships, wish'd well however to the Government, was anxious for the general Welfare of the whole Empire, and had a particular Regard for New England which had shown a very endearing Respect to his Family [with a memorial in Westminster Abbey to his elder brother killed during the French and Indian War]; That he was merely an independent Member of Parliament, desirous of doing what Good he could agreeable to his Duty in that Station; . . . that perhaps I might not be willing myself to have any direct Communication with this Ministry on this Occasion; that I might likewise not care to have it known that I had any indirect Communication with them, till I could be well asur'd of their good Dispositions; that being himself upon no ill Terms with them, he thought it not impossible that he might by conveying my Sentiments to them and theirs to me, be a means of bringing on a good Understanding without committing either them or me, if his Negociation should not succeed. And that I might rely on his keeping perfectly secret every thing I should wish to remain so.

I begg'd him in the first Place to give me Credit for a sincere Desire of healing the Breach between the two Countries; that I would chearfully and heartily do every thing in my small Power to accomplish it; but that I apprehended from . . . the Measures talk'd of as well as those already determin'd on, no Intention or Disposition of the kind existed in the present Ministry, and therefore no Accommodation could be expected till we saw a Change. That as to what his Lordship mentioned of the personal Injuries done me, those done my Country were so much greater that I did not think the others at this time worth mentioning; that besides it was a fix'd Rule with me not to mix my private Affairs with those of the publick; that I would join with my personal Enemy in serving the Publick, or, when it was for its Interest, with the Publick in serving that Enemy.[5] . . .

[Lord Chatham] call'd upon me in Cravenstreet. He brought with him his Plan transcrib'd, in the Form of an Act of Parliament, which he put into my Hands, requesting me to consider it carefully, and communicate to him such Remarks upon it as should occur to me. . . . Tho' he had considered the Business thoroughly in all its Parts, he was not so confident of his own Judgment, but that he came to set it right by mine, as Men set their Watches by a Regulator. . . . He concluded to offer it the Wednesday following; and therefore wish'd to see me upon it the preceding Tuesday, when he would again call upon me unless I could conveniently come to [his estate] Hayes. . . . I promis'd to be with him early, that we might have more time. He staid with me near two Hours, his Equipage waiting at the Door, and being there while People were coming from Church it was much taken notice of, as at that time was every little Circumstance that Men thought might possibly any way affect American Affairs. Such a Visit from, so great a Man, on so important a Business, flattered not a little my Vanity; and the Honour of it gave me the more Pleasure, as it happen'd on the very Day 12 month, that the Ministry had taken so much pains to disgrace me before the Privy Council.[6]

On Wednesday Lord Stanhope at Lord Chatham's Request call'd upon me and carry'd me down to the House of Lords, which was soon very full. Lord Chatham in a most excellent Speech, introduc'd, explain'd and supported his Plan. . . . But Lord Sandwich rose, and in a vehement petulant Speech oppos'd its being receiv'd at all, and gave his Opinion that it ought to be immediately REJECTED with the Contempt it deserv'd. That he could never believe it the Production of any British Peer. That it appear'd to him rather the Work of some American; and turning his Face towards me, who was leaning on the Bar, said, he fancied he had in his Eye the Person who drew it up, one of the bitterest and most mischievous Enemies this Country had ever known. This drew the Eyes of many Lords upon me; but as I had no inducement to take it to myself, I kept my Countenance as immoveable as if my Features had been made of Wood.

Lord Chatham, in his Reply to Lord Sandwich, took notice of his illiberal Insinuation that the Plan was not the Person's who propos'd it; declar'd that it was intirely his own. . . . That it had been hitherto reckon'd his Vice not to be apt to take Advice. But he made no Scruple to declare, that if he were the First Minister of this Country, and had the Care of Settling this momentous Business, he should not be asham'd of publickly calling to his Assistance a Person so perfectly acquainted with the whole of American Affairs, as the Gentleman alluded to and injuriously reflected on, one, he was pleas'd to say, whom all Europe held in high Estimation for his Knowledge and Wisdom, and rank'd with our Boyles and Newtons; who was an Honour not to the English Nation only but to Human Nature. I found it harder to stand this extravagant Compliment than the preceding equally extravagant Abuse, but kept as well as I could an unconcern'd Countenance, as not conceiving it to relate to me.[7]

> After Franklin had offered to pay for the tea dumped in Boston Harbor, Lord Howe, on 18 February, told him of a new plan. He wanted Franklin to assist as a friend and a secretary when his lordship should be commissioned to settle differences with America.

His Lordship then said, that he should not expect my Assistance without a *proper Consideration.* That the Business was of great Importance, and if he undertook it, he should insist on being enabled to make generous and ample Appointments for those he took with him, particularly for me; as well as a firm Promise of subsequent rewards; "and" says he, "that the Ministry may have an Opportunity of showing their good Disposition towards yourself, will you give me leave, Mr. Franklin, to procure for you previously some Mark of it, suppose the Payment here of the Arrears of your Salary as Agent for New England, which I understand they have stopt for some time past?" "My Lord," says I, "I shall deem it a great Honour to be in any shape join'd with your Lordship in so good a Work; but if you hope Service from any Influence I may be suppos'd to have, drop all Thoughts of procuring me any previous Favours from Ministers; my accepting them, would destroy the very Influence you propose to make use of; they would be considered as so many Bribes to betray the Interest of my Country: Only let me see the Propositions, and if I approve of them, I shall not hesitate a Moment, but will hold my self ready to accompany your Lordship at an hours Warning."[8]

Hearing nothing during all the following week . . . I mention'd his Silence occasionally to his Sister, adding that I suppos'd it owing to his finding what he had propos'd to me was not likely to take place; and I wish'd her to Desire him, if that was the Case, to let me know by a Line, that I might be at Liberty to take other Measures. She did so as soon as he return'd from the Country, . . . and I met his Lordship at the Hour appointed. He said that he had not seen me lately, as he expected daily to have something more material to say to me than had yet occurr'd. . . . That there was something in my verbal Message by Mrs. Howe, which perhaps she had apprehended imperfectly; it was the Hint of my Purpose to take other Measures. I answer'd, that having since I had last seen his Lordship, heard of the Death of my Wife at Philadelphia, in whose Hands I had left the Care of my Affairs there, it was become necessary for me to return thither as soon as conveniently might be; that what his Lordship had propos'd of my accompanying him to America, might if likely to take place, postpone my Voyage to suit his Conveniency, otherwise I should proceed by the first Ship.[9]

[A fortnight later] He began by saying, that I had been a better Prophet than himself; . . . and then said, that he hoped I would excuse the Trouble he had given me, as his Intentions had been good both towards me and the Publick; he was sorry that at present there was no Appearance of Things going into the Train he had wish'd; but that possibly they might yet take a more favourable Turn; and as he understood I was going soon to America, if he should chance to be sent thither on that important Business, he hop'd he might still expect my Assistance. I assur'd him of my Readiness at all times of co-operating with him in so good a Work. And so taking my Leave, and receiving his good Wishes, ended the Negociation with Lord Howe.[10]

During the whole my Time was otherwise much taken up, by Friends calling continually to enquire News from America, Members of both Houses of Parliament to inform me what passed in the Houses, and discourse with me on the Debates, and on the Motions made or to be made; Merchants of London and of the Manufacturing and Port Towns on their Petitions, the Quakers upon theirs, &c. &c. so that I had no time to take Notes of almost any thing. This Account is therefore chiefly from Recollection, in which doubtless much must have been omitted from deficiency of Memory; but what there is, I believe to be pretty exact; except that discoursing with so many different Persons about the same time on the same Subject, I may possibly have put down some things as said by or to one Person, which pass'd in Conversation with another.[11]

> During Franklin's decade in London, he had accumulated a host of close friends and followers in the British Isles and on the Continent, among them Voltaire, Adam Smith, David Hume, and Joseph Priestley along with such pioneers of the industrial revolution as James Watt and Matthew Boulton.[12] But in his long absence he lost Deborah Franklin: "My old and faithful Companion; and I every day become more sensible of the greatness of that loss; which cannot now be repair'd.[13]

28

FORGING INDEPENDENCE

1775–1785

One week after news of fighting at Lexington and Concord
reached Philadelphia, Franklin came home. He was
pressed into service on major committees of the Congress,
where delegates were debating whether to reconcile with
Britain until the King proclaimed a state of rebellion. They
immediately sent Franklin to Boston to confer with
Washington, to Montreal seeking Canadian support, to
Staten Island to meet his old friend Lord Howe, and to
France on a mission for financial aid. In July 1775 he found
Philadelphia in patriotic frenzy facing an uncertain future.

I found at my arrival all America from one End of the
12 united Provinces to the other, busily employed in learning the Use of Arms. The Attack upon the Country People
near Boston by the Army had rous'd every Body, and exas-
perated the whole Continent; the Tradesmen of this City,
were in the Field twice a day, at 5 in the Morning, and Six
in the Afternoon, disciplining with the utmost Diligence,
all being Volunteers. We have now three Battalions, a Troop
of Light Horse, and a Company of Artillery, who have made
surprizing Progress. The same Spirit appears every where
and the Unanimity is amazing.

The day after my Arrival, I was unanimously chosen by our Assembly, then sitting, an additional Delegate to the Congress, which met the next Week. The numerous Visits of old Friends, and the publick Business has since devoured all my time; for We meet at nine in the Morning, and often sit 'till four. I am also upon a Committee of Safety appointed by the Assembly, which meets at Six, and sits 'till near nine. The Members attend closely without being bribed to it, by either Salary, Place or Pension, or the hopes of any; which I mention for your Reflection on the difference, between a new virtuous People, who have publick Spirit, and an old corrupt one, who have not so much as an Idea that such a thing exists in Nature. There has not been a dissenting Voice among us in any Resolution for Defence, and our Army which is already formed, will consist of above 20,000 Men.

I am warm: and if a Temper naturally cool and phleg-matic can, in old age, which often cools the warmest, be thus heated, you will judge by that of the general Temper here, which is now little short of Madness. . . . I drop this disagreeable Subject; and will take up one, that I know must afford you and the good [Shipley] Family, as my Friends, some Pleasure. It is the State of my own Family, which I found in good Health; my Children affectionately dutifull and attentive to every thing that can be agreeable to me; with three very promising Grandsons, in whom I take great Delight. So that were it not for our publick Troubles, and the being absent from so many that I love in England, my present Felicity would be as perfect, as in this World one could well expect it. I enjoy however, what there is of it while it lasts, mindfull at the same time that its Continu-ance is like other earthly Goods, uncertain.[1]

In a letter widely circulated but not sent, Franklin expressed to his old friend Strahan a sense of the outrage only implied in other correspondence.

You are a Member of Parliament, and one of that Majority which has doomed my Country to Destruction. You have begun to burn our Towns, and murder our People. Look upon your Hands! They are stained with the Blood of your Relations! You and I were long Friends: You are now my Enemy, and I am, Yours, B Franklin.[2]

But a year later, to his London acquaintance, Lord Howe, now in America, he did express himself "very warmly."[3]

Long did I endeavour with unfeigned and unwearied Zeal, to preserve from breaking, that fine and noble China Vase the British Empire: for I knew that being once broken, the separate Parts could not retain even their Share of the Strength or Value that existed in the Whole, and that a perfect Re-Union of those Parts could scarce even be hoped for. Your Lordship may possibly remember the Tears of Joy that wet my Cheek, when, at your good Sister's in London, you once gave me Expectations that a Reconciliation might soon take place. I had the Misfortune to find those Expectations disappointed, and to be treated as the Cause of the Mischief I was labouring to prevent.

...I know your great Motive in coming hither was Hope of being instrumental in a Reconciliation; and I believe when you find *that* impossible on any Terms given you to propose, you will relinquish so odious a Command, and return to a more honorouble private Station.[4]

In late January 1777, with fellow-commissioner Arthur Lee, Franklin settled into a rented home in suburban Passy where he played the role of simple American.

Figure me in your mind as jolly as formerly, and as strong and hearty, only a few Years older, very plainly dress'd, wearing my thin gray strait Hair, that peeps out under my only Coiffure, a fine fur Cap, which comes down my Forehead almost to my Spectacles. Think how this must appear among the Powder'd Heads of Paris.[5]

> During the mission to France, Franklin was encumbered with colleagues impatient of his wily diplomacy and jealous of his popularity. He found Arthur Lee's paranoia particularly irritating and expressed his anger once more in a letter never sent but offering a window on life in the legation at Passy.

I hate Disputes. I am old, cannot have long to live, have much to do and no time for Altercation. If I have often receiv'd and borne your Magisterial Snubbings and Rebukes without Reply, ascribe it to the right Causes, my Concern for the Honour and Success of our Mission, which would be hurt by our Quarrelling, my Love of Peace, my Respect for your good Qualities, and my Pity of your Sick Mind, which is forever tormenting itself, with its Jealousies, Suspicions and Fancies that others mean you ill, wrong you, or fail in respect for you. If you do not cure your self of this Temper it will end in Insanity, of which it is the Symptomatick Forerunner, as I have seen in several Instances. God preserve you from so terrible an Evil; and for his sake pray suffer me to live in quiet.[6]

> Popularity meant other distractions. A French reporter noted: "Doctor Franklin is very much run after, and feted, not only by the savants but by all people who can get hold of him."[7] The *Pennsylvania Packet* (31 December 1777) reported that Parisians were paying for upstairs viewpoints just to watch him pass by in his carriage. There were also vicious rumors. New York's Tory newspaper, the *Royal Gazette* (7 March 1778) reported him killed by an assassin

at Bordeaux, a report not contradicted for sixty days. He took all that as occupational hazard, as he explained to daughter Sally in June 1779 when sending her a clay medallion.

The clay medallion was the first of its kind made in France. A variety of others have been made since of different sizes; some to be set in lids of snuff boxes, and some so small as to be worn in rings; and the numbers sold are incredible. These, with pictures, busts, and prints, (of which copies upon copies are spread every where) have made your father's face as well known as that of the moon, so that he durst not do any thing that would oblige him to run away, as his phiz would discover him wherever he should venture to show it. It is said by learned etymologists that the name Doll, for the images children play with, is derived from the word IDOL; from the number of dolls now made of him, he may be truly said, in that sense, to be i-doll-ized in this country.[8]

London's *Morning Post* for 12 June 1779 described Franklin's diplomacy as full of "vindictive subtlety, watchfulness, and political tricks." He did, in fact, enjoy as cover for clandestine activities the fashionable life of Parisian salons.

[I must explain] the Kindness of the French Ladies to me. This is the civilest Nation upon Earth. Your first Acquaintances endeavour to find out what you like, and they tell others. If 'tis understood that you like Mutton, dine where you will you find Mutton. Somebody, it seems, gave it out that I lov'd Ladies; and then every body presented me their Ladies (or the Ladies presented themselves) to be *embrac'd*, that is to have their Necks kiss'd. For as to kissing of Lips or Cheeks it is not the Mode here, the first is reckon'd rude, & the other may rub off the Paint. The French

Ladies have however 1000 other ways of rendering themselves agreable; by their various Attentions and Civilities, & their sensible Conversation. 'Tis a delightful People to live with.[9]

> To improve his French, septuagenarian Franklin exchanged sexually charged letters and billets doux with beautiful, young neighbor Anne-Louise Brillon. She called him, "Dear Papa" and insisted on being called his "daughter," but the difference in ages meant little to the gossips of Parisian salons. One of her letters complained, "People have the audacity to criticize my pleasant habit of sitting upon your knees, and yours of always asking me for what I always refuse." She also had no fear in correcting his logic as when she criticized his composition: "'When I was a young man,' you say, 'and enjoyed the favours of the sex more than at present, I had no gout.' 'Then,' one might reply to this, 'when I threw myself out of the window, I did not break my leg.'"[10]

When I was a young man, and enjoyed more of the favors of the fair sex than now, I did not have any gout. Therefore, if the ladies of Passy would have more of that sort of Christian charity which I have so often recommended to you in vain, I should not have had the gout now. It seems to me that this is good logic.[11]

> By summer 1781, exasperated by colleagues, niggling details, and other demands, Franklin pleaded with Congress to relieve him. He used ill health as an excuse but made clear to his daughter and to Robert Morris that he was just fed up. Not until mid-March 1784 did Congress even debate his release to enjoy "that repose in old age which a long series of years spent in the service of his country entitles him to expect."[12] And not until a year after

that did they grant him leave to return—even then over objections from Rhode Island and Massachusetts.[13] As he told Morris, public service must be its own reward.

The Publick is often niggardly, even of its Thanks, while you are sure of being censured by malevolent Criticks and Bug-Writers, who will abuse you while you are serving them, and wound your Character in nameless Pamphlets; thereby resembling those little dirty stinking Insects, that attack us only in the dark, disturb our Repose, molesting and wounding us while our Sweat and Blood is contributing to their Subsistence.[14]

To his daughter Sally Franklin he explained that he was just plain tired.

I find the Business too heavy for me, and too confining, being oblig'd to perform all the Functions of Consul, Judge of Admiralty, Merchant, Banker, &c. &c. besides that of Minister. I have borne the Burthen as long as I could; but I find that Age requires Rest. . . . My proper Situation indeed would be in my own House, with my Daughter to take care of me and nurse me in case of Illness, and with her Children to amuse me; but as this cannot well be at present, we must manage as we can.[15]

In January 1783, with peace virtually at hand, Franklin learned that his London landlady of many years had died and to her daughter lamented that the loss of friends is the cost of living long.

The last Year carried off my Friends Dr. Pringle, and Dr. Fothergill, Lord Kaims, and Lord le Despencer. This has begun to take away the rest and strike the hardest. Thus the Ties I had to that Country, and indeed to the World in general, are loosened one by one, and I shall soon have no Attachment left to make me unwilling to follow.[16]

With preliminaries of peace signed (21 January 1783), Franklin faced a new barrage of criticism that in negotiating he "favoured, or did not oppose" French designs against America. To colleague John Jay he described his best defense as a counteroffensive.

It is not my purpose to dispute any share of the honour of that treaty, which the friends of my colleagues may be disposed to give them; but, having now spent fifty years of my life in public offices and trusts, and having still one ambition left, that of carrying the character of fidelity at least to the grave with me, I cannot allow that I was behind any of them in zeal and faithfulness. I therefore think, that I ought not to suffer an accusation, which falls little short of treason to my country, to pass without notice, when the means of effectual vindication are at hand. . . . To you and my other colleagues I appeal, by sending to each a similar letter with this, and I have no doubt of your readiness to do a brother Commissioner justice, by certificates that will entirely destroy the effect of that accusation.[17]

A year later, he assured Jay that enemies could be put to use. "They point out to us our Faults; they put us upon our guard, and help us to live more correctly," as he himself had found.

I have, as you observe, some Enemies in England, but they are my Enemies as an *American*; I have also two or three in America, who are my Enemies as a *Minister;* but I thank God there is not in the whole world any who are my Enemies as a *Man;* for by his grace, thro' a long life, I have been enabled to conduct myself, that there does not exist a human Being who can justly say, "Ben Franklin has wrong'd me."[18]

Fascinated by experiments with balloons in Paris, Franklin urged British friends to conduct their own. To their objection, "What good are balloons?," he could have answered with the remark traditionally assigned to him: "What good is a new-born baby?" But now, he simply blamed them for being afraid of public ridicule.

I am sorry this experiment is totally neglected in England, where mechanic genius is so strong. I wish I could see the same emulation between the two nations as I have seen the two parties here. Your philosophy seems to be too bashful. In this country we are not so much afraid of being laughed at. If we do a foolish thing, we are the first to laugh at it ourselves, and are almost as much pleased with a bonmot or a good chanson, that ridicules well the disappointment of a project, as we might have been with its success. It does not seem to me a good reason to decline prosecuting a new experiment which apparently increases the power of a man over matter, till we can see to what use that power may be applied. When we have learnt to manage it, we may hope some time or other to find use for it, as men have done for magnetism and electricity, for which the first experiments were mere matters of amusement.[19]

News that the peace treaty had been ratified reached Paris by the end of March 1784, and while he waited to be relieved, Franklin returned to his memoirs and picked up correspondence with friends in England, and with his son William—who would spend his remaining days as a Loyalist refugee in London. Franklin wrote to him in mid-August 1784.

I received your Letter of the 22d past, and am glad to find that you desire to revive the affectionate Intercourse, that formerly existed between us. It will be very agreable to me; indeed nothing has ever hurt me so much and affected me with such keen Sensations, as to find myself deserted in my old Age by my only Son; and not only deserted, but to find him taking up Arms against me, in a Cause, wherein my good Fame, Fortune and Life were all at Stake. You conceived, you say, that your Duty to your King and Regard for your Country requir'd this. I ought not to blame you for differing in Sentiment with me in Public Affairs. We are Men, all subject to Errors. Our Opinions are not in our own Power; they are form'd and govern'd much by Circumstances, that are often as inexplicable as they are irresistible. Your Situation was such that few would have censured your remaining Neuter, *tho' there are Natural Duties which preceded political ones, and cannot be extinguish'd by them.*[20]

> He amused old friend George Whatley with musings on his condition now and hereafter, referring to an old song, "The Old Man's Wish," for "a warm House in a country Town, an easy Horse, some good old Authors, ingenious and cheerful Companions, a Pudding on Sundays, with stout Ale, and a Bottle of Burgundy," each stanza concluding with the refrain:

> > May I govern my Passions with an absolute sway,
> > Grow wiser and better as my Strength wears away,
> > Without Gout or Stone, by a gentle Decay.

But what signifies our Wishing? Things happen, after all, as they will happen. I have sung that *wishing Song* a thousand times, when I was young, and now find, at Fourscore, that the three Contraries have befallen me, being subject to the Gout and the Stone, and not being yet Master of all my Passions. Like the proud Girl in my country, who wished and resolv'd not to marry a Parson, nor a Presbyterian, nor an Irishman; and at length found herself married to an Irish Presbyterian Parson.

You see I have some reason to wish, that, in a future

State, I may not only be *as well as I was,* but a little better. And I hope it; ... for I *trust in God.* And when I observe, that there is great Frugality, as well as Wisdom, in his Works, since he has been evidently sparing both of Labour and Materials, for by the various wonderful Inventions of Propagation, he has provided for the continual peopling his World with Plants and Animals, without being at the Trouble of repeated new Creations; and by the natural Reduction of compound Substances to their original Elements, capable of being employ'd in new Compositions, he has prevented the Necessity of creating new Matter; so that the Earth, Water, Air, and perhaps Fire, which being compounded from Wood, do, when the Wood is dissolved, return, and again become Air, Earth, Fire, and Water; I say, that, when I see nothing annihilated, and not even a Drop of Water wasted, I cannot suspect the Annihilation of Souls, or believe, that he will suffer the daily Waste of Millions of Minds ready made that now exist, and put himself to the continual Trouble of making new ones. Thus finding myself to exist in the World, I believe I shall, in some Shape or other, always exist; and, with all the inconveniencies human Life is liable to, I shall not object to a new Edition of mine; hoping, however, that the *Errata* of the last may be corrected.[20]

At last, on 13 July 1785, he sent sister Jane Mecom welcome news. He was on his way home.

I left Passy, yesterday Afternoon, and am here in my Way to Havre de Grace a Seaport, in order to embark for America. I make Use of one of the Queen's Litters carried by Mules, who walk steadily and easily, so that I bear the Motion very well. I am to be taken on board a Philadelphia Ship on the Coast of England (Capt. Truxton) the beginning of next Month. . . . I have continu'd to work till late in the Day: tis time I should go home, and go to Bed.[21]

29

FREE AT LAST

1785–1790

In constant pain from a kidney stone, Franklin left Passy on the royal litter borne by mules to a ship for England. There, after parting from son William and old friends, he embarked for home. During the voyage, he composed papers on the gulf stream and smoking chimneys along with memoirs of negotiating with the British before and after the war. The hero's welcome in Philadelphia signaled his plunging at once into public service as governor of his state and delegate to the Constitutional convention of 1787. Too weak to speak, his appeal for compromise there was read by others. He would later require help in writing also, since he kept in touch with the scientific and intellectual community as well as old friends abroad. At home he continued to meet regularly with scientific and social clubs reminiscent of the old Junto and served as president of the society to abolish slavery, composing arguments, direct and allegorical, to mold public opinion as of old. Surrounded by daughter Sally's growing family, he died of the pleurisy that had plagued him off and on since he returned from England sixty-five years earlier.

Having stayed in France about eight years and a half, I

took leave of the Court and my friends, and set out on my return home, July 12, 1785, leaving Passy with my two grandsons [Benjamin Bache and William Temple Franklin], at four P.M.; arrived about eight o'clock at St. Germain. I found that the motion of the litter, lent me by the Duke de Coigny, did not much incommode me. It was one of the Queen's, carried by two large mules, the muleteer riding another; M. [Louis] LeVeillard and my children in a carriage. We drank tea . . . and went early to bed.

July 24.—We had a fair wind all night, and this morning at seven o'clock, being off Cowes, the captain represented to me the difficulty of getting there against the flood; and proposed that we should rather run up to Southampton, which we did, and landed there between eight and nine. Met my son, who had arrived from London the evening before. Wrote a letter to the Bishop of St. Asaph, acquainting him with my arrival, and he came with his lady and daughter, Miss Kitty, after dinner to see us; they talk of staying here as long as we do. Our meeting was very affectionate.

July 25.—The Bishop and family lodging in the same inn, the Star, we all breakfast and dine together. I went at noon to bathe in Martin's salt-water hot bath, and, floating on my back, fell asleep, and slept near an hour by my watch, without sinking or turning! a thing I never did before, and should hardly have thought possible. Water is the easiest bed that can be.

July 27.—Give a power to my son to recover what may be due to me from the British government. Hear from J. Williams that the ship is come. We all dine once more with the Bishop and family, who kindly accept our invitation to go on board with us. We go down in a shallop to the ship. The captain entertains us at supper. The company stay all night.

July 28.—When I waked in the morning found the company gone and the ship under sail.

Wednesday, September 14.—With the flood in the morning came a light breeze, which brought us above Gloucester Point, in full view of dear Philadelphia! when we again cast anchor to wait for the health officer, who, having made his visit and finding no sickness, gave us leave to land. My son-in-law came with a boat for us; we landed at Market Street wharf, where we were received by a crowd of people with huzzas, and accompanied with acclamations quite to my door. Found my family well. God be praised and thanked for all his mercies.[1]

> Hardly a fortnight later, elected to the state's executive council, Franklin found himself in the middle of a fight to curb the assembly's oligarchy, but he assured such English friends as the Bishop of St. Asaph and Polly Hewson that he was happy to be home.

As to my Domestic Circumstances, they are at present as happy as I could wish them. I am surrounded by my Offspring, a Dutiful and Affectionate Daughter in my House, with six Grandchildren. . . . What their Conduct may be, when they grow up and enter the important Scenes of Life, I shall not live to see, and I cannot *foresee.* I therefore enjoy among them the present Hour, and leave the future to Providence. . . . I still have Enjoyment in the Company of my Friends; and, being easy in my Circumstances, have many Reasons to like Living. But the Course of Nature must soon put a period to my present Mode of Existence. This I shall submit to with less Regret, as, having seen during a long Life a good deal of this World, I feel a growing Curiosity to be acquainted with some other; and can chearfully, with filial Confidence, resign my Spirit to the conduct of that great and good Parent of Mankind, who created it, and who has so graciously protected and prospered me from my Birth to the present Hour.[2]

The companions of my youth are indeed almost all departed, but I find an agreeable society among their children and grandchildren. I have public business enough to preserve me from ennui, and private amusement besides in conversation, books, my garden, and cribbage. Considering our well-furnished, plentiful market as the best of gardens, I am turning mine, in the midst of which my house stands, into grass-plots and gravel walks, with trees and flowering shrubs. Cards we sometimes play here, in long winter evenings; but it is as they play at chess, not for money, but for honour, or the pleasure of beating one another.... I have indeed now and then a little compunction in reflecting that I spend time so idly; but another reflection comes to relieve me, whispering: "You know that the soul is immortal; why then should you be such a niggard of a little time, when you have a whole eternity before you?" So, being easily convinced, and, like other reasonable creatures, satisfied with a small reason when it is in favour of doing what I have a mind to, I shuffle the cards again, and begin another game.

As to public amusements, we have neither plays nor operas, but we had yesterday a kind of oratorio;...and we have assemblies, balls, and concerts, besides little parties at one another's houses, in which there is sometimes dancing, and frequently good music; so that we jog on in life as pleasantly as you do in England; anywhere but in London, for there you have plays performed by good actors. That, however, is, I think, the only advantage London has over Philadelphia.[3]

Explaining to French friends his delay in continuing work

on his memoirs, he mentions the Convention to revise the federal Constitution.

You blame me for writing three pamphlets and neglecting to write the little history . . . they were written at sea, out of my own head; the other could not so well be written there for want of the documents that could only be had here. I hoped to do it this summer, having built an addition to my house, in which I have placed my library and where I can write without being disturbed by the noise of the children; but the General Assembly having lately desired my assistance in a great Convention to be held here in May next for amending the Federal Constitution, I begin to doubt whether I can make any progress in it till that business is over.[4]

> At the Convention, too feeble for his voice to be heard, he wrote out his last speech for compromise. It was so admired that it was reprinted in the press and recopied by Franklin himself for friends to use in persuading their own states' legislatures to ratify the Constitution.

I confess that I do not entirely approve of this Constitution at present, but Sir, I am not sure I shall never approve it: For having lived so long, I have experienced many Instances of being oblig'd, by better Information or fuller Consideration, to change Opinions even on important Subjects, which I once thought right, but found to be otherwise. It is therefore that the older I grow the more apt I am to doubt my own Judgment and to pay more Respect to the Judgment of others. Most Men indeed as well as most Sects in Religion, think themselves in Possession of all Truth, and that wherever others differ from them it is so far Error. [Sir Richard] Steele, a Protestant, in a Dedication tells the Pope, that the only difference between our two Churches in their Opinions of the Certainty of their Doctrine, is, the Romish Church is infallible, and the Church of England is never in the Wrong. But tho' many private Persons think almost as highly of their own Infallibility, as that of their Sect, few express it so naturally as a certain French lady, who in a little Dispute with her Sister, said, I don't know how it happens, Sister, but I meet with no body but myself that's *always* in the right. (Il n'y a que moi qui a toujours raison.)

I consent, Sir, to this Constitution because I expect no better, and because I am not sure that it is not the best. (The Opinions I have had of its Errors, I sacrifice to the Public Good.) Much of the Strength and Efficiency of any Government, in procuring & securing Happiness to the People depends on Opinion, on the general Opinion of the Goodness of that Government as well as of the Wisdom & Integrity of its Governors. I hope therefore that for our own Sakes, as Part of the People, and for the Sake of our Posterity, we shall act heartily & unanimously in recommending this Constitution, wherever our Influence may extend, and turn our Thoughts and Endeavours to the Means of having it well administered.

On the whole, Sir, I cannot help expressing a Wish, that every Member of the Convention, who may still have Objections to it, would with me on this Occasion doubt a little of his own Infallibility, and to make *manifest* our *Unanimity*, put his Name to this Instrument.[5]

In late November 1788 Franklin sent to Charles Thomson, who had been Congressional secretary since its inception but was now replaced, an oddly self-pitying letter about the ingratitude of Congress. Whether out of anxiety about his family's financial future or reacting to accusations that he had misspent funds while in France, he asked Thomson to pass on the attached document to Congress, where it was eventually received "but not read."[6]

I did hope, as it is customary in Europe to make some liberal provision for ministers when they return home from foreign service, during which their absence is necessarily injurious to their private affairs, the Congress would at least have been kind enough to have shewn their approbation of my conduct by a grant of some small tract of Land in their Western Country, which might have been of use and some honour to my Posterity. And I cannot but still think they will do something of the kind for me, whenever they shall be pleased to take my services into consideration, as I see by their minutes that they have allowed Mr. [Arthur] Lee handsomely for his service in England before his appointment to France, in which service I and Mr. [William] Bollan cooperated with him, and have had no such allowance; and since his return he has been very properly rewarded with a good place, as well as my friend Mr. [John] Jay; tho' these are trifling compensations in comparison with what was granted by the King to M. [Conrad] Gerard on his return from America.

But how different is what has happened to me! On my return from England [in 1775], the Congress bestowed on me the office of Postmaster-General, for which I was very thankful. It was indeed an office I had some kind of right to, as having previously greatly enlarged the Revenue of the post by regulations I had contrived and established, while I possessed it under the Crown. When I was sent to France, I left it in the hands of my Son-in-Law, who was to act as my Deputy. But soon after my departure it was taken from me and given to Mr. [Ebenezer] Hazard. When the English Ministry formerly thought fit to deprive me of the office, they left me, however, the privilege of receiving and sending my letters free of postage, which is the usage when a Postmaster is not displaced for misfeasance in the office; but in America I have ever since had the postage demanded of me, which, since my return from France, has amounted to about fifty pounds, much of it occasioned by my having acted as Minister there.

Considering [my grandson, William Temple Franklin] as brought up in the diplomatic line, and well qualified by his knowledge in that branch for the employ of a Secretary at least (in which opinion I was not alone, for three of my colleagues, without the smallest solicitation from me, chose him Secretary of the Commission for Treaties, which they had been empowered to do), I took the liberty of recommending him to the Congress for their protection. This was the only favour I ever asked of them; and the only answer I received was a Resolution superseding him, and appointing Colonel [David] Humphreys in his place, a gentleman who, tho' he might have indeed a good deal of military merit, certainly had none in the diplomatic line, and had neither the French language or the experience, or the address proper to qualify him for such an employment.

I have not, nor ever shall, make any public complaint; and even if I could have foreseen such unkind treatment from Congress, their refusing me thanks would not in the least have abated my zeal for the Cause and ardour in support of it. I know something of the nature of such changeable assemblies, and how little successors are inform'd of the services that have been rendered to the Corps before their admission, or feel themselves obliged by such services; and what effect in obliterating a sense of them, during the absence of the servant in a distant Country, the artful and reiterated malevolent insinuations of one or two envious and malicious persons may have on the minds of members, even of the most equitable, candid, and honourable dispositions. Therefore I would pass these reflections into oblivion.

SKETCH OF THE SERVICES OF B. FRANKLIN TO THE UNITED STATES OF AMERICA

In England he combated the Stamp Act, and his writings in the papers against it, with his examination in Parliament, were thought to have contributed much to its repeal.

He opposed the Duty Act; and, though he could not prevent its passing, he obtained of Mr. Townshend an omission of several articles, particularly salt.

In the subsequent difference he wrote and published many papers, refuting the claim of Parliament to tax the colonies.

He opposed all the oppressive acts.

He had two secret negotiations with the ministers for their repeal, of which he has written a narrative. In this he offered payment for the destroyed tea, at his own risk, in case they were repealed.

He was joined with Messrs. Bollan and Lee in all the applications to government for that purpose. Printed several pamphlets at his own considerable expense against the then measures of government, whereby he rendered himself obnoxious, was disgraced before the privy council, deprived of a place in the post-office of three hundred pounds sterling a year, and obliged to resign his agencies, viz.:

of Pennsylvania 500 pounds
Massachusetts 400 pounds
New Jersey 100 pounds
Georgia 200 pounds
1200 pounds

In the whole 1500 pounds sterling per annum.

Orders were sent to the King's governors not to sign any warrants on the treasury for the orders of his salaries; and though he was not actually dismissed by the colonies that employed him, yet, thinking the known malice of the Court against him rendered him less likely than others to manage their affairs to their advantage, he judged it to be his duty to withdraw from their service, and leave it open for less exceptionable persons, which saved them the necessity of removing him.

Returning to America, he encouraged the Revolution. He was appointed chairman of the Committee of Safety, where he projected the *chevaux de frise* for securing Philadelphia, then the residence of Congress.

He was sent by Congress to head-quarters near Boston with Messrs. [William] Harrison and [Thomas] Lynch, in 1775, to settle some affairs with the northern governments and General Washington.

In the spring of 1776 he was sent to Canada with Messrs. [Samuel] Chase and [Charles and John] Carroll, passing the Lakes while they were not yet free from ice. In Canada was, with his colleagues, instrumental in redressing sundry grievances, and thereby reconciling the people more to our cause. He there advanced to General [Benedict] Arnold and other servants of Congress, then in extreme necessity, 353 pounds in gold, out of his own pocket, on the credit of Congress, which was of great service at that juncture, in procuring provisions for our army.

Being at the time he was ordered on this service upwards of seventy years of age, he suffered in his health by the hardships of this journey; lodging in the woods, etc., in so inclement a season; but being recovered, the Congress in the same year ordered him to France. Before his departure he put all the money he could raise, between three and four thousand pounds, into their hands; which, demonstrating his confidence, encouraged others to lend their money in support of the cause.

He made no bargain for appointments, but was promised by a vote the *net* salary of five hundred pounds sterling per annum, his expense paid, and to be assisted by a secretary, who was to have one thousand pounds per annum, to include all contingencies.

When the Pennsylvania Assembly sent him to England in 1764, on the same salary, they allowed him one year's advance for his passage, and in consideration of the prejudice to his private affairs that must be occasioned by his sudden departure and absence. He has had no such allowance from Congress, was badly accommodated in a miserable vessel, improper for those northern seas (and which actually foundered in her return), was badly fed, so that on his arrival he had scarce strength to stand.

His services to the States as commissioner, and afterwards as minister plenipotentiary, are known to Congress, as may appear in his correspondence. His *extra services* may not be so well known, and therefore may be here mentioned. No secretary ever arriving, the business was in part before, and entirely when the other commissioners left him, executed by himself, with the help of his grandson, who at first was only allowed clothes, board, and lodging, and afterwards a salary, never exceeding three hundred pounds a year (except while he served as secretary to the Commissioners for peace), by which difference in salary, continued many years, the Congress saved, if they accept it, seven hundred pounds sterling a year.

He served as consul entirely several years, until the arrival of Mr. [Thomas] Barclay, and even after, as that gentleman was obliged to be much and long absent in Holland, Flanders, and England ... Constant frauds [were] attempted by presenting seconds and thirds for payment after the firsts had been discharged. As these bills were arriving more or less by every ship and every post, they required constant attendance. Mr. Franklin could make no journey for exercise, as had been annually his custom, and the confinement brought on a malady that is likely to afflict him while he lives.

In short, though he has always been an active man, he never went through so much business during eight years, in any part of his life, as during those of his residence in France; which, however, he did not decline till he saw peace happily made, and found himself in the eightieth year of his age; when, if ever, a man has some right to expect repose.[7]

Franklin seldom complained with such vigor but, after having retired as Pennsylvania's governor, he cloaked himself like an old Roman in Ciceronian leisure (*otium cum dignitate*).

I have now renounced all public business, and enjoy the *otium cum dignitate*. My friends indulge me with their frequent visits, which I have now leisure to receive and enjoy. The Philosophical Society, and the Society for Political Inquiries, meet at my house, which I have enlarged by additional building, that affords me a large room for those meetings, another over it for my library, now very considerable, and over all some lodging rooms. I have seven promising grandchildren by my daughter, who play with and amuse me, and she is a kind, attentive nurse to me when I am at any time indisposed; so that I pass my time as agreeably as at my age [83] a man may well expect, and have little to wish for except a more easy exit than my malady seems to threaten.[8]

> In bringing his old friend Catherine Greene up to date in March 1789, Franklin echoes the preamble to the memoirs he tried to compose under pressure from friends at home and abroad.

I am too old to follow printing myself, but, loving the business, I have brought up my grandson Benjamin [Bache] to it, and have built and furnished a printing-house for him, which he now manages under my eye. I have great pleasure in the rest of my grandchildren, who are now in number eight, and all promising, the youngest only six months old, but shows signs of great good nature. My friends here are numerous, and I enjoy as much of their conversation as I can reasonably wish; and I have as much health and cheerfulness, as can well be expected at my age, now eighty-three. Hitherto this long life has been tolerably happy; so that, if I were allowed to live it over again, I should make no objection, only wishing for leave to do, what authors do in a second edition of their works, correct some of my *errata*.[9]

> When Ezra Stiles of Yale asked about his religious beliefs, Franklin made this reply:

Here is my Creed. I believe in one God, Creator of the Universe. That he governs it by his Providence. That he ought to be worshipped. That the most acceptable Service we render to him is doing good to his other Children. That the Soul of Man is immortal, and will be treated with Justice in another Life respecting its Conduct in this. These I take to be the fundamental Principles of all sound Religion, and I regard them as you do in whatever Sect I meet with them.

As to Jesus of Nazareth . . . I think the System of Morals

and his Religion, as he left them to us, the best the World ever saw or is likely to see; but I apprehend it has received various corrupting Changes, and I have, with most of the present Dissenters in England, some Doubts as to his Divinity; tho' it is a question I do not dogmatize upon, having never studied it, and think it needless to busy myself with it now, when I expect soon an Opportunity of knowing the Truth with less Trouble. I see no harm, however, in its being believed, if that Belief has the good Consequence, as probably it has, of making his Doctrines more respected and better observed; especially as I do not perceive, that the Supreme takes it amiss, by distinguishing the Unbelievers in his Government of the World with any peculiar Marks of his Displeasure.

I have ever let others enjoy their religious Sentiments, without reflecting on them for those that appeared to me unsupportable and even absurd. All Sects here, and we have a great Variety, have experienced my good will in assisting them with Subscriptions for building their new Places of Worship; and, as I have never opposed any of their Doctrines, I hope to go out of the World in Peace with them all.[10]

In July 1788, Franklin drew up a will leaving his son William very little: "The part he acted against me in the late war, which is of public notoriety, will account for my leaving him no more of an estate he endeavoured to deprive me of." The following June he added a codicil prescribing the inscription for his grave ("Benjamin And Deborah Franklin 178–") and allocating funds as perennial seed money for "young married artificers" in Boston and Philadelphia such as he and Deborah had been sixty years earlier.

I was born in Boston, New England, and owe my first instructions in literature to the free grammar-schools es-

tablished there. I have, therefore, already considered these
schools in my will. But I am also under obligations to the
State of Massachusetts for having, unasked, appointed me
formerly their agent in England, with a handsome salary,
which continued some years; and although I accidentally lost
in their service, by transmitting Governor Hutchinson's letters, much more than the amount of what they gave me, I do
not think that ought in the least to diminish my gratitude.

I have considered that, among artisans, good apprentices are most likely to make good citizens, and, having
myself been bred to a manual art, printing, in my native
town, and afterwards assisted to set up my business in Philadelphia by kind loans of money from two friends there,
which was the foundation of my fortune, and of all the
utility in life that may be ascribed to me, I wish to be useful
even after my death, if possible, in forming and advancing
other young men, that may be serviceable to their country
in both these towns.[12]

> While at Passy, Franklin had developed a kidney stone that
> would torment the rest of his life. Back in Philadelphia he
> assured French friends that he could live with it—even
> joke about it.

I am sensible that it is grown heavier; but on the whole
it does not give me more pain than when at Passy, and except in standing, walking, or making water, I am very little
incommoded by it. Sitting or lying in bed I am generally
quite easy, God be thanked; and as I live temperately, drink
no wine, and use daily the exercise of the dumb-bell, I flatter myself that the stone is kept from augmenting so much
as it might otherwise do, and that I may still continue to
find it tolerable. People who live long, who will drink the
cup of life to the very bottom, must expect to meet with
some of the usual dregs, and when I reflect on the number

of terrible maladies human nature is subject to, I think
myself favoured in having to share only the stone and the
gout ....

I had sometimes wished I had brought with me from
France a balloon sufficiently large to raise me from the
ground. In my malady it would have been the most easy
carriage for me, being led by a string held by a man walking on the ground.[13]

> By November 1789, his Sisyphean stone was more than he
> could manage without medication of the worst sort.

I have tried so many things with so little effect, that I
am quite discouraged, and have no longer any faith in rem-
edies for the stone. The palliating system is what I am now
fixed in. Opium gives me ease when I am attacked by pain,
and by the use of it I still make life at least tolerable. Not
being able, however, to bear sitting to write, I now make
use of the hand of one of my grandsons, dictating to him
from my bed.[14]

> disturbed by early news of massacres in the French
> Revolution, Franklin still managed to jest with his old
> friend, French physicist Jean Baptiste LeRoy.

Are you still living? Or have the mob of Paris mistaken
the head of a monopolizer of knowledge, for a monopolizer of corn, and paraded it about the streets upon a pole.
Great part of the news we have had from Paris, for near a
year past, has been very afflicting.... The voice of *Philosophy* I apprehend can hardly be heard among those tumults.
... Our new Constitution is now established, and has an
appearance that promises permanency; but in this world
nothing can be said to be certain except death and taxes.[15]

> When sister Jane Mecom teased about the Boston press
> praising him, Franklin alludes to the joke attributed to

him about a Frenchman asking toll from a visiting Englishman in exchange for thrusting a hot iron up his backside. The visitor vigorously refuses. The Frenchman says, "At least give me something for heating my iron."[16]

I never see any Boston newspapers. You mention there being often something in them to do me honour. I am obliged to them. On the other hand, some of our papers here are endeavouring to disgrace me. I take no notice. My friends defend me. I have long been accustomed to receive more blame, as well as more praise, than I have deserved. It is the lot of every public man, and I leave one account to balance the other.

As you observe, there was no swearing in the story of the poker, when I told it. The late new dresser of it was, probably, the same, or perhaps akin to him, who, in relating a dispute that happened between Queen Anne and the Archbishop of Canterbury, . . . made both the Queen and the Archbishop swear three or four thumping oaths in every sentence of the discussion, and the Archbishop at last gained his point.

One present at this tale, being surprised, said, "But did the Queen and the Archbishop swear so at one another?"

"O, no, no," says the relator; "that is only my way of telling the story."[17]

In reporting that their old friend had died, 17 April 1790, Benjamin Rush told Richard Price about his last days, a report incorporated into his obituary and widely reprinted except for the final words.

A few days before he died, he rose from his bed and begged that it might be made up for him so that he might die "in a decent manner." His daughter told him that she hoped he would recover and live many years longer. He calmly replied, "He hoped not." Upon being advised to change his position in bed that he might breathe easy he said, "A dying man can do nothing easy.[18]

NOTES

ABBREVIATION

BF   Benjamin Franklin

INTRODUCTION

1. Smyth, *Writings,* 9:534.
2. Below, Chapter 18, p. 218.
3. Zall, *Wit and Wisdom,* 154–55.
4. Below, Chapter 19, p. 228.
5. Smyth, *Writings,* 10:493.
6. Bell, *Poor Richard's Almanacs,* i:xv.
7. Roosevelt, *Public Papers,* 7:214.
8. *Reader's Digest* (May 1976), p. 12. See Carla Mulford,"Figuring Benjamin Franklin in American Cultural Memory," *New England Quarterly* 72 (1999): 415–43.
9. Leo Lemay, ed. *The Oldest Revolutionary* (Philadelphia: Univ. Pennsylvania Press, 1976), 55-60.
10. Zall, *Franklin's Autobiography,* 68–69.
11. Below, Chapter 2, p. 44.
12. Lemay and Zall, *Genetic Text,* 205.
13. Smyth, *Writings,* 9:675–76.
14. Holograph, Huntington Library accession number HM 9999, ultimate source of the first-draft text, the basis of the present edition is the text in Lemay and Zall, *Genetic Text,* 1–170, edited as a text for students in Lemay and Zall, *Franklin's Autobiography,* and for general readers in Lemay, *Writings,* 1307–1469.
15. Franklin insisted upon "all the capitalling and italicking, that intimate the allusions and mark the emphasis of written discourses, to bring them as near as possible to those spoken" (Oberg 20:438). In the present edition, the inconsistency comes from sources other than Franklin's own printing or manuscripts.
16. Jefferson, "Autobiography," in *Writings,* ed. Merrill Peterson, 99–100.

1. GROWING UP BOSTONIAN

1. Epigraph from Zall, *Ben Franklin Laughing,* 113.

Notes

2. Lemay and Zall, *Genetic Text,* 5.
3. Starbuck, *History of Nantucket,* 740.
4. Lemay and Zall, *Genetic Text,* 8–9.
5. Franklin B. Dexter, ed. *Literary Diary of Ezra Stiles,* 3 vols. (N.Y. Scribners, 1901), 2: 375-76.
6. Tourtellot, *BF,* 152.
7. Lemay and Zall, *Genetic Text,* 6–7.
8. Tourtellot, *BF,* 157–58.
9. Lemay and Zall, *Genetic Text,* 7.
10. Oberg, *Papers,* 20:131.
11. Ibid., 20:133.
12. Lemay and Zall, *Genetic Text,* 8.
13. Lemay, *Writings,* 932.
14. Oberg, *Papers,* 20:286-87.
15. Lemay and Zall, *Genetic Text,* 11-16.

2. Becoming a Journalist

1. Lemay and Zall, *Genetic Text,* 17–20.

3. On the Road to Philadelphia

1. McKee, *Labor,* 64, 75.
2. Not to be confused with Governor William Keith, appearing later, George Keith in 1692 split Quakers over doctrine, politics, and law. As his supporter, Bradford had been imprisoned for seditious libel. Horle, *Lawmaking,* 1:44.
3. Casson, *Ships,* 193; Howard, *Boatmen,* 36.
4. Edwin Wolf II, *Book Culture of a Colonial American City* (Oxford: Clarendon Press, 1988), 188.
5. Cotton Mather's *Manuductio ad Ministerium* (1726) prescribed the water cure for fevers.
6. Oberg, *Papers,* 2:187n; Rogers, "Dr. John Brown," 1–6.
7. Lemay and Zall, *Genetic Text,* 20-22.

4. Settling at Philadelphia

1. Kelsey, "Early Description," 251–52; Wroth, *Colonial Printer,* 164–65.
2. Lemay and Zall, *Genetic Text,* 24–27.

5. A Prodigal's Return to Boston

1. Rush, *Effects of Spiritous Liquors,* 5.
2. Lemay and Zall, *Genetic Text,* 27–34.

Notes

6. Plotting to Deceive & Being Deceived

1. Tryon, *Way to Health*, 343.
2. *Dunciad*, Book 3:159.
3. Robinson, *British Mail*, 34, 44–45.
4. Lemay and Zall, *Genetic Text*, 34–42.
5. Horle, *Lawmaking*, 2:561–89.

7. Living in London

1. Defoe, *Tour*, 133, 144.
2. Lemay and Zall, *Genetic Text*, 43.
3. Oberg, *Papers*, 31:59.
4. Lemay and Zall, *Genetic Text*, 43.
5. Oberg, *Papers*, 31:59.
6. Lemay and Zall, *Genetic Text*, 43.
7. Ibid., 45-48, 49.
8. Oberg, *Papers*, 31:59.
9. Ibid., 1:54.
10. Lemay and Zall, *Genetic Text*, 43.
11. Ibid., 44-48.
12. Tatler, 1:252-55.
13. Orme, *Swimming*, 115–207.
14. Lemay and Zall, *Genetic Text*, 49–51.

8. Sailing Home

1. Lemay and Zall, *Genetic Text*, 51–52.
2. Oberg, *Papers*, 1:99–100.
3. Ibid., 1:72.
4. Defoe, *Tour*, 46.
5. Oberg, *Papers*, 1:79–81.
6. Ibid., 1:86.
7. Ibid., 1:90–91.
8. Ibid., 1:95–96.
9. Ibid., 1:96.
10. Ibid., 1:98–99.

9. Facing Uncertain Philadelphia Future

1. Lemay and Zall, *Genetic Text*, 52–54.
2. Ibid., 54–58.
3. Ibid., 61–62.
4. Ibid., 58–59.

Notes

10. Venturing into Business

1. Bezanson, *Prices,* 10–11, 320.
2. Lemay and Zall, *Genetic Text,* 59–60.
3. Ibid., 62.
4. Miller, *BF's Philadelphia Printing,* 2–3.
5. Lemay and Zall, *Genetic Text,* 63–64.
6. Ibid., 64–66.

11. Entering His Own Business

1. Lemay and Zall, *Genetic Text,* 66–69.
2. Ibid., 69-71.
3. Ibid., 75-76.

12. Finding Felicity in Philadelphia

1. Lemay and Zall, *Genetic Text,* 73.
2. Ibid., 72.
3. Ibid., 74–77.
4. Kalm, *Travels,* 20–24.
5. Lemay and Zall, *Genetic Text,* 77–78.
6. Ibid., 96.
7. Oberg, *Papers,* 2:85, 126.
8. Lemay and Zall, *Genetic Text,* 97.
9. Ibid., 78–87.
10. Ibid., 88–91.

13. Promoting a United Front

1. Lemay and Zall, *Genetic Text,* 91–94.
2. Lemay, *Writings,* 242–48.
3. Oberg, *Papers,* 1:197.
4. Ibid., 1:198.
5. Ibid., 1:198–99.
6. Ibid., 1:199.
7. Lemay and Zall, *Genetic Text,* 94–96.
8. Ibid., 96.
9. VanDoren, *Letters,* 43–44.
10. Lemay and Zall, *Genetic Text,* 98.

14. Taking Care of Business

1. Lemay and Zall, *Genetic Text,* 97–98.
2. Ibid., 99–100.
3. Ibid., 99.

Notes

4. Ibid., 101.
5. Oberg, *Papers*, 2:203.
6. Ibid., 2:204.
7. Lemay and Zall, *Genetic Text*, 101-102.
8. Ibid., 125.
9. Watson, *Annals of Philadelphia*, 1:211–12.
10. Lemay and Zall, *Genetic Text*, 128–29.

15. Promoting the Great Awakening

1. Lambert, *"Pedlar,"* 176–82.
2. Lemay and Zall, *Genetic Text*, 103-5.
3. Lemay and Zall, *Genetic Text*, 104–8.
4. Ibid., 116–17.

16. Promoting Provincial Defense

1. Lemay and Zall, *Genetic Text*, 108–09.
2. Oberg, *Papers*, 2:340.
3. Lemay and Zall, *Genetic Text*, 109–10.
4. Oberg, *Papers*, 3:269.
5. Lemay and Zall, *Genetic Text*, 110–12.
6. Levy, *Quakers*, 155.
7. Lemay and Zall, *Genetic Text*, 112–14.
8. Lemay and Zall, *Genetic Text*, 114–16.

17. Establishing an Academy

1. Smyth, *Writings*, 10:29.
2. Lemay and Zall, *Genetic Text*, 117–19.
3. Oberg, *Papers*, 2:409–10; Wroth, *The Colonial Printer*, 186.
4. Lemay and Zall, *Genetic Text*, 119.

18. Retiring to Public Service

1. Oberg, *Papers*, 4:199.
2. Lemay and Zall, *Genetic Text*, 119–20.
3. Brown, *Forum*, 1:236–37.
4. Lemay and Zall, *Genetic Text*, 120.
5. Ibid., 4:83.
6. Oberg, *Papers*, 3:474–75.
7. Ibid., 3:481–82.
8. Lemay and Zall, *Genetic Text*, 120.
9. Wallace, *Conrad Weiser*, 346.
10. Lemay and Zall, *Genetic Text*, 120–21.
11. Jennings, *BF, Politician*, 87–88.

Notes

12. Lemay and Zall, *Genetic Text*, 121.
13. Monboddo, *Antient Metaphysics,* 5.i.1.
14. Jefferson, 96.
15. Lemay and Zall, *Genetic Text*, 123-24.
16. Ibid., 130.

19. EXPERIMENTING WITH ELECTRICITY

1. Heilbron, *Electricity,* 324–25.
2. Lemay and Zall, *Genetic Text*, 152.
3. Oberg, *Papers,* 17:66.
4. Lemay, *Kinnersley,* 67–70.
5. Lemay and Zall, *Genetic Text*, 153.
6. Oberg, *Papers,* 3:115–18.
7. Ibid., 4:83.
8. Ibid., 22:263.
9. Lemay and Zall, *Genetic Text*, 153–54.
10. *Transactions of the Royal Society.* 47 (London, 1751-52), 203.
11. Heilbron, *Electricity,* 347–48.
12. Lemay and Zall, *Genetic Text*, 154–55.
13. Cohen, *Newton,* 91, 166; *Gentleman's Magazine* 26 (1756): 513–14.
14. Lemay and Zall, *Genetic Text*, 155.
15. Oberg, *Papers,* 4:366–69.
16. Lemay and Zall, *Genetic Text*, 155.
17. Oberg, *Papers,* 4:139.
18. Lemay and Zall, *Genetic Text*, 155–56.
19. Lemay and Rousseau, *Renaissance Man,* 16.
20. Oberg, *Papers,* 4:466–67.

20. PROMOTING A UNITED FRONT

1. Lemay and Zall, *Genetic Text*, 130–31.
2. Oberg, *Papers,* 5:417.
3. Lemay and Zall, *Genetic Text*, 132.
4. *Colonial Records* 6:135.
5. Lemay and Zall, *Genetic Text*, 132.
6. *Pennsylvania Archives,* 1s. (Philadelphia: Severn, 1852) 1:69, 76.
7. Lemay and Zall, *Genetic Text*, 132–33.
8. Oberg, *Papers,* 6:262.
9. Lemay and Zall, *Genetic Text*, 133–34.
10. Ibid., 136.
11. Oberg, *Papers,* 6:13n, 54–55.
12. Lemay and Zall, *Genetic Text*, 136.
13. Oberg, *Papers,* 6:54.

Notes

14. Lemay and Zall, *Genetic Text*, 136–38.
15. Hutson, "Pennsylvania Politics," 349–50.
16. Lemay and Zall, *Genetic Text*, 138–39.
17. Edmund B. O'Callaghan, ed., *Documents Relative to the Colonial History of the State of New York*, 15 vols. (Albany: Weed, Parsons, 1856-87), 17:272.
18. Lemay and Zall, *Genetic Text*, 140.
19. Ibid., 140–42.
20. *Pennsylvania Magazine of History and Biography* 17:272.
21. Moreau, *Memoire*, 242.
22. Lemay and Zall, *Genetic Text*, 142–44.
23. Oberg, *Papers*, 6:257n, 480–83.

21. Soldiering on the Frontier

1. Lemay and Zall, *Genetic Text*, 144–45.
2. Ibid., 145.
3. Oberg, *Papers*, 6:365.
4. Ibid., 6:357.
5. Lemay and Zall, *Genetic Text*, 145-46.
6. Page 75.
7. Lemay and Zall, *Genetic Text*, 147–48.
8. Ibid., 147–48.
9. Lemay and Zall, *Genetic Text*, 148.
10. Pargellis, *Military Affairs*, 169.
11. Nolan, *General BF*, 84.
12. Lemay and Zall, *Genetic Text*, 149.
13. Ibid., 150.
14. Ibid., 149.
15. Oberg, *Papers*, 7:13.
16. Lemay and Zall, *Genetic Text*, 150–51.
17. Oberg, *Papers*, 7:13–14.
18. Lemay and Zall, *Genetic Text*, 151.
19. Oberg, *Papers*, 7:14n; Middelkauff, *His Enemies*, 59.
20. Lemay and Zall, *Genetic Text*, 151–52.

22. Making a Mission to London

1. W. Smith, *Gentleman in London*, 6–7; Oberg, *Papers*, 7:111n.
2. Lemay and Zall, *Genetic Text*, 156–59.
3. Pargellis, *Military Affairs*, 384–85.
4. Lemay and Zall, *Genetic Text*, 159–60.
5. Huntington Library manuscript, Accession Number 5140.
6. Lemay and Zall, *Genetic Text*, 160–63.

Notes

7. Huntington Library manuscript, Accession Number LO 2:166-67.

8. Lemay and Zall, *Genetic Text*, 163.

9. Ibid., 163–66.

10. Oberg, *Papers of BF,* 7:243.

11. Lemay and Zall, *Genetic Text*, 166.

23. LOBBYING IN LONDON

1. Lemay and Zall, *Genetic Text*, 166–67.

2. Oberg, *Papers*, 7:273.

3. Ibid., 7:361–62.

4. Lemay and Zall, *Genetic Text*, 167–68.

5. Hutson, "Pennsylvania Politics," 43.

6. Oberg, *Papers*, 8: 313.

7. Lemay and Zall, *Genetic Text*, 168–70.

8. Oberg, *Papers*, 10:xxviii-ix.

24. SKIRMISHING WITH PARLIAMENT

1. Oberg, *Papers*, 12:158–60.

2. Ibid., 13:295n.

3. Ibid., 13:429.

4. Ibid., 13:169–70.

5. Ibid., 14:66, 67, 69–70.

6. Ibid., 14:73.

25. COPING IN A CALM

1. Oberg, *Papers*, 13:427.

2. Ibid., 17:342.

3. Ibid., 14:193–94.

4. Ibid., 19: 46-47.

5. Ibid., 14:241.

6. Ibid., 14:250-51.

7. Ibid., 14:252-53.

8. Ibid., 14:254–55.

9. Ibid., 15:272–73.

10. VanDoren, *Franklin's Autobiographical Writings*, 288.

11. Oberg, *Papers*, 17:314–15.

26. AGITATING FOR ALL AMERICANS

1. Oberg, *Papers*, 18:12–15.

2. Ibid., 18:14–16.

3. Ibid., 19:226.

Notes

4. Ibid., 19:257–59.
5. Ibid., 19:360.
6. Ibid., 20:437.
7. Ibid., 20:307.
8. Ibid., 20:387.
9. Ibid., 20:437–39.

27. Failing to Reconcile

1. Oberg, *Papers,* 21:546.
2. Ibid., 23:311.
3. Ibid., 21:550.
4. Ibid., 21:552.
5. Ibid., 21:565-67.
6. Ibid., 21:579.
7. Ibid., 21:581-82.
8. Ibid., 21:589-90.
9. Ibid., 21:593.
10. Ibid., 21:597.
11. Ibid., 21:597-98.
12. Crane, "Club of Honest Whigs," 210–33.
13. Oberg, *Papers,* 23:311.

28. Forging Independence

1. Oberg, *Papers,* 22:93-98.
2. Ibid., 22:85.
3. Ibid., 22:518.
4. Ibid., 22:520-21.
5. Ibid., 23:298-99.
6. Ibid., 26:223.
7. Aldridge, *Contemporaries,* 61–62.
8. Oberg, *Papers,* 29:613.
9. Oberg, *Papers,* 30:514.
10. Oberg, *Papers,* 34:25.
11. Ibid., 34:21.
12. *Journals of the Continental Congress,* 26:171.
13. Paul H. Smith, 22:157, 247, 252.
14. Oberg, *Papers,* 35:311-12.
15. Ibid., 35:59.
16. Fleming, *BF,* 357.
17. Smyth, *Writings,* 9:92
18. Ibid., 9:151.
19. Ibid., 9:117-18.

Notes

20. Ibid., 9:333-34.
21. Huntington ms., HM 22771.

29. FREE AT LAST

1. Smyth, *Writings,* 10:464-71.
2. Ibid., 9:490-91.
3. Ibid., 9:511-12.
4. Ibid., 9:559.
5. *Documentary History,* 13:213-14.
6. *Journals of the Continental Congress,* 34:603n.
7. Smyth, *Writings,* 9:692-97.
8. Ibid., 10:1-2.
9. Ibid., 10:4.
10. Ibid., 10:84-85.
11. Ibid., 10:502-3.
12. Ibid., 10:560–61.
13. Ibid., 9:560, 572.
14. Ibid., 10:49–50.
15. Ibid., 10:68–69.
16. Zall, *BF Laughing,* 33–34.
17. Smyth, *Writings,* 9:685.
18. Rush, *Letters,* 1:564.

SELECTED BIBLIOGRAPHY

American National Biography. Ed. John A. Garraty and Mark C. Carnes. New York: Oxford Univ. Press, 1999.

Adams, Charles Francis, ed. *Letters of Mrs. Adams.* 2 vols. Boston: Little Brown, 1840.

Aldridge, Alfred Owen. *Franklin and His French Contemporaries.* New York: New York Univ. Press, 1957.

Bell, Whitfield J., ed. *Complete Poor Richard's Almanacs.* 2 vols. Barre, Vermont: Imprint Society, 1970.

Bezanson, Anne, et al. *Prices in Colonial Pennsylvania.* Philadelphia: Univ. of Pennsylvania Press, 1935.

Brown, David Paul. *Forum; or, Fifty Years Full Practice at the Philadelphia Bar.* Philadelphia: R.H. Small, 1856.

Carlyle, Alexander. *Anecdotes and Characters of the Times.* Ed. James Kinsley. London: Oxford Univ. Press, 1973.

Carretta, Vincent, ed. *Satires Written by Mr. Whitehead.* Augustan Reprint Society, no. 223. Los Angeles: Clark Library, 1984.

Casson, Lionel. *Illustrated History of Ships.* Garden City: Doubleday, 1966.

Clark, Charles E., and Charles Wetherell. "The Measure of Maturity: The Pennsylvania Gazette, 1728–65." *William and Mary Quarterly* 3s. 46 (1989): 279–303.

Cohen, I. Bernard, ed. *Benjamin Franklin's Experiments.* Cambridge: Harvard Univ. Press, 1941.

———. *Franklin and Newton.* Philadelphia: American Philosophical Society, 1956.

Crane, Verner W. "The Club of Honest Whigs: Friends of Science and Liberty." *William and Mary Quarterly* 3s. 23(1966): 210–33.

Curti, Merle. *Learning for Ladies.* San Marino: Huntington Library, 1936.

Defoe, Daniel. *Tour thro' the Whole Island of Great Britain.* Ed. P.N. Fairbank and W.R. Owen. New Haven: Yale Univ. Press, 1991.

Documentary History of the Ratification of the Constitution. Ed. Merrill Jensen, et al. 18 vols. Madison: State Historical Society of Wisconsin, 1976–95.

Documents Relative to the Colonial History of New York. Ed. Edmund B. O'Callaghan, et al. 15 vols. Albany: Weed, Parsons, 1853–87.

Franklin, Benjamin. *Papers of Benjamin Franklin.* Ed. Barbara Oberg, Leonard Labarree, et al. New Haven: Yale Univ. Press, 1959–.

Heilbron, J.L. *Electricity in the 17th and 18th Centuries.* Berkeley: Univ. of California Press, 1979.

Horle, Craig W., et al. *Lawmaking and Legislators in Pennsylvania 1710–56.* Philadelphia: Univ. of Pennsylvania Press, 1997.

Howard, Robert W. *The Boatmen.* New York: Putnams, 1967.

Hutson, James H. "Benjamin Franklin and Pennsylvania Politics, 1751–55: A Reappraisal." *Pennsylvania Magazine of History and Biography* 93 (1969): 303–71.

Jefferson, Thomas. *Notes on the State of Virginia.* Ed. William Peden. Chapel Hill: Univ. of North Carolina Press, 1955.

———. *Writings.* Ed. by Merrill Peterson. New York: Library of America, 1984.

Jennings, Francis. *Benjamin Franklin Politician.* New York: Norton, 1996.

Journals of the Continental Congress 1774–89. 35 vols. Washington: Library of Congress, 1907–76.

Kalm, Peter. *Travels in North America.* Ed. Adolph B. Benson. New York: Wilson-Erickson, 1937.

Kelsey, R.W. "An Early Description of Pennsylvania." *Pennsylvania Magazine of History and Biography* 45 (1921): 243–54.

Lambert, Frank. *"Pedlar in Divinity": George Whitefield and the Transatlantic Revivals, 1737–70.* Princeton: Princeton Univ. Press, 1994.

Lemay, J.A. Leo. "Chronology." http://www.english.udel.edu/lemay/franklin.

———. *Ebenezer Kinnersley: Franklin's Friend.* Philadelphia: Univ. of Pennsylvania Press. 1964.

Lemay, J.A. Leo, and George Rousseau. *Renaissance Man in the 18th Century.* Los Angeles: Clark Library, 1978.

Lemay, J.A. Leo, and P.M. Zall, eds. *Autobiography of Benjamin Franklin: A Genetic Text.* Knoxville: Univ. of Tennessee Press, 1981.

———. *Benjamin Franklin's Autobiography: Norton Critical Edition.* New York: Norton, 1986.

Lemay, J.A. Leo, ed. *Writings.* New York: Library of America, 1987.

Levy, Barry. *Quakers and the American Family.* New York: Oxford Univ. Press, 1988.

McKee, Samuel, Jr. *Labor in Colonial New York.* New York: Columbia Univ. Press, 1935.

Selected Bibliography

Middelkauff, Robert. *Benjamin Franklin and His Enemies*. Berkeley: Univ. of California Press, 1996.

Miller, William C. *Benjamin Franklin's Philadelphia Printing*. Philadelphia: American Philosophical Society, 1974.

Monboddo, James Burnett. *Antient Metaphysics*. 6 vols. Edinburgh: J. Balfour, 1779–99.

Moreau, Jacob. *Memoire Contenant le Precis des Faits, avec leur Pieces*. Paris, 1756; tr. Philadelphia: Chattin, 1757.

Nolan, J. Bennett. *Benjamin Franklin in Scotland and Ireland*. Philadelphia: Univ. of Pennsylvania Press, 1938.

———. *General Benjamin Franklin*. Philadelphia: Univ. of Pennsylvania Press, 1936.

Oberg, Barbara, et al., eds. *Papers of Benjamin Franklin*. New Haven: Yale Univ. Press, 1959—.

Orme, Nicholas. *Early English Swimming*. Exeter: Univ. of Exeter, 1983.

Pargellis, Stanley, ed. *Military Affairs in North America, 1748–65*. New York: Appleton, 1936.

Robinson, Howard. *Carrying British Mail Overseas*. London: Allen and Unwin, 1964.

Rogers, Fred B. "Dr. John Browne: Friend of Benjamin Franklin," *Bulletin of the History of Medicine* 30 (1956): 1–6.

Roosevelt, Franklin Delano. *Public Papers and Addresses*. 13 vols. New York: Macmillan, 1938–50.

Rush, Benjamin. *Effects of Spiritous Liquors*. Boston: Thomas and Andrews, 1790.

———. *Letters*. Ed. Lyman Butterfield. 2 vols. Princeton: Princeton Univ. Press, 1951.

Skemp, Sheila L. *William Franklin: Son of a Patriot, Servant of a King*. New York: Oxford Univ. Press, 1990.

Smith, Carleton Sprague. *Broadsides and their Music in Colonial America: Music in Colonial Massachusetts*. Boston: Colonial Society of Massachusetts, 1980.

Smith, Paul H., ed. *Letters of Delegates to the Continental Congress, 1774–89*. 25 vols. Washington: Library of Congress, 1977–98.

Smith, William. *Letter from a Gentleman in London, to His Friend in Pennsylvania*. London: J. Scott, 1756.

Smyth, Albert H., ed. *Writings of Benjamin Franklin*. 10 vols. New York: Macmillan, 1907.

Starbuck, Alexander. *History of Nantucket*. Boston: Goodspeed, 1924.

Steele, Richard. *The Tatler.* Ed. Donald F. Bond. 3 vols. New York: Oxford Univ. Press, 1987.

Tourtellot, Arthur Benson. *Benjamin Franklin: The Shaping of Genius.* Garden City: Doubleday, 1977.

Tryon, Thomas. *Way to Health, Long Life, and Happiness.* London: A. Sowle, 1683.

VanDoren, Carl, ed. *Franklin's Autobiographical Writings.* New York: Viking, 1945.

———. *Letters of Benjamin Franklin and Jane Mecom.* Princeton: American Philosophical Society, 1950.

Wallace, Paul A.W. *Conrad Weiser.* Philadelphia: Univ. of Pennsylvania Press, 1945.

Warden, Gerard B. *Boston, 1689–1776.* Boston: Little Brown, 1970.

Watson, John F. *Annals of Philadelphia and Pennsylvania in the Olden Time.* Rev. Willis P. Hazard. 3 vols. Philadelphia: Stuart, 1899.

Williamson, Peter. *French and Indian Cruelty Exemplified in the Life and various Vicissitudes of Fortune, of Peter Williamson, a Disbanded Soldier.* 2d ed. York: 1758.

Wroth, Lawrence C. *The Colonial Printer.* Portland, Maine: Southworth-Anthoenson, 1938.

Zall, Paul M. *Ben Franklin Laughing.* Berkeley: Univ. of California Press, 1980.

———. *Franklin's Autobiography: A Model Life.* Boston: G.K. Hall, 1989.

———. *Wit and Wisdom of the Founding Fathers.* Hopewell, N.J.: ECCO Press, 1996.

INDEX

Only Franklin's texts are indexed.
His name is abbreviated BF.

Index

Index

Index

constitution for academy, 157

fund-raising: for academy, 157-58; hospital, 165-67; library, 105; Tennent seeks advice on, 167-68

Gentleman's Magazine: prints BF's experiments, 173

Gnadenhut: BF arrives at, 196-97; buries dead, 197; massacre at, 195

Godfrey, Thomas: joins Junto, 86; lodges with BF, 89; wife plays matchmaker, 99-100

Gordon, Patrick: succeeds Keith as governor, 79

Grace, Robert: BF's benefactor, 93, 94; casts stove, 144; joins Junto, 86

Granville, John First Earl: lectures BF on colonial law, 219-20

Greenwood, James: BF reads grammar, 25

Hall, David: BF takes as partner, 158-59, 233

Hamilton, Andrew: BF has cabin of, 56; tells of conspiracy, 58; tenders patronage in Delaware, 96; and Philadelphia, 92-93

Hamilton, James: appoints BF to Albany commission, 179; serves as governor of Pennsylvania, 181; vacates cabin on ship, 56

Harry, David: at Barbadoes, 98; fails in business, 99; Keimer employs, 81; returns to farming, 98

Harvard: grants MA to BF, 168

Health, of BF: dreads venereal disease, 100; suffers: flu, 220; gout, 268, 285; kidney stone, 268, 284; takes opiate for pain, 285; thinks pleurisy terminal, 80; travel good for, 234; tolerable, 162; of Francis F., smallpox, 133-34; of parents, 13

Hemphill, Samuel: BF writes for, 108; preaches heterodoxy, 108-9

Hillsborough, Wills Hill, Lord: grants BF interview, 240-44; loses office, 245; visited repeatedly, 245-46; worst "double and deceitful" man, 245

Holmes, Robert (brother-in-law): offers BF advice, 41-42; urges return home, 41

Hospital, Pennsylvania: Bond wants credit for, 165; fund raising for, 165-67

House, George: brings first customers, 89

Howe, Lady Caroline: invites chess matches, 251-52, 256

Howe, Viscount Richard,

Index

Index

Market Street wharf, first
and final landings at, 35, 272
Plato: quoted, 73
Plutarch's *Lives*: in Josiah F's
library, 18
Poor Richard's Almanac: drama-
tizes Father Abraham,124;
substitutes for books, 123;
traditional proverbs in, 124
Pope, Alexander: quoted, 87;
ruins Ralph as poet, 54, 207
popularity, BF's: in Paris, 263; in
militia, 202-3, 229; reelected,
161, 227; return from
France acclaimed, 272
Port Royal Academy: early
textbook of BF, 24
post office: BF as comptroller,
168; deputy postmaster-
general at Philadelphia, 134;
for British North America,
168; career in summarized,
168, 237; Collins clerks in
Boston, 44; inspection tours
by BF, 227; urged dismissal,
203, 237-38; terminated, 168
Potts, Stephen: at Keimer's, 81; in
Junto, 86
Pownall, John: secretary to
secretaries of state, 240-42,
246; takes part in interview,
240-44; praises William F,
246
prayer: BF's private, 114; from
Thomson's *Seasons*, 114
Pringle, Sir John: dies, 265;

Queen's physician, 234;
travels with BF, 234-35
printing: BF apologizes for, 125-
27; at Delaware, 96; at New
Jersey, 84; casts type,
engraves, 82, 84; has own
shop, 89; joins chapel, 64-65;
proud of, 238; raises
grandson to, 282; works at
Keimer's, 39-40, 81-83;
Palmer's, 60-63; Watts's, 63-
68; Philadelphia needs, 49
Proprietors, of Pennsylvania:
obstruct defense, 193. *See
also* Penn, Thomas
proverbs: kindness obliges, 133;
of Solomon, 106, 114; on
thriving with wife, 101; on
upright sacks, 124; in Poor
Richard's Almanac, 124
public service, BF's: agent for
Georgia, 241; Massachusetts,
241; Pennsylvania, 207;
alderman, 161; clerk of
Assembly, 132, 149-50, 161;
congressman, 260; justice of
peace, 161; military service,
149, 201-2; militia commission, 227; minister to France,
261-69; committee of safety,
260; speaker of Assembly,
229; summary of career, 278-
81; urban renewal, 135-36;
vs. private interest, 238, 253

Quakers: BF exempts, 193, 201;

312

Index

first meeting, 37; in Assembly, 152-53; on pacifism, 149-54; prints history, 90; services petitions, 257

Ralph, James, relations with BF: BF corrupts, 87; conspires in poetry contest, 53-54; hears late news of, 207; inscribes pamphlet to, 60; keeps broke, 68; takes name, 62; with in ship, 56; in London, 59-62, 63; ruined by Pope, 54, 207; ruins Mrs T, 62-63
razor, value of, 137
Read, John: as BF's landlord, 37; Deborah F's father, ruined, 58
Read, Sarah (mother-in-law): acknowledges error, 100; forbids marriage, 52
reason: convenient, 51; infected, 87; no reason, 235; pseudo-, 116
religion, BF's: abandons formal, 107-8; as necessitarian, 88; creed, 106, 122, 282; deist in youth, 87; evades, 23; ignores revealed, 88; in plan for moral perfection, 116, 122; non sectarian, 135-36; praises Dunkers, 154; God's conservation of energy, 269; prepares private prayers, 108, 114; values Jesus, 282-83
revolution: American, 180, 229-

30; French, 285
Richardson, Samuel: BF praises dramatic style of, 32
Riddlesden, William: as villain, 58
Rogers, John: deserts Deborah Read, 79-80; rumored bigamist, 100-101
Royal Society: awards BF medal, 176; grants free membership,176; reviews experiments, 175; ridicules, 172
rum, chaplain distributes, 198; Indian orator praises, 164-65

Saint Asaph, Jonathan Shipley, Bishop of, visits BF, 271
Sancho Panza: anecdote of, 183
Seller, John: BF reads on navigation, 24
Shirley, General William: prefers low seat, 212-13; succeeds Braddock, 191
Shirley, William, Jr.: killed with Braddock, 189
Sloane, Hans: buys BF's asbestos, 61
Society for Political Inquiries: meets at BF's house, 281
Society of Free and Easy, 122-23, 131-32
Socrates: BF practices method, 25; urges imitation of (appearance of humility), 111

313

Index